Debt Information for Teens

TEEN FINANCE SERIES

First Edition

Debt
Information
for Teens

Tips for a Successful Financial Life

*Including Facts about Money, Interest Rates, Loans,
Credit Cards, Finance Charges, Predatory Lending Practices,
Preventing and Resolving Debt-Related Problems, and More*

◆

Edited by Karen Bellenir

Omnigraphics

P.O. Box 31-1640, Detroit, MI 48231-1640

Bibliographic Note

Because this page cannot legibly accommodate all the copyright notices, the Bibliographic Note portion of the Preface constitutes an extension of the copyright notice.

Edited by Karen Bellenir

Teen Finance Series

Karen Bellenir, *Managing Editor*
Elizabeth Collins, *Research and Permissions Coordinator*
Cherry Stockdale, *Permissions Assistant*
EdIndex, Services for Publishers, *Indexers*

* * *

Omnigraphics, Inc.

Matthew P. Barbour, *Senior Vice President*
Kay Gill, *Vice President—Directories*
Kevin Hayes, *Operations Manager*

* * *

Peter E. Ruffner, *Publisher*

Copyright © 2008 Omnigraphics, Inc.
ISBN 978-0-7808-0989-5

Library of Congress Cataloging-in-Publication Data

Debt information for teens : tips for a successful financial life including
facts about money, interest rates, loans, credit cards, finance charges,
predatory lending practices, preventing and resolving debt-related problems,
and more / edited by Karen Bellenir.
    p. cm. -- (Teen finance series)
    Summary: "Provides information for teens about obtaining and using credit,
managing debt, and avoiding predatory lending"--Provided by publisher.
    Includes bibliographical references and index.
    ISBN 978-0-7808-0989-5 (hardcover : alk. paper) 1. Teenagers--Finance,
Personal. 2. Consumer credit. I. Bellenir, Karen.
    HG179.D379 2007
    332.024'020835--dc22

                                                                2007031021

This book is printed on acid-free paper meeting the ANSI Z39.48 Standard. The infinity symbol that appears above indicates that the paper in this book meets that standard.

Printed in the United States

Table Of Contents

Part One: Money And The Economy: How The Big Picture Affects Your Wallet

Part Two: Using Credit

Part Three: Credit And Debit Cards

Part Four: Predatory And Problematic Lending Practices

Part Five: Preventing And Resolving Debt-Related Problems

Part Six: If You Need More Information

Preface

About This Book

For many of today's teens, the milestones that mark the journey toward adulthood include debt and other financial obligations. They eagerly look forward to their first credit card or taking on the responsibility of car payments. Those who learn how to manage their finances responsibly and make smart decisions about purchases can gain experience and skills that will serve them for a lifetime. Those who falter, however, can find themselves trapped in a cycle of increasing debt.

Debt Information For Teens explains the economic fundamentals that govern the use of debt as a financial tool. It talks about the uses and abuses of credit and describes how everyday transactions serve to create a person's credit history. Different types of loans, including vehicle loans, loans for education, business loans, and mortgages are described. A special section on credit and debit cards outlines the advantages and disadvantages of using plastic. Another section on predatory and problematic lending practices focuses on the types of credit often associated with exceptionally high interest rates and other abuses, including payday and title loans, refund anticipation loans, and advance-fee loan scams. Information on preventing and resolving debt-related problems is also included, and the book concludes with a directory of resources for additional information and suggestions for further reading.

How To Use This Book

This book is divided into parts and chapters. Parts focus on broad areas of interest; chapters are devoted to single topics within a part.

Part One: Money And The Economy: How The Big Picture Affects Your Wallet describes the interconnection between monetary policies and personal finances. It looks at the history of money, the development of different types of currency, and the processes by which money came to play such an important role in society. It also explains the tools used by government policy makers to manage the availability, cost, and value of money.

Part Two: Using Credit discusses the nature of credit and how it can be used or abused. It explains the process of building and maintaining a good credit history and the consequences of credit-related missteps. Individual chapters focus on the most commonly used types of credit. Some of these, such as vehicle financing and student loans, will be of immediate interest to teens. Other information provides a foundation of knowledge for future stages of life.

Part Three: Credit And Debit Cards explains the principles that govern the use of credit and debit cards and describes their respective advantages and disadvantages. It offers suggestions on evaluating credit card offers, understanding the terms and conditions that accompany the use of a credit card, and avoiding such common problems as unanticipated interest and finance charges, mushrooming balances, and credit card fraud.

Part Four: Predatory And Problematic Lending Practices offers facts about types of debt associated with high interest rates and fees, the kinds of loans that tend to trap unwary consumers in cycles of growing indebtedness, and methods of offering credit that may signal potential fraud.

Part Five: Preventing And Resolving Debt-Related Problems gives tips for managing personal finances and avoiding costly money-handling mistakes. It offers suggestions for budgeting, saving, and spending wisely. For teens who do encounter problems in the years ahead, the part also provides facts that will help them understand their rights and responsibilities related to debt collection practices, credit counseling, credit repair, and bankruptcy.

Part Six: If You Need More Information includes statistics about the use of consumer credit in the United States, a directory of organizations that can help teens learn about money and money management, and suggestions for further reading.

Bibliographic Note

This volume contains documents and excerpts from publications issued by the following government agencies: Administrative Office of the U.S. Courts; Federal Deposit Insurance Corporation (FDIC); Federal Trade Commission (FTC); U.S. Bureau of Engraving and Printing; U.S. Bureau of the Public Debt; U.S. Census Bureau; U.S. Department of Education; U.S. Department of Housing and Urban Development (HUD); U.S. Department of the Treasury; U.S. Government Accountability Office; and the U.S. Securities and Exchange Commission (SEC).

In addition, this volume contains copyrighted documents and articles produced by the following organizations: America Saves; American Bankruptcy Institute; Asian Women in Business; Balance; Bankrate.com; Bond Market Foundation; Center for Responsible Lending; Colorado State University Cooperative Extension; Consumer Federation of America; Debtors Anonymous General Service Board, Inc.; Department of Banking, State of Connecticut; Federal Reserve Bank of Atlanta; Federal Reserve Bank of Chicago; Federal Reserve Bank of Dallas; Federal Reserve Bank of Minneapolis; Federal Reserve Bank of San Francisco; Federal Reserve Board of Governors; Government National Mortgage Association (Ginnie Mae); Maryland Office of the Attorney General; National Consumer Law Center; National Consumers League; New Jersey Coalition for Financial Education; Northwestern Mutual Life Insurance Company; South Carolina Appleseed Legal Justice Center; and WGBH Educational Foundation (NOVA-PBS).

Full citation information is provided on the first page of each chapter. Every effort has been made to secure all necessary rights to reprint the copyrighted material. If any omissions have been made, please contact Omnigraphics to make corrections for future editions.

Acknowledgements

In addition to the organizations listed above, special thanks are due to research and permissions coordinator Elizabeth Collins and to editorial assistants Elizabeth Bellenir and Nicole Salerno.

Part One

Money And The Economy:
How The Big Picture Affects Your Wallet

Chapter 1

The History Of Money

Consider this problem: You catch fish for your food supply, but you're tired of eating it every day. Instead you want to eat some bread. Fortunately, a baker lives next door. Trading the baker some fish for bread is an example of barter, the direct exchange of one good for another.

However, barter is difficult when you try to obtain a good from a producer that doesn't want what you have. For example, how do you get shoes if the shoemaker doesn't like fish? The series of trades required to obtain shoes could be complicated and time consuming.

Early societies faced these problems. The solution was money. Money is an item, or commodity, that is agreed to be accepted in trade. Over the years, people have used a wide variety of items for money, such as seashells, beads, tea, fish hooks, fur, cattle, and even tobacco.

Coins: Most early cultures traded precious metals. In 2500 BC the Egyptians produced metal rings for use as money. By 700 BC, a group of seafaring people called the Lydians became the first in the Western world to make

About This Chapter: This chapter begins with an undated document titled "The History of Money," reprinted with permission from the Federal Reserve Bank of Minneapolis, www.minneapolisfed.org. Text under the heading "A Money Timeline" is excerpted and reprinted with permission from "The History of Money," NOVA, PBS, from WGBH Educational Foundation, Copyright © 2002 WGBH/Boston. Text under the heading "Digital Cash" is by Brad Puffer, and is also reprinted with permission from NOVA, PBS, from WGBH Educational Foundation, Copyright © 2002 WGBH/Boston.

coins. The Lydians used coins to expand their vast trading empire. The
Greeks and Romans continued the
coining tradition and passed it on
to later Western civilizations. Coins
were appealing since they were du-
rable, easy to carry and contained
valuable metals.

During the 18th century, coins
became popular throughout Europe
as trading grew. One of the most
widely used coins was the Spanish
8-reale. It was often split into pieces
or bits to make change. Half a coin
was 4 bits, a quarter was 2 bits, a
term still used today.

> ♣ **It's A Fact!!**
>
> Money serves three purposes:
>
> - **Medium Of Exchange:** People
>   accept money in trade for goods
>   and services.
>
> - **Standard Of Value:** The value
>   of a good or service can be mea-
>   sured with money. For example,
>   a car with a price of $2,000 is
>   worth twice as much as a car
>   with a price of $1,000.
>
> - **Store Of Value:** Money can be
>   saved and used in the future.
>
> Source: Federal Reserve Bank of
> Minneapolis.

Coins containing precious metals are an example of "commodity money."
The item was traded because it held value. For example, the value of the coin
depended upon the amount of gold and silver it contained.

Paper Currency: The Chinese were the first to use paper money, beginning in the T'ang Dynasty (618–907 AD). During the Ming Dynasty in 1300
AD, the Chinese placed the emperor's seal and signatures of the treasurers on
a crude paper made from mulberry bark.

Representative money is tokens or pieces of paper that are not intrinsically
valuable themselves, but can be exchanged for a specific commodity, such as
gold or silver. In 1715 Maryland, North Carolina, and Virginia issued a "tobacco note" which could be converted to a certain amount of tobacco. This type
of money was easier to make large payments and carry than coin or tobacco
leaves. In the late 1800s, the U.S. government issued gold and silver certificates.

Fiat money is similar to representative money except it can't be redeemed
for a commodity, such as gold or silver. The Federal Reserve notes we use
today are an example of fiat money. In 1967 Congress authorized the U.S.

Treasury to stop redeeming silver certificates in silver dollars or bullion beginning the following year. By 1970 silver was removed from the production of coins. The old coins were gradually removed from circulation and replaced with new copper-cored coins that were faced or "clad" with layers of an alloy of 75 percent copper and 25 percent nickel—the same alloy used in nickels.

People are willing to accept fiat money in exchange for the goods and services they sell only because they are confident it will be honored when they buy goods and services. The Federal Reserve is responsible for maintaining the integrity of U.S. currency by setting monetary policy—controlling the amount of money in circulation—to keep prices stable. If prices remain stable, people have confidence that the dollar they use to buy goods and services today will buy a similar amount in the future.

A Money Timeline

In The Beginning: Barter

Barter is the exchange of resources or services for mutual advantage, and may date back to the beginning of humankind. Some would even argue that it's not purely a human activity; plants and animals have been bartering—in symbiotic relationships—for millions of years. In any case, barter among humans certainly pre-dates the use of money. Today individuals, organizations, and governments still use, and often prefer, barter as a form of exchange of goods and services.

9,000–6,000 BC: Cattle

Cattle, which include anything from cows, to sheep, to camels, are the first and oldest form of money. With the advent of agriculture came the use of grain and other vegetable or plant products as a standard form of barter in many cultures.

1,200 BC: Cowrie Shells

The first use of cowries, the shell of a mollusk that was widely available in the shallow waters of the Pacific and Indian Oceans, was in China. Historically, many societies have used cowries as money, and even as recently as the middle of this century, cowries have been used in some parts of Africa. The cowrie is the most widely and longest used currency in history.

1,000 BC: First Metal Money And Coins

Bronze and copper cowrie imitations were manufactured by China at the end of the Stone Age and could be considered some of the earliest forms of metal coins. Metal tool money, such as knife and spade moneys, was also first used in China. These early metal moneys developed into primitive versions of round coins. Chinese coins were made out of base metals, often containing holes so they could be put together like a chain.

500 BC: Modern Coinage

Outside of China, the first coins developed out of lumps of silver. They soon took the familiar round form of today, and were stamped with various gods and emperors to mark their authenticity. These early coins first appeared in Lydia, which is part of present-day Turkey, but the techniques were quickly copied and further refined by the Greek, Persian, Macedonian, and later the Roman empires. Unlike Chinese coins which depended on base metals, these new coins were made from precious metals such as silver, bronze, and gold, which had more inherent value.

118 BC: Leather Money

Leather money was used in China in the form of one-foot-square pieces of white deerskin with colorful borders. This could be considered the first documented type of banknote.

800–900 AD: The Nose

The phrase "To pay through the nose" comes from Danes in Ireland, who slit the noses of those who were remiss in paying the Danish poll tax.

806 AD: Paper Currency

The first paper banknotes appeared in China. In all, China experienced over 500 years of early paper money, spanning from the ninth through the fifteenth century. Over this period, paper notes grew in production to the point that their value rapidly depreciated and inflation soared. Then beginning in 1455, the use of paper money in China disappeared for several hundred years. This was still many years before paper currency would reappear in Europe, and three centuries before it was considered common.

1500s: Potlach

"Potlach" comes from a Chinook Indian custom that existed in many North American Indian cultures. It is a ceremony where not only were gifts exchanged, but dances, feasts, and other public rituals were performed. In some instances potlach was a form of initiation into secret tribal societies. Because the exchange of gifts was so important in establishing a leader's social rank, potlach often spiraled out of control as the gifts became progressively more lavish and tribes put on larger and grander feasts and celebrations in an attempt to out-do each other.

1535: Wampum

The earliest known use of wampum, which are strings of beads made from clam shells, was by North American Indians in 1535. Most likely, this monetary medium existed well before this date. The Indian word "wampum" means white, which was the color of the beads.

1816: The Gold Standard

Gold was officially made the standard of value in England in 1816. At this time, guidelines were made to allow for a non-inflationary production of standard banknotes which represented a certain amount of gold. Banknotes had been used in England and Europe for several hundred years before this time, but their worth had never been tied directly to gold. In the United States, the Gold Standard Act was officially enacted in 1900, which helped lead to the establishment of a central bank.

✎ What's It Mean?

Currency: Money.

Note: A written promise to pay.

Source: © 2007 Government National Mortgage Association (Ginnie Mae). The Home Zone. http://www.ginniemae.gov/homezone/index.html. Reprinted with permission.

1930: End Of The Gold Standard

The massive Depression of the 1930s, felt worldwide, marked the beginning of the end of the gold standard. In the United States, the gold standard was revised and the price of gold was devalued. This was the first step in ending the relationship altogether. The British and international gold standards soon ended as well, and the complexities of international monetary regulation began.

Digital Cash

In the last few years scores of companies have been formed, sporting appropriately cyber-sounding names, all aiming to be a part of the future of money. Some use the internet to facilitate secure transactions through credit card sales. Others, through complex algorithms, convert your bank dollars to digital code—complete with your digital signature—which can be sent to online vendors. Still others are setting up independent systems of electronic money which use their own network of vendors and users.

What is digital money, and where is it taking us?

Digital cash acts much like real cash, except that it's not on paper. Money in your bank account is converted to a digital code, stored on a microchip, a pocket card, or on the hard drive of your computer, and can be used for anonymous transactions by any vendor who accepts it. Your special bank account code can be used over the internet to purchase a new CD, or can be presented in card form at the local supermarket for food. Everybody involved in the transaction, from the bank to the user to the vendor, all agree to recognize its worth, and thus create this new form of exchange.

The internet may be the natural environment in which digital cash will flourish. In fact, if the internet is to continue to grow, many experts argue that it must become commercial. But fears that credit card numbers and other personal information could be snatched away by a clever hacker make many users apprehensive about buying goods over the internet.

To bring consumers to the internet, many corporations have rushed into developing new technologies to create secure and efficient transactions over the World Wide Web. Many of the new technologies depend on systems, like credit card purchases, that are already familiar to users. By pre-registering your credit card numbers in a secure computer, users can send a special code over the internet to authorize use of your number. The card number itself never travels over the internet and you even receive an e-mail confirming your purchase. Another system uses a complex encryption method so that if someone did manage to steal your number, the number would be completely useless to them. These forms of electronic transactions are the first, and most familiar step, for commercializing the web and beginning the process of electronic monetary exchange.

But the use of digital cash, though convenient, may bring with it complex problems. Because digital money is anonymous, criminals could use untraceable digital money to evade taxes or launder money. Money could flow instantly between countries without being traced. Computer hackers could break into digital cash systems and instantly download the wealth of thousands of customers.

The potential problems go beyond those posed by anonymity. If your hard drive crashes, would you lose not only a hard drive and valuable information, but all of your digital cash as well? Could digital cash wreak havoc on traditional bank and government-controlled monetary systems? Would large private companies take power away from traditional banks by controlling and regulating large holdings of digital cash? And will digital cash be available to those who cannot afford personal computers?

Along with potential problems, digital cash brings with it clear advantages over traditional money. For the user, electronic money is precise, simple, and convenient. For banks, it could mean the elimination of thousands of paper transactions and, in turn, the reduction in user fees. For corporations, it could mean the ability to circumvent banks entirely to create direct company to company transfers. Most experts believe that the use of the internet for electronic transactions and the use of digital cash will rapidly increase over the next ten to twenty years, but it won't replace the real cash you can crinkle in your hand any time soon.

Chapter 2

U.S. Currency

Money

Money is what we buy things with. You exchange money for goods and services. When most people speak of money, they are talking about paper money and coins. This is called currency.

In the United States, currency consists of coins and bills. There are six types of coins: pennies (one cent), nickels (five cents), dimes (10 cents), quarters (25 cents), half-dollars (50 cents), and dollars (100 cents). There are seven denominations of bills: one dollar, two dollars, five dollars, 10 dollars, 20 dollars, 50 dollars, and 100 dollars.

The government stopped making the $500, $1,000, $5,000, and $10,000 bills in 1946.

The Federal Reserve System controls the amount of money in the United States. The Federal Reserve System consists of a Board of Governors based in Washington D.C. and 12 regional banks. The banks are in Boston, New York, Philadelphia, Cleveland, Richmond, Atlanta, Chicago, St. Louis,

About This Chapter: This chapter begins with "Money," © 2007 Government National Mortgage Association (Ginnie Mae). The Home Zone. http://www .ginniemae.gov/homezone/index.html. Reprinted with permission. Text under the headings "Facts About Dollar Bills," "Frequently Asked Questions about Currency," "U.S. Currency: A Time Line" are from the U.S. Department of the Treasury, Bureau of Engraving and Printing, 2006.

Minneapolis, Kansas City, Dallas, and San Francisco. President Woodrow Wilson created the Federal Reserve in 1913.

The U.S. Mint makes all the coins that are circulated in the United States. Paper money is made at the U.S. Bureau of Engraving and Printing in Washington, D.C. The facilities that make coins are located in Denver and Philadelphia.

U.S. currency is printed by the engraved intaglio steel plate method, a procedure that gives the money an embossed feel and other features that are hard to counterfeit. Pennies are made of zinc. Nickels are made of an alloy of copper and nickel. The other coins are made from the same alloy as nickels and a core of copper.

Inflation And The Value Of A Dollar

You may have heard your parents or grandparents say that a dollar used to buy more than it does today. For example, a soft drink that costs $1 now may have cost 50 cents when your parents were younger. This is called inflation. Inflation is an increase in the level of prices, or a decrease in the value of a dollar. The U.S. Department of Labor measures inflation by something called the Consumer Price Index.

The Department of Labor developed the Consumer Price Index by surveying people to determine about 400 common items that they all typically buy. This imaginary collection of items is called the market basket. The Consumer Price Index is based on the amount everyone would have to pay to buy everything in the market basket. The change in the price of the market basket is expressed as a percent. The percent is the rate of inflation (if the cost goes up) or deflation (if the cost goes down.)

✎ **What's It Mean?**

Intaglio Printing: The kind of printing used to create U.S. paper currency. The intaglio process involves printing money from an engraved hard surface. Money is printed from a steel plate.

Source: © 2007 Government National Mortgage Association (Ginnie Mae). The Home Zone. http://www.ginniemae.gov/homezone/index.html. Reprinted with permission.

Facts About Dollar Bills

The basic face and back designs of all denominations of United States paper currency, except the backs of the $1 and $2 denominations in general circulation today, were adopted in 1928.

The front of the bills feature portraits of famous, deceased American statesmen: George Washington on the $1, Thomas Jefferson on the $2, Abraham Lincoln on the $5, Alexander Hamilton on the $10, Andrew Jackson on the $20, Ulysses Grant on the $50, and Benjamin Franklin on the $100. Notes of higher denominations, while no longer produced featured William McKinley on the $500, Grover Cleveland on the $1000, James Madison on the $5000, and Salmon Chase on the $10,000.

Faceplace Numbers and *Letters* are the small numbers and letters that can be found in the lower right and upper left corners of a bill. In the left corner is the *Note Position Number*. This consists of the *Note Position Letter* and a quadrant number. The combination indicates the position of the note on the plate from which it was printed. In the lower right corner, the *Note Position Letter* is followed by the *Plate Serial Number*. This identifies the plate from which the note was printed. The *Plate Serial Number* for the reverse (back) side of the note is in the lower-right corner, just inside the ornamental border on the reverse of the bill.

The backs of the bills feature images reflective of the history of our nation: The Great Seal of the United States on the $1, the signing of the Declaration of Independence on the $2, the Lincoln Memorial on the $5, the Treasury Building on the $10, the White House on the $20, the Capitol on the $50, and Independence Hall on the $100. Denominations higher than $100 feature ornate impressions of the numerical value of the note, such as an ornate "500."

A popular and often asked question about design concerns the one that appears on the back of the $1 note, the Great Seal of the United States. The front of the seal shows an American bald eagle behind our national shield. The eagle holds an olive branch, which symbolizes peace, with 13 berries and 13 leaves. In the left talon, the eagle holds 13 arrows; this represents war. The 13 leaves represent the original colonies. The eagle's head is turned toward the olive branch, showing a desire for peace.

The Exchange Rate

Different countries have different currencies. If you travel to another country, you will probably exchange your U.S. money for the money that is used in that country. In some countries—all things considered—the equivalent of the U.S. dollar will buy less than it does at home; in other countries, it will buy more. The rate at which one country's currency can be converted to another is called the exchange rate. The U.S. exchange rate is based on the dollar.

Here are the names of basic currencies in other parts of the world:

- Algeria: Dinars
- Argentina: Pesos
- Australia: Dollars
- Austria: Schillings
- Bahamas: Dollars
- Barbados: Dollars
- Belgium: Francs
- Bermuda: Dollars
- Brazil: Real
- Bulgaria: Lev
- Canada: Dollars
- Chile: Pesos
- China: Yuan Renmimbi
- Cyprus: Pounds
- Czech Republic: Koruna
- Denmark: Kroner
- Egypt: Pounds
- Europe: Euro
- Fiji: Dollars
- Finland: Markka
- France: Francs
- Germany: Deutsche Marks
- Greece: Drachmas
- Hong Kong: Dollars
- Hungary: Forint
- Iceland: Krona
- India: Rupees
- Indonesia: Rupiah
- Ireland: Punt
- Israel: New Shekels
- Italy: Lira
- Jamaica: Dollars
- Japan: Yen
- Jordan: Dinar
- Korea (South): Won
- Lebanon: Pounds
- Malaysia: Ringgit
- Mexico: Pesos
- Netherlands: (Dutch) Guilders
- New Zealand: Dollars
- Norway: Kroner
- Pakistan: Rupees
- Philippines: Pesos
- Poland: Zloty
- Portugal: Escudo
- Romania: Leu
- Russia: Rubles
- Saudi Arabia: Riyal
- Singapore: Dollars
- Slovakia: Koruna
- South Africa: Rand
- Spain: Pesetas
- Sudan: Dinar
- Sweden: Krona
- Switzerland: Francs
- Taiwan: Dollars
- Thailand: Baht
- Trinidad and Tobago: Dollars
- Turkey: Lira
- United Kingdom: Pound
- Venezuela: Bolivar
- Zambia: Kwacha

Note that the dollars in other countries are not the same thing as dollars in the United States.

Source: © 2007 Government National Mortgage Association (Ginnie Mae). Reprinted with permission.

The top of the shield represents the Congress, the head of the eagle the Executive branch, and the nine tail feathers the Judiciary branch of our government. The 13-letter motto, "E Pluribus Unum," on the ribbon held in the eagle's beak means "Out of Many, One."

On the reverse of the seal is a pyramid with 1776 in Roman numerals at the base. The pyramid stands for permanence and strength. The pyramid is unfinished, signifying the United States' future growth and goal of perfection. A sunburst and an eye are above the pyramid, representing the overseeing eye of a deity. The 13-letter motto, "Annuit Coeptis" means "He has favored our undertakings." Below the pyramid the motto, "Novus Ordo Seclorum" means "A new order of the ages," standing for the new American era.

The motto "In God We Trust" first appeared on U.S. coins in 1864. However, it was not until 1955 that a law was passed which stated that thereafter all new designs for coins and currency would bear that inscription.

Frequently Asked Questions About Currency

What denominations of currency are in circulation today? Will any new denominations be produced?

The present denominations of our currency in production are $1, $2, $5, $10, $20, $50 and $100. The purpose of the United States currency system is to serve the needs of the public and these denominations meet that goal. Present currency in circulation satisfies the public at large, and the Bureau of Engraving and Printing (BEP) has no plans to change the denominations in use today.

What was the largest currency denomination ever produced?

The largest denomination of currency ever printed by the Bureau of Engraving and Printing (BEP) was the $100,000 Series 1934 Gold Certificate featuring the portrait of President Wilson. These notes were printed from December 18, 1934 through January 9, 1935 and were issued by the Treasurer of the United States to Federal Reserve Banks only against an equal amount of gold bullion held by the Treasury Department. The notes were used only for official transactions between Federal Reserve Banks and were not circulated among the general public.

What denominations of currency notes is the Treasury Department no longer printing?

On July 14, 1969, David M. Kennedy, the 60th Secretary of the Treasury, and officials at the Federal Reserve Board announced that they would immediately stop distributing currency in denominations of $500, $1,000, $5,000 and $10,000. Production of these denominations stopped during World War II. Their main purpose was for bank transfer payments. With the arrival of more secure transfer technologies, however, they were no longer needed for that purpose. While these notes are legal tender and may still be found in circulation today, the Federal Reserve Banks remove them from circulation and destroy them as they are received.

Did the Treasury Department ever produce a $1 million currency note? I have one that I want to know about.

The Treasury Department receives many inquiries asking if a $1 million currency note was ever produced. People have sent in copies of these notes, and they were found to be nonnegotiable platinum certificates known as a "One Million Dollar Special Issue." These notes were from a special limited copyrighted art series originally sold by a Canadian firm for $1.00 each as a collectible item. They are not official United States currency notes manufactured by our Bureau of Engraving and Printing (BEP). As such, they are not redeemable by the Department of the Treasury.

♣ It's A Fact!!

The origin of the "$" sign has been variously accounted for. Perhaps the most widely accepted explanation is that it is the result of the evolution of the Mexican or Spanish "P's" for pesos, or piastres, or pieces of eight. This theory, derived from a study of old manuscripts, explains that the "S," gradually came to be written over the "P," developing a close equivalent to the "$" mark. It was widely used before the adoption of the United States dollar in 1785.

Source: U.S. Department of the Treasury, Bureau of Engraving and Printing, 2006.

♣ It's A Fact!!
The Euro

In the United States, the unit of currency is the dollar. Of course, virtually all other countries have monetary systems and their own currencies. For example, Italy uses the lira and France uses the franc. A recent major development in the world is the creation of the Euro, which is a currency that is shared by 11 European nations.

Since January 1, 1999, the Euro has co-existed with the 11 national currencies in the countries where it is in use. The 11 countries and their currencies are the Austrian schilling, Belgian franc, Dutch guilder, Finnish markka, French franc, German mark, Irish punt, Italian lira, Luxembourg franc, Portuguese escudo, and Spanish peseta.

The currency was placed in full circulation in 2002. The Euro was created to ease financial relationships among European nations themselves and with the rest of the world. Some economists warn that if the Euro runs into trouble it could create more widespread problems than if an individual country had a problem with its currency.

Source: © 2007 Government National Mortgage Association (Ginnie Mae). The Home Zone. http://www.ginniemae.gov/homezone/index.html. Reprinted with permission.

You may be interested to know that the BEP learned of these certificates in the spring of 1982. All related correspondence was forwarded to the United States Secret Service to decide if there were any violations of Federal currency laws. The Secret Service subsequently advised, however, that these certificates did not violate any United States law.

Why did the Treasury Department remove the $2 bill from circulation?

The Treasury Department receives many letters asking why the $2 bill is no longer in circulation. Contrary to the impression of many people, the

Treasury Department did not stop circulating the $2 bill. On September 12, 1996, Robert E. Rubin, the 70th Secretary of the Treasury, was presented with a new series $2 bill. The Series 1995 notes were printed at the Bureau of Engraving and Printing's (BEP) Western Currency Facility and bear the seal of the Federal Reserve Bank of Atlanta.

The $2 bill remains one of our circulating currency denominations. According to BEP statistics, 590,720,000 Series 1976 $2 bills were printed and as of February 28, 1999, there was $1,166,091,458 worth of $2 bills in circulation worldwide.

The key for successfully circulating the two-dollar bill is for retailers to use them just like any other denomination in their daily operations. In addition, most commercial banks will readily supply their retail customers with these bills if their customers request them in sufficient volume to justify stocking them in their vaults. However, neither the Treasury Department nor the Federal Reserve System can force the distribution or use of any denomination of currency on banks, businesses or individuals.

♣ It's A Fact!!

United States coins and currency (including Federal reserve notes and circulating notes of Federal reserve banks and national banks) are legal tender for all debts, public charges, taxes, and dues. Foreign gold or silver coins are not legal tender for debts.

However, there is no Federal statute which mandates that private businesses must accept cash as a form of payment. Private businesses are free to develop their own policies on whether or not to accept cash unless there is a State law which says otherwise.

Source: U.S. Department of the Treasury, Bureau of Engraving and Printing, 2006.

I thought that United States currency was legal tender for all debts. Some businesses or governmental agencies say that they will only accept checks, money orders, or credit cards as payment, and others will only accept currency notes in denominations of $20 or smaller. Isn't this illegal?

The pertinent portion of law that applies to your question is the Coinage Act of 1965, specifically Section 31 U.S.C. [U.S. Code; the official compilation of federal laws] 5103, entitled "Legal tender," which states: "United States coins and currency (including Federal reserve notes and circulating notes of Federal reserve banks and national banks) are legal tender for all debts, public charges, taxes, and dues."

This statute means that all United States moneys as identified above are a valid and legal offer of payment for debts when tendered to a creditor. There is, however, no Federal statute mandating that a private business, a person, or an organization must accept currency or coins as for payment for goods and/or services. Private businesses are free to develop their own policies on whether or not to accept cash unless there is a State law which says otherwise. For example, a bus line may prohibit payment of fares in pennies or dollar bills. In addition, movie theaters, convenience stores, and gas stations may refuse to accept large denomination currency (usually notes above $20) as a matter of policy.

What are United States notes and how are they different from Federal Reserve notes?

United States notes (characterized by a red seal and serial number) were the first national currency, authorized by the Legal Tender Act of 1862 and began circulating during the Civil War. The Treasury Department issued these notes directly into circulation, and they are obligations of the United States Government. The issuance of United States notes is subject to limitations established by Congress. It established a statutory limitation of $300 million on the amount of United States notes authorized to be outstanding and in circulation. While this was a significant figure in Civil War days, it is now a very small fraction of the total currency in circulation in the United States.

Both United States notes and Federal Reserve notes are parts of our national currency and both are legal tender. They circulate as money in the same way. However, the issuing authority for them comes from different statutes. United States notes were redeemable in gold until 1933, when the United States abandoned the gold standard. Since then, both currencies have

---

♣ It's A Fact!!
Circulation Of Money

The amount of cash in circulation in the United States increased dramatically during the 20th century, as shown in Table 2.1. (Figures are from statements published by the Treasury Department.)

Table 2.1. Cash In Circulation

Date	Amount Of Cash In Circulation	Amount Of Cash Per Capita*
June 30, 1910	$3,148,700,000	$34.07
June 30, 1920	$5,698,214,612	$53.18
June 30, 1930	$4,521,987,962	$36.74
June 30, 1940	$7,847,501,324	$59.40
June 30, 1950	$27,156,290,042	$179.03
June 30, 1960	$32,064,619,064	$177.47
June 30, 1970	$54,350,971,661	$265.39
June 30, 1980	$127,097,192,148	$570.51
June 30, 1990	$266,902,367,798	$1,062.86
June 30, 2000	$571,121,194,344	$2,075.63

*In the United States

How Money Circulates: The Treasury Department ships new paper money and coins to the Federal Reserve Banks; the Reserve Banks pay it out to commercial banks, savings and loan associations, and other depository institutions. Customers of these institutions withdraw cash as they need it. Once people spend their cash at department stores, grocery stores, and so on, most of this money is eventually redeposited in depository institutions. As notes wear out or become dirty or damaged, depository institutions redeposit them at the Reserve Banks.

served essentially the same purpose, and have had the same value. Because United States notes serve no function that is not already adequately served by Federal Reserve notes, their issuance was discontinued, and none have been placed in to circulation since January 21, 1971.

When Money Wears Out: Money wears out from handling and is sometimes accidentally damaged or destroyed. The average life span of a $1 bill, for example, is about 18 months. The $10 bill has about the same life span. For a $5 bill the average life is 15 months, and for a $20, two years. The $50 and $100 notes don't circulate as often as the smaller denominations, so they last longer—the $50 bill, about five years, and the $100, eight and a half years. The average life of a coin is 25 years.

Banks send old, worn, torn, or soiled notes to a Federal Reserve Bank to be exchanged for new bills. The Reserve Banks sort the money they receive from commercial banks to determine if it is "fit" or "unfit." Fit (reusable) money is stored in their vaults until it goes out again through the commercial banking system. Reserve Banks destroy unfit currency and return damaged and worn coins to the Treasury.

Redeeming Damaged Money: Paper money that has been mutilated or partially destroyed may in some cases be redeemable at full face value. Any badly soiled, defaced, torn, or worn-out currency that is clearly more than half of the original note can be exchanged at a commercial bank, which processes the note through a Federal Reserve Bank. More seriously damaged notes—those with clearly less than half of the original surface or those requiring special examination to determine their value—must be sent to the Department of the Treasury for redemption.

The redemption value of mutilated coins depends on their type, denomination, and the extent of their mutilation. Redemption of mutilated coins is handled by the U.S. Mint in Philadelphia. Coins that are merely bent or worn slick through natural wear are not considered mutilated and are exchangeable at full face value.

Source: From "Dollars and Cents: Fundamental Facts About U.S. Money," 2006. Reprinted with permission from the Federal Reserve Bank of Atlanta, www.frbatlanta.org.

The Federal Reserve Act of 1913 authorized the production and circulation of Federal Reserve notes. Although the Bureau of Engraving and Printing (BEP) prints these notes, they move into circulation through the Federal Reserve System. They are obligations of both the Federal Reserve System and the United States Government. On Federal Reserve notes, the seals and serial numbers appear in green.

What are Federal Reserve notes and how are they different from United States notes?

Federal Reserve notes are legal tender currency notes. The twelve Federal Reserve Banks issue them into circulation pursuant to the Federal Reserve Act of 1913. A commercial bank belonging to the Federal Reserve System can obtain Federal Reserve notes from the Federal Reserve Bank in its district whenever it wishes. It must pay for them in full, dollar for dollar, by drawing down its account with its district Federal Reserve Bank.

Federal Reserve Banks obtain the notes from our Bureau of Engraving and Printing (BEP). It pays the BEP for the cost of producing the notes, which then become liabilities of the Federal Reserve Banks, and obligations of the United States Government.

Congress has specified that a Federal Reserve Bank must hold collateral equal in value to the Federal Reserve notes that the Bank receives. This collateral is chiefly gold certificates and United States securities. This provides backing for the note issue. The idea was that if the Congress dissolved the Federal Reserve System, the United States would take over the notes (liabilities). This would meet the requirements of Section 411, but the government would also take over the assets, which would be of equal value. Federal Reserve notes represent a first lien on all the assets of the Federal Reserve Banks, and on the collateral specifically held against them.

Federal Reserve notes are not redeemable in gold, silver, or any other commodity, and receive no backing by anything This has been the case since 1933. The notes have no value for themselves, but for what they will buy. In another sense, because they are legal tender, Federal Reserve notes are "backed" by all the goods and services in the economy.

History Of U.S. Currency

1690: The Massachusetts Bay Colony, one of the Thirteen Original Colonies, issued the first paper money to cover costs of military expeditions. The practice of issuing paper notes spread to the other Colonies.

1739: Benjamin Franklin's printing firm in Philadelphia printed colonial notes with nature prints—unique raised impressions of patterns cast from actual leaves. This process added an innovative and effective counterfeit deterrent to notes, not completely understood until centuries later.

1764: Following years of restrictions on colonial paper currency, Britain finally ordered a complete ban on the issuance of paper money by the Colonies.

1775: The Continental Congress issued paper currency to finance the Revolutionary War. Continental currency was denominated in Spanish milled dollars. Without solid backing and easily counterfeited, the notes quickly lost their value, giving rise to the phrase "not worth a Continental."

1781: Congress chartered the Bank of North America in Philadelphia as the first national bank, creating it to support the financial operations of the fledgling government.

1785: Congress adopted the dollar as the money unit of the United States.

1791: Congress chartered the Bank of the United States for a 20-year period to serve as the U.S. Treasury's fiscal agent. The bank was the first to perform central bank functions for the government and operated until 1811, when Congress declined to renew the bank's charter. Recognizing that a central banking system was still necessary to meet the nation's financial needs, Congress chartered a second Bank of the United States in 1816 for another 20-year period.

1792: The Coinage Act of 1792 created the U.S. Mint and established a federal monetary system, set denominations for coins, and specified the value of each coin in gold, silver, or copper.

1861: The first general circulation of paper money by the federal government occurred in 1861. Pressed to finance the Civil War, Congress authorized the U.S. Treasury to issue non-interest-bearing Demand Notes. These notes acquired the nickname "greenback" because of their color. Today all U.S. currency issued since 1861 remains valid and redeemable at full face value.

1861: The first $10 notes were Demand Notes, issued in 1861 by the Treasury Department. A portrait of President Abraham Lincoln appeared on the face of the notes.

1862: By 1862, the design of U.S. currency incorporated fine-line engraving, intricate geometric lathework patterns, a Treasury seal, and engraved signatures

---

♣ It's A Fact!!
Types Of U.S. Paper Money

Currency In Circulation: More than 99 percent of the total dollar amount of paper money in circulation in the United States today is made up of Federal Reserve notes. The other small part of circulating currency consists of U.S. notes or legal tender notes still in circulation but no longer issued.

Federal Reserve notes are printed and issued in denominations of $1, $2, $5, $10, $20, $50, and $100. The $500, $1,000, $5,000, and $10,000 denominations have not been printed since 1946.

The Federal Reserve Act requires that adequate backing be pledged for all Federal Reserve notes in circulation. U.S. Treasury securities, acquired through open market operations, are the most important form of collateral and provide backing for most of the value of the currency in circulation. Some other types of collateral the Federal Reserve holds are gold certificates and certain eligible instruments such as notes, drafts, and bills of exchange.

The Federal Reserve System, established by Congress in 1913, issues Federal Reserve notes through its 12 Federal Reserve Districts. Every district has its main office in a major city, and all but two have branches in other large cities. Each district is designated by a number and the corresponding letter of the alphabet.

to aid in counterfeit deterrence. Since that time, the U.S. Treasury has continued to add features to thwart counterfeiting.

1863: Congress established a national banking system and authorized the U.S. Treasury to oversee the issuance of National Bank Notes. This system established Federal guidelines for chartering and regulating "national" banks and authorized those banks to issue national currency secured by the purchase of United States bonds.

1865: The United States Secret Service was established as a bureau of the Treasury for the purpose of controlling the counterfeiters whose activities were destroying the public's confidence in the nation's currency.

The Bureau of Engraving and Printing, a division of the U.S. Treasury Department, produces currency for the Federal Reserve System to replace damaged or worn notes or to support economic growth. Federal Reserve Banks issue currency according to the need in their districts. The district letter and number on the face of a note identify the issuing Reserve Bank.

Types No Longer Issued: Besides the denominations of U.S. notes, from $1 to $10,000, that were issued before 1929, several other types of U.S. paper money no longer issued have circulated within the past 75 years. National Bank notes were issued by national banks from 1863 to 1929. Gold certificates, authorized in 1865 and issued by the Treasury Department in exchange for gold coin and bullion, circulated until 1933. Silver certificates, authorized in 1878 and issued in exchange for silver dollars, accounted for nearly all of the $1 notes in circulation until November 1963, when the first $1 Federal Reserve notes were issued.

Source: From "Dollars and Cents: Fundamental Facts About U.S. Money," 2006. Reprinted with permission from the Federal Reserve Bank of Atlanta, www.frbatlanta.org.

1877: The Department of the Treasury's Bureau of Engraving and Printing began printing all U.S. currency.

1905: The last U.S. paper currency printed with background color was the $20 Gold Certificate, Series 1905, which had a golden tint and a red seal and serial number.

1913: The Federal Reserve Act of 1913 created the Federal Reserve as the nation's central bank and provided for a national banking system that was more responsive to the fluctuating financial needs of the country. The Federal Reserve Board issued new currency called Federal Reserve notes.

1914: The first $10 Federal Reserve notes were issued. These notes were larger than today's notes and featured a portrait of President Andrew Jackson on the face.

1929: The first sweeping change to affect the appearance of all paper money occurred in 1929. In an effort to lower manufacturing costs, all currency was reduced in size by about 30 percent. In addition, standardized designs were instituted for each denomination across all classes of currency, decreasing the number of different designs in circulation. This standardization made it easier for the public to distinguish between genuine and counterfeit notes.

1957: The use of the National Motto "In God We Trust" on all currency has been required by law since 1955. It first appeared on paper money with the issuance of the $1 Silver Certificates, Series 1957, and began appearing on Federal Reserve notes with the 1963 Series.

1990: A security thread and microprinting were introduced to deter counterfeiting by advanced copiers and printers. The features first appeared in Series 1990 $100 notes. By Series 1993, the features appeared on all denominations except $1 and $2 notes.

1996: In the first significant design change in 67 years, U.S. currency was redesigned to incorporate a series of new counterfeit deterrents. The new notes were issued beginning with the $100 note in 1996, followed by the $50 in 1997, the $20 in 1998 and the $10 and $5 notes in 2000. The Bureau of

Engraving and Printing announced that new designs would be undertaken every 7–10 years to stay ahead of currency counterfeiters.

2003: Protecting the security of the dollar against counterfeiting takes its place side-by-side with other homeland security efforts, as the U.S. Secret Service is integrated into the new U.S. Department of Homeland Security.

2003: To stay ahead of currency counterfeiters, the U.S. government announces new designs to be issued. For the first time since the Series 1905 $20 Gold Certificate, the new currency will feature subtle background colors, beginning with the new $20 note in October 2003. Different colors will be used for different denominations. This will help everyone—particularly those who are visually impaired—to tell denominations apart. The new $20 note features subtle background colors of green, peach, and blue, as well as images of the American eagle.

2004: The currency redesigns continue with the $50 note, which was issued on September 28, 2004. Similar to the redesigned $20 note, the new $50 note features subtle background colors and highlights historical symbols of Americana. Specific to the $50 note are background colors of blue and red and images of a waving American flag and a small metallic silver-blue star.

2006: A redesigned Series 2004A $10 note was issued on March 2, 2006. The "A" in the series designation indicates a change in some feature of the note, in this case, a change in the Treasurer's signature. Like the new $20 and $50 notes, the redesigned $10 note features subtle shades of color and Symbols of Freedom. Specific to the $10 note are background colors of orange, yellow, and red along with images of the Statue of Liberty's torch and the words "We the People" from the United States Constitution.

2006: On June 29, 2006, the U.S. government announced that it will redesign the $5 note as part of ongoing efforts to enhance the security of U.S. currency. The government currently expects the $5 note to be issued in early 2008.

Chapter 3

Banks, Thrifts, And Credit Unions

Banks And Our Economy

"Bank" is a term people use broadly to refer to many different types of financial institutions. What you think of as your "bank" may be a bank and trust company, a savings bank, a savings and loan association, or other depository institution.

What Is A Bank?

Banks are privately owned institutions that, generally, accept deposits and make loans. Deposits are money people leave in an institution with the understanding that they can get it back at any time or at an agreed-upon future time. A loan is money let out to a borrower to be generally paid back with interest. This action of taking deposits and making loans is called financial intermediation. A bank's business, however, does not end there.

Most people and businesses pay their bills with bank checking accounts, placing banks at the center of our payments system. Banks are the major source of consumer loans—loans for cars, houses, education—as well as main lenders to businesses, especially small businesses.

Banks are often described as our economy's engine, in part because of these functions, but also because of the major role banks play as instruments of the government's monetary policy.

How Banks Create Money

Banks can't lend out all the deposits they collect, or they wouldn't have funds to pay out to depositors. Therefore, they keep primary and secondary reserves. Primary reserves are cash, deposits due from other banks, and the reserves required by the Federal Reserve System. Secondary reserves are securities banks purchase, which may be sold to meet short-term cash needs. These securities are usually government bonds. Federal law sets requirements for the percentage of deposits a bank must keep on reserve, either at the local Federal Reserve Bank or in its own vault. Any money a bank has on hand after it meets its reserve requirement is its excess reserves.

It's the excess reserves that create money. This is how it works (using a theoretical 20% reserve requirement): You deposit $500 in YourBank. YourBank keeps $100 of it to meet its

♣ It's A Fact!!
A Short History

The first American banks appeared early in the 18th century, to provide currency to colonists who needed a means of exchange. Originally, banks only made loans and issued notes for money deposited. Checking accounts appeared in the mid-19th century, the first of many new bank products and services developed through the state banking system. Today banks offer credit cards, automatic teller machines, NOW [negotiable order of withdrawal] accounts, individual retirement accounts, home equity loans, and a host of other financial services.

In today's evolving financial services environment, many other financial institutions provide some traditional banking functions. Banks compete with credit unions, financing companies, investment banks, insurance companies and many other financial services providers. While some claim that banks are becoming obsolete, banks still serve vital economic goals. They continue to evolve to meet the changing needs of their customers, as they have for the past two hundred years. If banks did not exist, we would have to invent them.

reserve requirement, but lends $400 to Ms. Smith. She uses the money to buy a car. The Sav-U-Mor Car Dealership deposits $400 in its account at TheirBank. TheirBank keeps $80 of it on reserve, but can lend out the other $320 as its own excess reserves. When that money is lent out, it becomes a deposit in a third institution, and the cycle continues. Thus, in this example, your original $500 becomes $1,220 on deposit in three different institutions. This phenomenon is called the multiplier effect. The size of the multiplier depends on the amount of money banks must keep on reserve.

The Federal Reserve can contract or expand the money supply by raising or lowering banks' reserve requirements. Banks themselves can contract the money supply by increasing their own reserves to guard against loan losses or to meet sudden cash demands. A sharp increase in bank reserves, for any reason, can create a "credit crunch" by reducing the amount of money a bank has to lend.

How Banks Make Money

While public policy makers have long recognized the importance of banking to economic development, banks are privately owned, for-profit institutions. Banks are generally owned by stockholders; the stockholders' stake in the bank forms most of its equity capital, a bank's ultimate buffer against losses. At the end of the year, a bank pays some or all of its profits to its shareholders in the form of dividends. The bank may retain some of its profits to add to its capital. Stockholders may also choose to reinvest their dividends in the bank.

Banks earn money in three ways:

- They make money from what they call the spread, or the difference between the interest rate they pay for deposits and the interest rate they receive on the loans they make.

- They earn interest on the securities they hold.

- They earn fees for customer services, such as checking accounts, financial counseling, loan servicing and the sales of other financial products (for example, insurance and mutual funds).

Banks earn an average of just over 1% of their assets (loans and securities) every year. This figure is commonly referred to as a bank's "return on assets," or ROA.

Banks And Public Policy

Our government's earliest leaders struggled over the shape of our banking system. They knew that banks have considerable financial power. Should this power be concentrated in a few institutions, they asked, or shared by many? Alexander Hamilton argued strongly for one central bank; that idea troubled Thomas Jefferson, who believed that local control was the only way to restrain banks from becoming financial monsters.

We've tried both ways, and our current system seems to be a compromise. It allows for a multitude of banks, both large and small. Both the federal and state governments issue bank charters for "public need and convenience," and regulate banks to ensure that they meet those needs. The Federal Reserve controls the money supply at a national level; the nation's individual banks facilitate the flow of money in their respective communities.

Since banks hold government-issued charters and generally belong to the federal Bank Insurance Fund, state and federal governments have considered banks as instruments of broad financial policy beyond money supply. Governments encourage or require different types of lending; for instance, they enforce nondiscrimination policies by requiring equal opportunity lending. They promote economic development by requiring lending or investment in banks' local communities, and by deciding where to issue new bank charters. Using banks to accomplish economic policy goals requires a constant balancing of banks' needs against the needs of the community. Banks must be profitable to stay in business, and a failed bank doesn't meet anyone's needs.

Banks, Thrifts, And Credit Unions—What's The Difference?

There are three major types of depository institutions in the United States. They are commercial banks, thrifts (which include savings and loan associations and savings banks), and credit unions.

These three types of institutions have become more like each other in recent decades, and their unique identities have become less distinct. They still differ, however, in specialization and emphasis, and in their regulatory and supervisory structures.

Commercial banks are the traditional "department stores" of the financial services world. Thrift institutions and credit unions are more like specialty shops that, over time, have expanded their lines of business to better compete for market share.

Commercial Banks

Commercial banks are generally stock corporations whose principal obligation is to make a profit for their shareholders. Basically, banks receive deposits, and hold them in a variety of different accounts, extend credit through loans and other instruments, and facilitate the movement of funds. While commercial banks mostly specialize in short-term business credit, they also make consumer loans and mortgages, and have a broad range of financial powers. Their corporate charters and the powers granted to them under state and federal law determine the range of their activities.

States and the federal government each issue bank charters. State-chartered banks operate under state supervision and, if they fail, are closed under provisions of state as well as federal law. National banks are chartered and regulated by the Office of the Comptroller of the Currency (OCC), a division of the Treasury Department. Banks can choose between a state or a federal charter when starting their business, and can also convert from one charter to another after having been in business. Commercial banks receive deposit insurance from the Federal Deposit Insurance Corporation (FDIC) through the Bank Insurance Fund (BIF). All national banks, and some state-chartered banks, are members of the Federal Reserve System.

Savings And Loans/Savings Banks

Savings and loan associations and savings banks specialize in real estate lending, particularly loans for single-family homes and other residential properties. They can be owned by shareholders ("stock" ownership) or by their depositors and borrowers ("mutual" ownership). These institutions are referred to as "thrifts," because they originally offered only savings accounts, or time deposits. Over the past two decades, however, they have acquired a wide range of financial powers, and now offer checking accounts (demand deposits) and make business and consumer loans as well as mortgages.

Both savings and loan associations and savings banks may be chartered by either the federal Office of Thrift Supervision (OTS) or by a state government regulator. Generally, savings and loan associations are insured by the Savings Association Insurance Fund (SAIF), and savings banks are insured by the Bank Insurance Fund (BIF).

Savings institutions must hold a certain percentage of their loan portfolio in housing-related assets to retain their charter, as well as their membership in the Federal Home Loan Bank System. This is called the "qualified thrift lender" (QTL) test. Savings institutions must maintain 65% of their portfolio in housing-related or other qualified assets to maintain their status. Recent liberalization of the QTL test has allowed thrifts to use some non-housing assets to meet this requirement.

The number of thrifts declined dramatically in the late 1980s and early 1990s. The savings and loan crisis of the 1980s forced many institutions to close or merge with others, at an extraordinary cost to the federal government. However, there has been a resurgence of interest in the thrift charter in recent years. The recapitalization of the thrift fund, a revitalized industry and legislative changes have made the charter—once thought doomed to extinction—an appealing route to financial modernization for some. Due to liberalization of the qualified thrift lender test, many insurance companies and securities firms, as well as commercial firms, are now able to qualify as unitary thrift holding companies and to own depository institutions, bypassing prohibitions in the Glass Steagall Act and the Bank Holding Company Act. Critics of a revitalized thrift charter have said that it has advantaged a certain class of financial institutions, highlighting the need for broader financial modernization through federal legislation.

Credit Unions

Credit unions are cooperative financial institutions, formed by groups of people with a "common bond." These groups of people pool their funds to form the institution's deposit base; the group owns and controls the institution together. Membership in a credit union is not open to the general public, but is restricted to people who share the common bond of the group that created the credit union. Examples of this common bond are working for the same

✤ It's A Fact!!

Credit unions were first chartered in the U.S. in 1909, at the state level. The federal government began to charter credit unions in 1934 under the Farm Credit Association, and created the National Credit Union Administration (NCUA) in 1970. States and the federal government continue to charter credit unions; almost all credit unions are insured by the National Credit Union Share Insurance Fund, which is controlled by the NCUA.

employer, belonging to the same church or social group, or living in the same community. Credit unions are nonprofit institutions that seek to encourage savings and make excess funds within a community available at low cost to their members.

Credit unions accept deposits in a variety of accounts. All credit unions offer savings accounts, or time deposits; the larger institutions also offer checking and money market accounts. Credit unions' financial powers have expanded to include almost anything a bank or savings association can do, including making home loans, issuing credit cards, and even making some commercial loans. Credit unions are exempt from federal taxation and sometimes receive subsidies, in the form of free space or supplies, from their sponsoring organizations.

Banks And Their Regulators

Bank regulation, or supervision, involves four federal agencies and fifty state agencies. At first glance this regulatory scheme seems hopelessly complicated, but it's not that hard to understand once you know what each agency does.

State And Federal Charters

You may have seen or heard the term "dual banking system." This refers to the fact that both states and the federal government issue bank charters for the need and convenience of their citizens. The Office of the Comptroller of the Currency (OCC) charters national banks; the state banking departments charter state banks. In addition, the Office of Thrift Supervision (OTS) charters federal savings banks and savings associations. The words "national," "federal" or "state" in a institution's name have nothing to do with where it operates; rather they refer to the type of charter the bank holds.

Chartering agencies ensure that new banks have the necessary capital and management expertise to meet the public's financial needs. The charterer is an institution's primary regulator, with front-line duty to protect the public from unsafe and unsound banking practices. Chartering agencies conduct on-site examinations to assess banks' condition and monitor compliance with banking laws. They issue regulations, take enforcement actions, and close banks if they fail.

The Deposit Insurer

The Federal Deposit Insurance Corporation (FDIC) insures the deposits of banks up to a maximum of $100,000 per account holder. All states

---

♣ It's A Fact!!

How did we get so many regulators?

Many people have said that we would never design our current regulatory system as it is if we were starting from scratch. But our current system has evolved with the country and has changed with the country's needs.

The states were the first to charter banks in the United States. The Federal government chartered the First and Second Banks of the United States in the early 19th century. These were the first national banks, and they performed functions similar to today's Federal Reserve System. From 1837, when the Second Bank's charter expired, to 1863 there were no national banks and no federal regulators.

The National Bank Act of 1863 created the Office of the Comptroller of the Currency, and authorized it to charter national banks. The original purpose of both the OCC and national banks was to circulate a universal currency, thus making tax collection easier and helping to finance the Civil War. The dual banking system took shape in the late 19th century as states reformed their chartering policies and regulatory systems in response to the National Bank Act.

A series of money shortages early in the 20th century made it clear that the country needed some central authority to monitor and control the money supply. The Federal Reserve Act of 1913 established this authority through a network of twelve Federal Reserve Banks, overseen by a Board of Governors. The Federal Reserve System had regulatory authority over all its member banks; this was the first time a federal agency had direct authority over state-chartered banks, although state bank membership in the Federal Reserve was voluntary.

require newly chartered state banks to join the FDIC before they can accept deposits from the public. Under the 1991 Federal Deposit Insurance Corporation Improvement Act (FDICIA), both state-chartered and national banks must apply to the FDIC for deposit insurance; previously, national banks had received insurance automatically with their new charters.

The FDIC is the federal regulator of the approximately 5,000 state-chartered banks that do not belong to the Federal Reserve System. It cooperates with state banking departments to supervise and examine these banks, and has considerable authority to intervene to prevent unsafe and unsound banking

The FDIC was created by the Banking Act of 1933 in response to the avalanche of bank failures that followed the stock market crash of 1929. The FDIC originally insured deposits up to $5,000. The 1933 Banking Act required all state-chartered banks to join the Federal Reserve within a certain period of time or lose their deposit insurance, but this requirement was eventually repealed. The FDIC established its own standards for state nonmember bank acceptance into the fund.

Bank holding companies were new corporate entities that began appearing in the 1940s. The banks were all regulated, but no one regulated the holding company subsidiaries that weren't banks, and no one watched the flow of resources among affiliates within the holding company. The Bank Holding Company Act of 1956 gave the Federal Reserve regulatory responsibility for these companies, while leaving the supervision of banks within holding companies in the hands of their traditional regulators.

In 1989, the Financial Institutions Reform, Recovery, and Enforcement Act (FIRREA) expanded the FDIC's supervisory and enforcement authority, and extended its responsibilities to include the thrift deposit insurance role held by the former Federal Savings and Loan Insurance Corporation (FSLIC).

Most recently, 1991's FDICIA also expanded the authority of federal regulators to intervene in troubled institutions. FDICIA also mandated specific enforcement actions for unhealthy institutions—the first time prescribed "early intervention" provisions had been included in federal statutes.

practices. The FDIC also has backup examination and regulatory authority over national and Fed-member banks.

The FDIC deals with failed institutions by either liquidating them or selling the institutions to redeem insured deposits.

The Central Bank

The Federal Reserve System ("the Fed") controls the flow of money in and out of banks by raising or lowering its requirements for bank reserves and by buying and selling federal securities. It lends money to banks at low interest rates (the "discount rate") to help banks meet their short-term liquidity needs, and is known as the "lender of last resort" for banks experiencing liquidity crises. Together, the FDIC and the Federal Reserve form the federal safety net that protects depositors when banks fail.

Membership in the Federal Reserve System is required for national banks and is optional for state banks. While many large state banks

> ✔ **Quick Tip**
> You can find more deposit insurance information at the Federal Deposit Insurance Corporation (FDIC) website, http://www.fdic.gov.

have become Fed members, most state banks have chosen not to join. The Federal Reserve is the federal regulator of about 1,000 state-chartered member banks and cooperates with state bank regulators to supervise these institutions.

The Federal Reserve also regulates all bank holding companies. Its regulatory focus is not so much on the banks within a holding company as on the umbrella structure of the holding company itself. Holding companies must apply to the Federal Reserve to acquire new subsidiaries or to engage in new activities. The Fed monitors the capital condition and general financial health of holding companies, and may take enforcement actions against them. The Federal Reserve is also responsible for federal oversight of foreign banks operating in the United States.

Chapter 4

What Determines Interest Rates?

Interest rates can significantly influence people's behavior. When rates decline, home owners rush to buy new homes and refinance old mortgages, automobile buyers scramble to buy new cars, the stock market soars, and people tend to feel more optimistic about the future.

But even though individuals respond to changes in rates, they may not fully understand what interest rates represent, or how different rates relate to each other. Why, for example, do interest rates increase or decrease? And in a period of changing rates, why are certain rates higher, while others are lower?

Levels Of Interest

The Price Of Credit

To understand the economic forces that drive (and sometimes are driven by) interest rates, we first need to define interest rates. An interest rate is a price, and like any other price, it relates to a transaction or the transfer of a good or service between a buyer and a seller. This special type of transaction is a loan or credit transaction, involving a supplier of surplus funds (that is, a lender or saver) and a demander of surplus funds (that is, a borrower).

About This Chapter: Reprinted from "Points of Interest: What Determines Interest Rates?" an online financial education publication of the Federal Reserve Bank of Chicago, http://www.chicagofed.org, 2006.

In a loan transaction, the borrower receives funds to use for a period of time, and the lender receives the borrower's promise to pay at some time in the future.

The borrower receives the benefit of the immediate use of funds. The lender, on the other hand, gives up the immediate use of funds, forgoing any current goods or services those funds could purchase. In other words, lenders loan funds they have saved—surplus funds they do not need for purchasing goods or services today.

Because these lenders/savers sacrifice the immediate use of funds, they ask for compensation in addition to the repayment of the funds loaned. This compensation is interest, the price the borrower must pay for the immediate use of the lender's funds. Put more simply, interest rates are the price of credit.

✎ What's It Mean?

Bonds: Loans that investors make to corporations or governments. It is a type of investment where the issuer (the corporation or government) pays a specified amount of interest on a regular basis, plus the full value of the loan when it matures.

Collateral: Property you pledge to guarantee somebody you'll pay back money that you borrow. If you don't pay back the money, the lender can take your collateral property.

Consumer Price Index: A number to show the price of a imaginary basket of goods that tells if the price of things we buy is getting more expensive (inflation) or getting less expensive (deflation).

Interest: A charge for borrowing money. Usually a percentage of the amount owed.

Risk: The possibility of loss.

Yield: The rate at which money you invest grows over time. Yield is usually expressed in terms of how much interest your investment earns in a year.

Source: Source: © 2007 Government National Mortgage Association (Ginnie Mae). The Home Zone. http://www.ginniemae.gov/homezone/index.html. Reprinted with permission.

Supply And Demand

Remember!!

As the demand for credit increases, interest rates rise. As the supply for credit increases, interest rates fall.

Source: Federal Reserve Bank of Chicago, 2006.

As with any other price in our market economy, interest rates are determined by the forces of supply and demand, in this case, the supply of and demand for credit. If the supply of credit from lenders rises relative to the demand from borrowers, the price (interest rate) will tend to fall as lenders compete to find use for their funds. If the demand rises relative to the supply, the interest rate will tend to rise as borrowers compete for increasingly scarce funds. The principal source of the demand for credit comes from our desire for current spending and investment opportunities.

The principal source of the supply of credit comes from savings, or the willingness of people, firms, and governments to delay spending. Depository institutions such as banks, thrifts, and credit unions, as well as the Federal Reserve, play important roles in influencing the supply of credit.

Let's examine these sources.

The Source Of Demand

Consumption: At one time or another, virtually all consumers, businesses, and governments demand credit to purchase goods and services for current use. In these loans, borrowers agree to pay interest to a lender/saver because they prefer to have the goods or services now, rather than waiting until some time in the future when, presumably, they would have saved enough for the purchase. To describe this preference for current consumption, economists say that borrowers have a high rate of time preference. Expressed simply, people with high rates of time preference prefer to purchase goods now, rather than wait to purchase future goods—an automobile now rather than an automobile at some time in the future, a current vacation opportunity rather than a future opportunity, and present goods or services rather than those in the future.

Although lenders/savers generally have lower rates of time preference than borrowers, they too tend to prefer current goods and services. As a result, they ask for the payment of interest to encourage the sacrifice of immediate consumption. As a lender/saver, for example, one would prefer not to spend $100 now only if the money was not needed for a current purchase and one could receive more than $100 in the future.

Investment: In the use of funds for investment, on the other hand, time preference is not the sole factor. Here consumers, businesses, and governments borrow funds only if they have an opportunity they believe will earn more—that is, create a larger income stream—than they will have to pay on the loan, or than they will receive in some other activity.

Say, for example, a widget manufacturer sees an opportunity to purchase a new machine that can reasonably be expected to earn a 20 percent return (that is, produce income from the manufacture of widgets equal to 20 percent of the cost of the machine). The manufacturer will borrow funds only if they can be obtained at an interest rate less than 20 percent.

What borrowers are willing to pay, then, depends principally on time preferences for current consumption and on the expected rate of return on an investment.

The Source Of Supply

The supply of credit comes from savings—funds not needed or used for current consumption. When we think of savings, most of us think of money in savings accounts, but this is only part of total savings.

All funds not currently used to purchase goods and services are part of total savings. For example, insurance premiums,

☞ Remember!!

Savings includes all funds not currently used to purchase goods and services. This includes savings accounts, but it also includes money in checking accounts, insurance premiums, pension fund contributions, stocks and bonds, and social security contributions.

Source: Federal Reserve Bank of Chicago, 2006.

♣ It's A Fact!!
Banks And Deposit Creation

Depository institutions, which for simplicity we will call banks, are different from other financial institutions because they offer transaction accounts and make loans by lending deposits. This deposit creation activity, essentially creating money, affects interest rates because these deposits are part of savings, the source of the supply of credit.

Banks create deposits by making loans. Rather than handing cash to borrowers, banks simply increase balances in borrowers' checking accounts. Borrowers can then draw checks to pay for goods and services. This creation of checking accounts through loans is just as much a deposit as one we might make by pushing a ten-dollar bill through the teller's window.

With all of the nation's banks able to increase the supply of credit in this fashion, credit could conceivably expand without limit. Preventing such uncontrolled expansion is one of the jobs of the Federal Reserve System (the Fed), our central bank and monetary authority. The Fed has the responsibility of monitoring and influencing the total supply of money and credit.

Source: Federal Reserve Bank of Chicago, 2006.

---

contributions to pension funds and social security, funds set aside to purchase stocks and bonds, and even funds in our checking accounts are savings.

Since most of us use funds in checking accounts to pay for current consumption, we may not consider them savings. However, funds in checking accounts at any time are considered savings until we transfer them out to pay for goods and services.

Most of us keep our savings in financial institutions—like insurance companies and brokerage houses—and in depository institutions, such as banks, savings and loan associations, credit unions, and mutual savings banks. These financial institutions then pool the savings and make them available to people who want to borrow.

This process is called financial intermediation. This process of bringing together borrowers and lenders/savers is one of the most important roles that financial institutions perform.

The General Level Of Rates

The general level of interest rates is determined by the interaction of the supply and demand for credit. When supply and demand interact, they determine a price (the equilibrium price) that tends to be relatively stable. However, we have seen that the price of credit is not necessarily stable, implying that something shifts the supply, the demand, or both. Let's examine several factors that influence these shifts.

Expected Inflation: As we have already seen, interest rates state the rate at which borrowers must pay future dollars to receive current dollars. Borrowers and lenders, however, are not as concerned about dollars, present or future, as they are about the goods and services those dollars can buy, the purchasing power of money.

Inflation reduces the purchasing power of money. Each percentage point increase in inflation represents approximately a 1 percent decrease in the quantity of real goods and services that can be purchased with a given number of dollars in the future. As a result, lenders, seeking to protect their purchasing power, add the expected rate of inflation to the interest rate they demand. Borrowers are willing to pay this higher rate because they expect inflation to enable them to repay the loan with cheaper dollars.

If lenders expect, for example, an eight percent inflation rate for the coming year and otherwise desire a four percent return on their loan, they would likely charge borrowers 12 percent, the so-called nominal interest rate (an eight percent inflation premium plus a four percent "real" rate).

Borrowers and lenders tend to base their inflationary expectations on past experiences which they project into the future. When they have experienced inflation for a long time, they gradually build the inflation premium into their rates. Once people come to expect a certain level of inflation, they may have to experience a fairly long period at a different rate of inflation before they are willing to change the inflation premium.

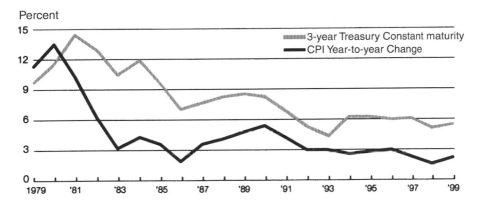

Figure 4.1. Effect of Inflation Premium.

The effect of an inflation premium can be seen in Figure 4.1. Although the chart tracks the consumer price index or CPI and the constant maturity 3-year Treasury note rate, one could use almost any inflation measure and interest rate and see a similar pattern. As inflation rose through the late 1970s, it came to be "expected" by lenders as well as borrowers. This "inflation expectation" can be seen by the fact that investors in Treasury notes were demanding a relatively high inflation premium in the early 1980s, even after inflation reached its apex. This was partially due to the fact that relatively high levels of inflation were fresh in the memories of borrowers and lenders, and there was uncertainty as to how serious policy makers would be in pursuing lower levels of inflation. In 1984, for example, it took only a slight increase in inflation to cause a relatively rapid increase in interest rates.

For most of the 1980s, inflation was relatively low and interest rates continued their downward trend with the gap between rates and inflation narrowing. As the memory of high inflation receded, so did pressure for a high inflation premium, as indicated by the relatively modest rise in rates when inflation flared in 1990. Inflationary expectations had been reduced, a goal sought by many monetary policy makers. Indeed, former Fed Chairman Alan Greenspan has stated that price stability would be achieved when the expectation of future price changes plays no role in the decision making of businesses and households.

Economic Conditions: All businesses, governmental bodies, and households that borrow funds affect the demand for credit. This demand tends to vary with general economic conditions.

When economic activity is expanding and the outlook appears favorable, consumers demand substantial amounts of credit to finance homes, automobiles, and other major items, as well as to increase current consumption. With this positive outlook, they expect higher incomes and as a result are generally more willing to take on future obligations. Businesses are also optimistic and seek funds to finance the additional production, plants, and equipment needed to supply this increased consumer demand. All of this makes for a relative scarcity of funds, due to increased demand.

> ✔ **Quick Tip**
>
> To help understand inflation, consider that an ice cream cone may have cost a nickel in 1945. That same cone may have cost 95 cents in 1995. The increase in price is due to inflation. What do you think an ice cream cone will cost in 2045?
>
> Source: Federal Reserve Bank of Chicago, 2006.

On the other hand, when sales are sluggish and the future looks grim, consumers and businesses tend to reduce their major purchases, and lenders, concerned about the repayment ability of prospective borrowers, become reluctant to lend. As a result, both the supply of and demand for credit may fall. Unless they both fall by the same amount, interest rates are affected.

Federal Reserve Actions: As we have seen, the Fed acts to influence the availability of money and credit by adjusting the level and/or price of bank reserves. The Fed affects reserves in three ways: by setting reserve requirements that banks must hold, as we discussed earlier; by buying and selling government securities (usually U.S. Treasury bonds) in open market operations; and by setting the "discount rate," which affects the price of reserves banks borrow from the Fed through the "discount window."

These "tools" of monetary policy influence the supply of credit, but do not directly impact the demand for credit. Because the Fed directly affects only one side of the supply and demand relationship, it cannot totally control interest rates. Nevertheless, monetary policy clearly does affect the general level of interest rates.

Fiscal Policy: Federal, state, and local governments, through their fiscal policy actions of taxation and spending, can affect either the supply of or the demand for credit. If a governmental unit spends less than it takes in from taxes and other sources of revenue, as many have in recent years, it runs a budget surplus, meaning the government has savings. As we have seen, savings are the source of the supply of credit. On the other hand, if a governmental unit spends more than it takes in, it runs a budget deficit, and must borrow to make up the difference. The borrowing increases the demand for credit, contributing to higher interest rates in general.

Interest Rate Predictions

The level of interest rates influences people's behavior by affecting economic decisions that determine the well-being of the nation: how much people are willing to save and how much businesses are willing to invest.

With so many important decisions based on the level of interest rates, it is not surprising that people want to know which way rates are going to move. However, with so many diverse elements influencing rates, it is also not surprising that people are not able to predict the direction of these movements precisely.

☞ Remember!!

Even though we are not able to predict accurately and consistently how interest rates will move, these movements are clearly not random. To the contrary, they are strictly controlled by the most calculating master of all—the economic forces of the market.

Source: Federal Reserve Bank of Chicago, 2006.

Different Interests

As we have seen, certain factors affect the general level of interest rates. But why do the rates vary for different transactions? For example, on a typical day at a local financial institution, a lending officer might approve a $20,000 loan to the local school board for emergency repairs on the school's furnace and charge the board 8 percent interest for the use of the funds. Later, the banker might approve a used-car loan for $4,000, at 11 percent interest, to be paid in three years, and a small business loan for $17,000, at 8.5 percent interest, for a term of four years.

Meanwhile, the bank's investment officer submits a bid for a two-year Treasury note on which the bank wants to receive 6 percent interest, and purchases a 15-year general obligation municipal bond issued by the local city government. The bank will receive 8 percent interest on this bond. At the next desk, the new accounts officer opens an interest-paying checking account, which will pay a customer 1.5 percent interest.

Credit Transactions

As different as all these transactions may at first appear, they are the same in one respect—they all involve borrowing and lending funds. Each transaction has a lender, who exchanges funds for an asset in the form of an IOU or credit, and a borrower who exchanges the IOU for funds. Because credit, the IOU, is being bought and sold, these are called credit transactions. Most of us can easily see that the loan officer is providing credit—the bank is lending money to the school board, the person buying the used car, and the businessperson.

The other transactions are also credit transactions, although we generally think of them in different terms. We usually refer to the purchase of a Treasury note or a municipal bond as making an investment, but they are credit transactions because the bank is loaning money to the federal and city governments. By investing in the note and bond, the bank makes funds available directly to the government (or indirectly by replacing the previous holder of the government's debt). The bank, in return, receives interest payments from the government.

> ### ♣ It's A Fact!!
>
> Some of the most important factors that cause interest rates to differ include the following:
>
> • Different levels and kinds of risk
>
> • Different rights granted to borrowers and lenders
>
> • Different tax considerations
>
> Source: Federal Reserve Bank of Chicago, 2006.

When the new accounts officer opened the checking account for the customer, the bank gained the use of funds. This, too, is a credit transaction in which the customer is the lender and the bank is the borrower. To compensate for the use of funds, the bank pays interest.

Degrees Of Interest

Although all the transactions at the bank that morning were credit transactions, they all involved different interest rates, different prices of credit. As with other prices in a free market system, interest rates are determined by many factors. As we've seen, some factors are more or less the same for all credit transactions. General economic conditions, for example, cause all interest rates to move in the same direction over time.

Other factors vary for different kinds of credit transactions, causing their interest rates to differ at any one time. Some of the most important of these factors are different levels and kinds of risk, different rights granted to borrowers and lenders, and different tax considerations. Let's examine each of these.

Levels Of Risk

Risk refers to the chance that something unfavorable may happen. If you go skydiving, the risks you assume are obvious. When you purchase a financial asset, say by lending funds to a corporation by purchasing one of its bonds, you also take a risk—a financial risk. Something unfavorable could happen to your money—you could lose all of it if the company issuing the security goes bankrupt, or you could lose part of it if the asset's price goes down and you have to sell before maturity.

Different people are willing to accept different levels of risk. Some people will not go skydiving under any circumstances, while others will go at the drop of a hat. In credit transactions, too, people are willing to accept different levels of risk. However, most people risk are averse; that is, they prefer not to increase risks with their money unless they receive increased compensation.

To illustrate, let's say we have a choice of buying two debt securities, which are bonds or IOUs issued by corporations or governments seeking to borrow funds. One security pays (meaning, we will receive) a certain five percent interest, while the other has a 50 percent chance of paying eight percent interest and a 50 percent chance of paying two percent. Which security should we buy? If we are risk averse investors/lenders, we would choose the security paying the certain five percent, because would not view the uncertain return on the second security as an advantage.

If, on the other hand, the second security has a 50 percent chance paying 15 percent interest and 50 percent chance of paying two percent, we might be inclined to buy it because we might consider the higher potential return to be worth the risk.

Even though lenders are willing to accept different levels of risk, they want to be compensated for taking the risk. Therefore, as securities differ in level of risk, their interest rates tend to differ. Generally, interest rates on debt securities are affected by three kinds of risk:

- default risk
- liquidity risk
- maturity risk

Default Risk

For any number of reasons, even the most well-intentioned borrowers may not be able to make interest payments or repay borrowed funds on time. If borrowers do not make timely payments, they are said to have defaulted on loans. When borrowers do not make interest payments, lenders' returns (the interest they receive) are reduced or wiped out completely; when borrowers do not repay all or part of the principal, the lenders' return is actually negative.

All loans are subject to default risk since borrowers may die, go bankrupt, or be faced with unforeseen problems that prevent payments. Of course, default risk varies with different people and companies; nevertheless, no one is free from risk of default.

While investors/lenders accept this risk when they loan funds, they prefer to reduce the risk. As a result, many borrowers are compelled to secure their loans; meaning, they give the lender some assurances against default. Frequently, these assurances are in the form of collateral, some physical object the lender can possess and then sell in the event of default. For automobile loans, for example, the car usually serves as collateral. Other assurances could include a cosigner, another person willing to make payment if the original borrower defaults. Generally speaking, because secured loans are comparatively less risky, they carry a lower interest rate than unsecured loans.

As a borrower, the federal government offers firm assurances against default. As a result of the power to tax and authority to coin money, payments of principal and interest on loans made to (or securities purchased from) the U.S. government are, for all practical purposes, never in doubt, making U.S. government securities virtually default-risk free. Since investors tend to be risk averse and U.S. government securities are all but free from default risk, they generally carry a lower interest rate than securities from corporations.

Similarly, other types of borrowers represent different levels of risk to the lender. In each case, the lender needs to evaluate what are commonly called "the three Cs" of character, capital, and capacity. Character represents the borrower's history with previous loans. A history containing bankruptcies, repossessions, consistently late or missed payments, and court judgments may indicate a higher risk potential for the lender. Capital represents current financial condition. Is the borrower currently debt-free, or relatively so in comparison with assets? They may represent a party with "thrifty" habits, who can take on additional debt without imposing an undue burden on other assets. Capacity represents the future ability to service the loan (that is, make principal and interest payments). Income, job stability, regular promotions, and raises are all indicators to be considered.

Liquidity Risk

In addition to default risk, liquidity risk affects interest rates. If a security can be quickly sold at close to its original purchase price, it is highly liquid; meaning, it is less costly to convert into money than one that cannot be sold at a price close to its purchase price. Therefore, it is less risky than one with a wide spread between its purchase price and its selling price.

To illustrate, let's say that we have a choice between purchasing an infrequently traded security of an obscure company, and a broadly traded security of a well-known company, which we know we can sell easily at a price close to our purchase price. If we are risk averse, we would choose the security from the well-known company if both were paying the same interest rate.

To encourage us to buy its security, the obscure company must pay a higher rate to compensate us for the difficulty we will experience if we want to sell.

Maturity Risk

Credit transactions usually involve lending/borrowing funds for an agreed upon period of time. At the end of that time the loan is said to have matured and must be repaid. The length of maturity is a source of another kind of risk—maturity risk.

Long-term securities are subject to more risk than short-term securities because the future is uncertain and more problems can arise the longer the security is outstanding. These greater risks usually, but not always, result in higher rates for long-term securities than for short-term securities.

To illustrate, let's examine U.S. government securities—Treasury bills (with original maturities of one year or less), Treasury notes (with original maturities of two to ten years), and Treasury bonds (with original maturities of over ten years). These securities are quite similar, except in length of maturity. As we have seen, U.S. government securities are virtually default-risk free, and because there is such a large and active market for them, they are also virtually liquidity risk free.

If default and liquidity were the only kinds of risk in holding government securities, we would be inclined to think that they all would have the same interest rate. However, because of maturity risk, short-term Treasury bills usually pay less (have a lower interest rate) than longer-term Treasury notes and bonds.

♣ It's A Fact!!
Tax Considerations

In addition to the level and kinds of risk and the different rights granted by different debt securities, taxes also play a significant role in affecting rates of return.

To illustrate, let's say you borrow $1,000 for a year at 10 percent interest. At the end of the year, you pay the $1,000 principal plus $100 interest. However, if the lender is in a 25 percent tax bracket, the lender will pay $25 in taxes on that $100. Thus, the lender's actual after-tax yield is reduced from 10 percent to 7.5 percent.

Different debt securities carry different tax considerations. Corporate bonds (loans to corporations) are subject to local, state, and federal taxes. U.S. government securities are subject to federal taxes, but exempt from local and state taxes. Municipal bonds are exempt from federal taxes, and in some states, exempt from local taxes.

Taking taxes into consideration, a lender will receive more after-tax interest income from a municipal bond paying 10 percent than from a corporate bond paying the same rate. This special tax-exempt status of municipal bonds enables state and local governments to raise funds at a relatively lower interest cost.

On the other hand, for corporations to attract lenders, they must pay a higher rate of interest to compensate for taxes.

Source: Federal Reserve Bank of Chicago, 2006.

Different Rights

Risk is not the only reason credit transactions can have different rates of interest. As we have seen, certain assurances, such as securing loans, also affect rates. Typically, borrowers write these assurances into their debt securities specifying the rights of both borrower and lender. Because these rights differ, debt securities tend to pay different rates of interest. Let's look at some of these rights in the more common debt securities.

Coupon And Zero-Coupon Bonds: Most debt securities promise to repay the amount borrowed (the principal) at the end of the length of the loan and also pay interest at specified times, such as every six months, throughout the term of the loan. Some of these bonds are issued with attached coupons, which lenders can clip and send every six months or year to collect the interest that is due.

Zero-coupon bonds, however, make no interest payments throughout the life of the loan. Rather than pay interest, these bonds are sold at a price well below their stated face value. Although not usually thought of in such terms, a savings bond is like a zero-coupon bond in that it renders one payment at maturity.

Even though zero-coupon bonds make no interest payments, investors/lenders still need to know the return on these bonds so they can compare it to the return on a coupon bond or other alternative investment. To figure the return, or yield, investors compare the difference between their purchase price and selling price.

Since zero-coupon bonds provide lenders no compensation until the end of the loan period, borrowers issuing these bonds tend to pay a higher rate than borrowers issuing coupon bonds.

Convertible Bonds: Some borrowers sell bonds that can be converted into a fixed number of shares of common stock. With convertible bonds, a lender (bondholder) can become a part owner (stockholder) of the company by converting the bond into the company's stock. Because investors generally view this right as desirable, borrowers can sell convertible bonds at a lower interest rate than they would otherwise have to pay for a similar bond that was not convertible.

Call Provisions: Some bonds are callable after a specified date; that is, the borrower has the right to pay off part or all of it before the scheduled maturity date. Unlike convertible bonds which give certain rights to the lenders, call provisions give borrowers certain rights, the right to call the bond. As a result, borrowers must pay a higher interest rate than on similar securities without a call provision.

Of course, borrowers will call (redeem) only when it is to their benefit. For example, when the general level of interest rates falls, the borrower can call the bonds paying high rates of interest and reborrow funds at the lower rate.

As partial compensation to the lender, the borrower often has to pay a penalty to call a bond. Naturally, a borrower will call a bond only if the advantages of doing so outweigh the penalty. In other words, interest rates would have to fall sufficiently to compensate for the penalty before a borrower would call a bond.

Municipal Bonds: Municipal bonds are debt securities issued by local and state governments. Usually these governmental bodies issue either general obligation bonds or revenue bonds.

General obligation bonds, the more common type, are issued for a wide variety of reasons, such as building schools and providing social services. They are secured by the general taxing power of the issuing government.

Revenue bonds, on the other hand, are issued to finance a specific project—building a tollway, for example. The interest and principal are paid exclusively out of the receipts that the project generates.

Both kinds of municipal bonds are considered safe. However, because general obligation bonds are secured by the assets of the issuing government and the power of that government to tax, they are usually considered safer than revenue bonds, whose payments must come out of receipts of the specific project for which the bond is issued. As a result, general obligation bonds usually pay a lower rate of interest than revenue bonds.

Efficient Allocation

With so many different interest rates and so many different factors affecting them, it may seem that borrowing and lending would be hopelessly complicated and inefficient. In reality, however, the variety of interest rates reflects the efficiency of the market in allocating funds.

In analyzing investment opportunities, lenders look for an interest rate high enough to account for all their risks, rights, and taxes, as we have discussed. If the project will not pay that rate, they will look for other investments. For their part, borrowers will undertake only projects with returns high enough to cover at least the cost of borrowed funds.

The market, then, serves to assure that only worthwhile projects will be funded with borrowed funds. In other words, market forces and differences in interest rates work together to foster the efficient allocation of funds.

Chapter 5

Public Debt: When The Government Owes Money

Debt As An Asset

We all know what debt is when it is our own—we owe money to someone else. On the other hand, it may not be so easy to understand that many of our financial assets are someone else's debts. For example, to a consumer a savings account at a bank is an asset. However, to the bank it is a debt.

The bank owes us the money that is in our account. We let the bank hold the money for us because it promises to pay us back with interest. The bank then uses our money to make loans and to invest in other debt, including the government's.

Like the savings account, most of us think of the $25 savings bond we received from grandma as a financial asset. However, it is also a debt our government owes us.

About This chapter: This chapter begins with "Debt As An Asset" and "Government Debt Instruments," excerpted from "Public Debt: Private Asset," a publication of the Federal Reserve Bank of Chicago, http://www.chicagofed.org, 1999. "Public Debt And The National Economy" and "Pros And Cons Of Federal Borrowing" are excerpted from "Federal Debt: Answers to Frequently Asked Questions," Government Accountability Office, Pub. No. GAO-04-485SP, March 2004.

Just as there must be a buyer for every seller in a sales transaction, for every debt incurred someone acquires a financial asset of equal value. Debt, then, is considered an asset of the creditor, and a claim against the assets and earnings of the debtor.

In terms of the national debt, every dollar of the government's debt is someone's asset. Corporations, brokerage houses, bond-trading firms, foreign nationals, and U.S. citizens, both here and abroad, are all willing to loan money to the U.S. government. They view the loan as an investment, an asset that increases their wealth.

Government Debt Instruments

When the federal government spends more than its revenues, it finances its deficit by selling debt instruments that compete for investors' money with instruments of other issuers of debt. The instruments the government sells

---

✤ It's A Fact!!

What is the national debt?

The term national debt refers to direct liabilities of the United States Government. There are several different concepts of debt that are at various times used to refer to the national debt:

• Public debt is defined as public debt securities issued by the U.S. Treasury. U. S. Treasury securities primarily consist of marketable Treasury securities (bills, notes and bonds), savings bonds, and special securities issued to state and local governments (State and Local Government Series securities, or SLGS). A portion is debt held by the public and a portion is debt held by government accounts.

• Debt held by the public excludes the portion of the debt that is held by government accounts.

• Gross federal debt is made up of public debt securities and a small amount of securities issued by government agencies.

are called Treasury securities. For many people, the most familiar of these securities are savings bonds, like the one from grandma. They are nonmarketable, meaning that the owner cannot sell them to anyone. Of course, savings bonds can be liquidated before maturity by redeeming them at a prescribed price.

Despite their familiarity, however, savings bonds do not account for most of the government's debt. That distinction goes to marketable Treasury securities: Treasury bills (T-bills), Treasury notes (T-notes), and Treasury bonds (T-bonds, not to be confused with savings bonds).

These marketable securities are distinguished from each other by their length of maturity and denomination. T-bills are issued with 3-, 6-, or 12-month maturities. T-notes have maturities from two to ten year. T-bonds mature in more than ten years. As of 1998, all Treasury securities have a minimum denomination of $1,000.

What is the difference between the debt and the deficit?

The deficit is the fiscal year difference between what the United States Government (Government) takes in from taxes and other revenues, called receipts, and the amount of money the Government spends, called outlays. The items included in the deficit are considered either on-budget or off-budget.

You can think of the total debt as accumulated deficits plus accumulated off-budget surpluses. The on-budget deficits require the U.S. Treasury to borrow money to raise cash needed to keep the Government operating. The Government borrows the money by selling securities like Treasury bills, notes, bonds and savings bonds to the public.

Source: Excerpted from "FAQs: National Debt," an undated document produced by the U.S. Department of the Treasury, and "Frequently Asked Questions about the Public Debt," Bureau of the Public Debt, U.S. Department of the Treasury, February 2007.

Public Debt And The National Economy

Members of the Congress, other public officials, and many citizens have recognized that rising federal debt has serious consequences for the nation. Large deficits and rising federal debt constrain future economic growth and living standards by reducing the amount of saving in the United States available for private investment. Federal borrowing to finance deficits may also put upward pressure on interest rates, which increases household borrowing costs for such things as homes, cars, and college loans.

In addition to these economic consequences, the budgetary effects of deficits and growing debt reduce the federal government's flexibility in funding various programs and activities. Spending on interest cannot be directly controlled—interest costs are determined by the amount of past borrowing and interest rates. In fiscal year 2003, net interest spending was the sixth largest item in the federal budget—about 7 percent of total federal spending was primarily used to pay interest on debt held by the public rather than to finance other public priorities. With debt held by the public increasing and interest rates expected to rise, interest spending is bound to increase in the near future. Spending for interest payments accompanied with the growth in mandatory programs over the longer term will decrease budgetary flexibility in financing discretionary programs.

Table 5.1. Interest Expense On Outstanding Public Debt

Year	Fiscal Year End
2006	$405,872,109,315.83
2005	$352,350,252,507.90
2004	$321,566,323,971.29
2003	$318,148,529,151.51
2002	$332,536,958,599.42
2001	$359,507,635,242.41
2000	$361,997,734,302.36
1995	$332,413,555,030.62
1990	$264,852,544,615.90

Source: Bureau of the Public Debt, U.S. Department of the Treasury, March 2007.

Pros And Cons Of Federal Borrowing

Federal borrowing has both advantages and disadvantages that vary depending upon economic circumstances. In addition, views of federal borrowing generally vary with its size in relation to the economy and stage of the business cycle. Borrowing, in lieu of higher taxes or lower government spending, may be viewed as appropriate during times of economic recession, war, and other temporary challenges or national needs. Borrowing during a recession can help to maintain household income and spending levels and reduce the severity of a recession. Similarly, borrowing in times of war can finance increased defense spending without reducing other government spending or enacting large tax increases that could be disruptive to the economy. Further, borrowing can finance higher government spending in response to other temporary challenges or national needs, such as large natural disasters or the terrorist attacks of September 11, 2001. Borrowing for such short-term circumstances can permit the government to hold tax rates relatively stable and avoid economic disruptions.

Federal borrowing might also be viewed as appropriate for federal investment, such as building roads, training workers, and conducting scientific research, contributing to the nation's capital stock and productivity. Public facilities, such as transportation systems and water supplies, are vital to meeting immediate as well as long-term public demands for safety, health, and improved quality of life.

Any judgment about borrowing involves trade-offs and the costs of borrowing could outweigh the benefits. Borrowing for additional spending or lower taxes aimed at maintaining current consumption improves short-term well-being for today's workers and taxpayers but does not enhance the ability to repay the borrowing in the future. Although reducing federal deficits is the surest way to increase national saving available for private investment, the composition of federal spending also matters. At some point, reducing federal deficits at the expense of federal investment spending raises concerns about the outlook for the nation's infrastructure, future workers' skills, technological advancement, and thus economic growth. For any given fiscal policy path, policy makers can strive to allocate a greater share of federal spending on well-chosen investment activities aimed at enhancing long-term productivity.

In the near term, federal borrowing absorbs scarce savings available for private investment and can exert upward pressure on interest rates. When the economy is operating near full capacity, government borrowing can be large enough to affect overall interest rates, making borrowing more expensive for individuals and families who take out loans for homes, cars, and college. Or, the United States has been able to invest more than it saves by borrowing from abroad. Over the long term, the costs of federal borrowing will be borne by tomorrow's workers and taxpayers. Higher saving and investment in the nation's capital stock—factories, equipment, and technology—increase the nation's capacity to produce goods and services and generate higher income in the future. Increased economic capacity and rising incomes would allow future generations to more easily bear the burden of the federal government's debt. Persistent deficits and rising levels of debt, however, reduce funds available for private investment in the United States and abroad. Over time, lower productivity and GDP [gross domestic product] growth ultimately may reduce or slow the growth of the living standards of future generations.

♣ **It's A Fact!!**
The Debt:
To The Penny
And Who Holds It

Current and historical data about the public debt can be obtained online at http://www.treasurydirect.gov/govt/govt.htm. The numbers that follow are from June 25, 2007:

- Debt Held by the Public: $4,950,662,396,067.18

- Intragovernmental Holdings: $3,856,239,279,801.68

- Total Public Debt Outstanding: $8,806,901,675,868.86

Source: Bureau of the Public Debt, U.S. Department of the Treasury, June 2007.

Part Two
Using Credit

Chapter 6

Why Should You Care About Credit?

What is credit?

Getting credit is when a bank, credit union, or other financial institution, even a local department store, makes you a loan—either when they issue you a credit card or when they give you a check for a certain amount in the form of a loan. When you get a credit card or a loan it means that you're borrowing money from them with the understanding that you will pay them back:

- a certain amount—either part of, or the entire amount,
- at a certain time—when your payment is due, typically on a monthly basis,
- at a certain cost—how much interest.

What does credit cost?

One of the most important things to know about using credit is that it will cost you money. In addition to the annual fee that most credit cards charge you for using their card, you also need to know about something called interest. When a bank or a department store or a credit union or a car dealership approves you for a credit card or gives you a loan they will charge you a fee, called interest, for borrowing their money. That's why it's so important that you not borrow or charge more than you can afford to pay back. And it's important that you understand the terms of the agreement—how long you have to pay the loan back and how much interest you'll be charged on the loan.

Here's how interest works. Say you have a credit card. If you pay your bill in full, every month, you will not be charged any interest. If, however, you pay only a portion of your bill, the credit card company will charge you a percentage of the money you owe for the balance outstanding. For example, say your credit card carries an interest rate, also called the annual percentage rate (APR), of 16%. (You can find the APR for your credit card under the "Terms" section on the back of your monthly bill.) If you owe $1,000 on a credit card charging you 16% APR you'll end up owing them approximately an additional $160 a year or about $13 in interest every month. You can find the APR on your monthly bill under a section entitled "Finance Charges." The important thing to remember is that interest compounds. Let's say that you've accumulated $3,500 in credit card debt at 16% APR. If you don't charge anything else and make $120 in payments every month it will take you 37 months—more than 3 years—to pay your bill off completely. And you would have paid nearly $4,430—or about $930 in interest.

Let's look at another example. Let's say that you've signed a car loan to buy a new car from a local dealership. You take out a three-year loan for $18,000 charging 10%. That works out to a monthly repayment of $580. In this case the interest you'll pay on the loan is fixed—meaning that every month you'll pay off a certain amount of the original $18,000 you borrowed plus a certain amount of interest. At the end of three years, you will have paid nearly $2,900 in interest. In other words, you will have paid the bank nearly $2,900 for borrowing their money for three years.

Understanding what credit is and how much it can possibly cost you is important.

> **♣ It's A Fact!!**
> Bad credit can affect your ability to get more credit. Did you know it also can affect your ability to get or keep a job? Employers often use a credit report when they hire and evaluate employees for promotion, reassignment, or retention.
>
> Source: Excerpted from "Negative Credit Can Squeeze A Job Search," Federal Trade Commission (www.ftc .gov), May 2006.

So why is it important to have good credit?

Managing your credit is extremely important to your financial future. Having good credit means that you have a history of paying back your debts and paying off your bills in a timely manner. It shows banks, stores, and other institutions that you're responsible with money—that you are willing and able to pay your bills and pay off your debts. Your history of paying your bills on time and paying your debt off is compiled into something called a credit report. Think of it as a report card on your credit habit. Every time you accept a credit card offer, take on a student loan, or sign up for a utility like electrical or phone services, those accounts are recorded by the three major credit reporting companies: TransUnion, Equifax, and Experian.

Your credit habits—good and bad—are then reported by the credit card companies, utilities, etc. to these three companies. So if you regularly pay your credit card bills on time or if you default on your student loan or if you pay the minimum amount of your credit card every month, all of that is recorded by the credit reporting companies. Even things like how often you move, change jobs, whether or not you own a home are all tracked on your credit report.

Why is that important to know? Because when you go to apply for a loan, such as a car loan or home mortgage, the bank or the car dealership will get a copy of your credit report and use it as part of how they decide whether or not to approve you for a loan. Employers and insurance companies can also access and use your credit report as a way of determining whether or not to hire you or to approve you for an insurance policy.

The dangers of accumulating a lot of credit debt.

Tania and Juan got married when they were 23. They always intended to be wise with their money but let their credit card spending get out of control quickly. At first they were just charging large items like furniture for their apartment, but then they started using their credit cards for smaller, everyday purchases like dinners out, groceries, dry cleaning, and renting movies. Add in unexpected bills like car repair or doctors' bills and pretty soon instead of paying their bills off in full, they could only pay only a portion, or even sometimes just the minimum amount due. Using their credit cards became a habit. They started charging things without realizing that by charging them instead of paying cash they were accumulating a lot of debt. They didn't think about how much it was costing them in interest payments to charge things that they should have been paying cash for.

After a few years they wanted to buy a home. They sat down to figure out how much savings they had and how much debt they were carrying. They were shocked to realize that they owed over $11,500 just in credit card debt. At an interest rate of 16% if they pay off just $100 a month it would take them 115 months—that's 9½ years!—to pay their card off completely. And they would be charged $7,781.67 in interest to pay a total of $19,281.67!

According to http://www.cardweb.com, Americans carry, on average, $5,800 in monthly credit card debt. To pay that off by making only the minimum monthly payment, it would take 30 years to pay off. And that amount would include having to pay an additional $15,000 in interest.

Tania and Juan are among thousands of Americans who have discovered the three main dangers of accumulating a lot of debt:

- Accumulating debt affects your ability to qualify for future loans or your future buying power. If you carry a lot of debt or you're unable to pay back existing debt it will show up on your credit report. If you have poor credit (for example, a history of late payments or failing to pay back a loan) it takes 7 years before it will be cleared from your record. Filing bankruptcy will stay on your record for 10 years. Why should you care about a poor credit report? Banks, lenders, car dealerships, and other financial institutions use those reports to determine whether or not they'll loan you money. A negative report affects your ability to get approved for a future loan to buy a car, a home, etc.

- Accumulating debt can compound beyond your control. Credit cards carry interest rates. Interest, or the money you owe on your debt, compounds, or multiplies. Interest compounds quickly. Without realizing it, you can find yourself with debt that has grown out of your control.

♣ It's A Fact!!
Your Rights As A Credit Consumer

You have rights as a credit consumer! By law, the Equal Credit Opportunity Act (ECOA) prohibits credit discrimination on the basis of sex, race, marital status, religion, national origin, age, or receipt of public assistance. Even if you're asked for this information, by law creditors can't use it to deny you a loan. You also cannot be denied a loan or credit card, or charged a higher interest rate simply because, for example, you are a Latino American or a woman. If you are denied a loan you have the right to find out why. Lenders are also prohibited from charging you a higher interest rate on your loan because of your race.

For more information on your rights as a consumer, check out the following link to the Federal Trade Commission's website: www .ftc.gov/bcp/conline/pubs/credit/ecoa.htm.

Source: © 2007 The Bond Market Foundation.
All rights reserved.

• Accumulating debt drains your ability to save and invest for your future. Every dollar that you owe toward debt is a dollar that you're not able to save and invest. The sooner you're able to begin saving and investing the more money you'll make toward your financial goals such as homeownership or retirement.

Note: Remember that when you co-sign a loan or for a credit card for a family member it means that you're responsible for paying that debt if he/she doesn't. The bank will expect you to pay off their debt. If you get divorced, or are in the process of divorce, you'll want to make sure that you and your spouse have clearly separated your financial responsibilities, or you can be held responsible for your spouse's debt.

How To Establish Good Credit

Used wisely, credit cards can help you establish a good credit history, which can help you down the line if you want to apply for a loan.

If You Have Credit Cards

- Pay your bills on time;

- Pay your bills in full or at least pay more than the minimum amount due; and

- Reduce the number of credit cards or accounts you have open...in other words, pay off a few of those cards, cut them up and then send a note to the company that you want to close the account. It's not a bad idea to send a copy of the letter to the three major credit bureaus so they know you've closed the account.

Getting A Credit Card For The First Time

You probably get a credit card offer in the mail almost every day. Be careful before signing up. You need to read the fine print carefully. Remember that what you're signing is a legally binding agreement between you and the credit company. You're agreeing to pay back the company on their terms. So you need to know what the terms are! Here are some things to look for:

- **The Interest Rate:** Some will offer in big letters on the envelope an outrageously low interest rate. Often that's called a "teaser", introductory, or promotional rate. This is a very low rate of interest that only lasts for a short period of time (like 30 to 90 days), and then it's jacked up to a much higher interest rate of 15, 18, 21% or more. If you don't look at your bill carefully you may not notice the jump in interest charged until your debt has accumulated substantially. Cards can also carry different interest rates for purchases and cash advances.

- **Fees:** Credit cards can charge annual fees, cash advance fees, and late fees: (1) Annual fees. This is a fee charged for just having the card. Some cards charge no annual fee. Others can charge $35, $50, even

$100 just for the privilege of using the card. These fees are automatically added in to your monthly bill so you may not notice if you're not looking carefully. (2) Cash advance fee. The fee charged for withdrawing money from a bank or ATM charged to your credit card. You are typically given a cash advance limit less than your total credit limit and may be charged a higher interest rate, in addition to a fee, for using the cash advance privilege. (3) Late fee. If you are late, or delinquent, in making your payment, you will be charged a fee and your APR may also be raised.

- **Credit And Cash Advance Limit:** How much is the maximum you're allowed to charge, or borrow, using the card? How much cash are you allowed to withdraw using the card?

Many credit cards will now offer additional benefits such as online access where you can check your account on the internet, free gifts when you open an account, and perks like earning frequent flyer miles or offers for services like insurance policies.

There are several ways to find a credit card—through your local bank or credit union; online; or through a mail offer. Depending on whether or not you have used credit in the past you will be offered a secured or unsecured line of credit. A secured credit card means that you'll need to give the bank or company a deposit of up to a few hundred dollars. If you fail to pay your bill they'll take money out of the deposit to make the payment. An unsecured credit card means you won't be required to make a deposit as a guarantee of payment.

Ideally you want a credit card with a low guaranteed interest rate, no deposit required, and no annual fee required for using the card. For more information on applying for, and comparing credit card interest rates check out the following websites:

- http://www.creditsourceonline.com
- http://www.consumer-shopping-guide.com
- www.bankrate.com/esp
- http://www.cardweb.com

✔ Quick Tip

Tips For Keeping Your Credit Habits Under Control

- Try to have only one or two major credit cards.

- Unless you're trying to establish credit for the first time, don't get cards for individual store accounts.

- Shop around for the best, lowest-cost credit card. By doing some online research you can find cards that offer low interest rates, no annual fees, and benefits such as insurance, frequent flyer programs and more. If you've been a consistent bill payer, call your credit card company and ask them to lower your interest rate or even drop any fees associated with your card.

- If you don't pay your bill in full after three months, cut your cards up or stick them in the freezer. By the time they thaw out your urge to buy may have subsided!

- Itemize your credit card charges in your checkbook—every time you make a charge, enter it into your check register. That way you'll have accounted for all your charges and can pay off the bill in full at the end of the month.

- Nix the cash advance privilege—getting cash by using the cash advance privilege on your credit card can be an extremely expensive way to get cash quickly. Depending on the terms of your credit card, you may be charged a different or higher interest rate for the cash you borrow. Try limiting use of the cash advance privilege to emergency uses only.

- Ask a friend or a family member to keep you "in check." If you have a trusted friend or family member who is good with money, consider asking them to help you out by going over your credit card bills every month. There's nothing better to motivate some people to keep their spending under control if they know someone else will be taking a look at their bill!

- The key to remember is that credit is not a source of free money! Establishing and maintaining good credit is an important part of wisely planning for your, and your family's, financial future.

Source: © 2007 The Bond Market Foundation. All rights reserved.

Establishing Nontraditional Credit

You can build good credit without having to apply for, or get, a credit card. It's called establishing a nontraditional credit history. There are several ways you can begin establishing a good credit habit:

- Stay with your current job for a few years.

- Pay your utility bills, phone bills, and rent on time. Keep records and receipts of the timely payments.

- Open a checking or savings account through your local bank and maintain a more than minimum balance.

- Apply for a line of credit through a small local store (such as a local department store, clothing store, appliance store, etc.) and pay your bills in full and on time.

Chapter 7

The ABCs Of Credit Reports

What is a credit report?

A credit report is a summary of your financial reliability—for the most part, your history of paying debts and other bills. It is prepared by credit bureaus (also known as credit reporting agencies) primarily for use by lenders, employers, and others who, under the federal Fair Credit Reporting Act (FCRA), have a legitimate need for the information—such as when you apply for a loan, insurance policy, apartment, or job. The wealth of information gathered by credit bureaus, coupled with the speed of today's computer systems, explains why consumers can quickly get loans and other services, including approvals of certain credit applications in minutes.

What is in my credit report?

In general, your credit report has four components:

- Identifying information, such as your name, Social Security number, current and previous addresses, telephone number, birth date, and employer. This information helps ensure that your credit report is accurate and doesn't mistakenly include details about another person (perhaps someone with the same name).

About This Chapter: Text in this chapter is excerpted from "Credit History 101: The ABCs of Credit Reports and Credit Scores," *FDIC Consumer News*, Federal Deposit Insurance Corporation (FDIC), Winter 2002/2003.

- Public record information, generally gathered from local courthouses, including bankruptcy records, foreclosures, tax liens, court-ordered payments, and late child-support payments. This information is used to determine if you have previous defaults or legal judgments against you. For example, a mortgage lender will want to know if you've had a past foreclosure before granting a home loan. Derogatory information can generally remain on your credit report for up to seven years, except for bankruptcy information, which may be reported for 10 years.

- Other credit history information, such as a list of your credit cards and loans, and whether payments were on time. Here, too, negative information about your credit relationships, such as late payments or defaults, will remain on your report for up to seven years, and bankruptcy information may appear on your report for 10 years.

- "Inquiries," a section of your report that lists the creditors, insurance companies, or other parties that have requested your credit report, usually when considering an application you submitted. Inquiries typically can remain on your credit report for two years.

✔ Quick Tip

The three nationwide consumer reporting companies have set up a central website, a toll-free telephone number, and a mailing address through which you can order your free annual report.

To order, visit http://www.annualcreditreport.com, call 877-322-8228, or complete the Annual Credit Report Request Form and mail it to: Annual Credit Report Request Service, P.O. Box 105281, Atlanta, GA 30348-5281. You can print the form from http://www.ftc.gov/credit.

Do not contact the three nationwide consumer reporting companies (Equifax, Experian and TransUnion) individually. They are providing free annual credit reports only through http://www.annualcreditreport.com, 877-322-8228, and Annual Credit Report Request Service, P.O. Box 105281, Atlanta, GA 30348-5281.

Source: "Your Access to Free Credit Reports," Federal Trade Commission, September 2005.

What is NOT in your credit report?

Your credit report typically does not contain information about your checking and savings account balances, brokerage accounts, medical history, race, sex, religion, national origin, or your driving record.

How do credit bureaus get their information?

According to David Lafleur, a Policy Analyst at the FDIC, "Lenders voluntarily supply the information to credit bureaus on an ongoing basis; no federal laws require companies to submit the data." Why? Because having access to current and reliable information about you helps lenders make informed decisions and offer you financial products and services very quickly. Lenders, landlords, and other users of credit reports also may want to know about events such as lawsuits and bankruptcies, so credit bureaus obtain this information from courthouses and public records.

Can anyone get my credit report?

No. The Fair Credit Reporting Act (FCRA) contains rules about who can get your credit report. Generally, a third party can access your credit report when considering an application you've made, such as for a loan, a job, insurance, or an apartment. The law also allows entities to access your report as part of an ongoing business relationship. Suppose you already have an auto loan at the bank and you miss a payment or you move and don't provide a forwarding address. In this situation, the bank has the right to obtain a copy of your latest credit report.

But even if you are paying on a loan or credit card as agreed, the institution where you have the account can obtain your credit report as part of its regular maintenance of the account, and that includes looking for warning signs that you may have problems fulfilling your obligations in the future. "For example, it is not uncommon for credit card issuers to review their cardholders' credit reports on a regular basis and raise their APR (annual percentage rate) or lower their credit limit if there are signs of trouble, even if someone has been diligently paying the card issuer," says FDIC Consumer Affairs Specialist Howard Herman.

An exception to the ongoing relationship would be for employers, who would first need to obtain the employee's permission each time before requesting a credit report.

How often should I get my credit report?

Many financial advisors suggest that you review your credit report for inaccuracies or omissions about once a year. It's especially important to review your credit report before making a major purchase, such as a home or a car, so you can correct an error before it slows down your credit approval or prevents you from getting the best possible loan terms.

What kinds of problems could I encounter?

While federal law requires lenders and other companies providing information to credit bureaus to give accurate information, mistakes do happen. So, when you look at your report check it carefully:

- Make sure it accurately reflects how you have paid your bills. If you always pay your credit card and other loans on time, but your credit report erroneously shows late payments, you'll want to correct that.

- Verify that all the accounts listed are yours, especially if you have a common name or you share a name with a relative (such as John Doe, Jr.). You also want to be careful that an identity thief hasn't opened new accounts in your name to commit financial fraud.

- Look for accounts you don't use and may have forgotten. You may be able to raise your credit score by closing unnecessary credit card accounts (although having long-standing accounts in good order can actually help your credit score).

Can I correct wrong or incomplete information in my credit report?

The FCRA gives you the right to dispute inaccuracies or omissions, and it requires credit bureaus to investigate your complaint (generally within 30 days), send you a prompt response, and correct any errors. The law also requires the source of inaccurate information (such as a bank) to correct the record at the credit bureaus to which it initially provided the erroneous information. [See Chapter 8 for more information about disputing errors on credit reports.]

♣ It's A Fact!!

The Federal Trade Commission (FTC), the nation's consumer protection agency, wants you to know that, if you want to order your free annual credit report online, there is only one authorized website: http://www.annualcreditreport.com.

Many other websites claim to offer "free credit reports," "free credit scores," or "free credit monitoring." But, be careful. These sites are not part of the official annual free credit report program. And in some cases, the "free" product comes with strings attached. For example, some sites sign you up for a supposedly "free" service that converts to one you have to pay for after a trial period ends. If you don't cancel during the trial period, you may be agreeing to let the company start charging fees to your credit card.

These sites often look like the official site at http://www.annualcreditreport.com. Some use terms like "free report" in their names; others have website names that purposely misspell annualcreditreport.com in the hope that you will mistype the name of the official site. Some of these "impostor" sites direct you to other sites that try to sell you something or collect your personal information.

Source: Excerpted from "Want a Free Annual Credit Report?" U.S. Federal Trade Commission, May 2006.

What if I have a question or complaint involving a credit bureau?

First, try to resolve the matter with the credit bureau directly. If you're not satisfied, contact the FTC (http://www.ftc.gov). The FTC does not resolve individual disputes, but it does provide useful information that may help consumers resolve their problems. Awareness of consumer complaints also enables the FTC to spot patterns of problems that may trigger an enforcement action.

What is a credit score and why is it important?

A credit score is a number calculated by a credit bureau, a lender, or another company intended for use in making a decision on a loan application or other product or service. (For example, many lenders use a system developed by Fair Isaac and Company called the "FICO score.") Think of credit scoring as a point system based on your credit history, designed to help predict how likely you are to repay a loan or make payments on time. Everyone with a credit record also has a credit score. Different lenders and other companies may use different scoring systems, so your score (and the products or services you're offered as a result) may vary significantly from one source to another. [See Chapter 9 for more information about credit scoring.]

✔ **Quick Tip**

If you get an e-mail or see a pop-up ad claiming it's from annualcreditreport.com or any of the three nationwide consumer reporting companies, do not reply or click on any link in the message—it's probably a scam. The official website for annual credit reports (http://www.annualcreditreport.com) will NEVER send you an e-mail solicitation for your free annual credit report, use pop-up ads, or call you to ask for personal information. Forward any e-mail that claims to be from annualcreditreport.com or any of three consumer reporting companies to the FTC's database of deceptive spam at spam@uce.gov.

Source: Excerpted from "Want a Free Annual Credit Report?" U.S. Federal Trade Commission, May 2006.

Chapter 8

How To Dispute Credit Report Errors

Your credit report contains information about where you live, how you pay your bills, and whether you've been sued, arrested, or filed for bankruptcy. Consumer reporting companies sell the information in your report to creditors, insurers, employers, and other businesses that use it to evaluate your applications for credit, insurance, employment, or renting a home or apartment. The federal Fair Credit Reporting Act (FCRA) promotes the accuracy and privacy of information in the files of the nation's consumer reporting companies. Some financial advisors and consumer advocates suggest that you review your credit report periodically.

Correcting Errors

Under the FCRA, both the consumer reporting company and the information provider (that is, the person, company, or organization that provides information about you to a consumer reporting company) are responsible for correcting inaccurate or incomplete information in your report. To take advantage of all your rights under this law, contact the consumer reporting company and the information provider.

Step One

Tell the consumer reporting company, in writing, what information you think is inaccurate. Include copies (NOT originals) of documents that

About This Chapter: Text in this chapter is from "How to Dispute Credit Report Errors," Federal Trade Commission (http://www.ftc.gov), May 2006.

✔ Quick Tip

An amendment to the Fair Credit Reporting Act requires each of the nationwide consumer reporting companies—Equifax, Experian, and TransUnion—to provide you with a free copy of your credit report, at your request, once every 12 months. These three nationwide consumer reporting companies have set up one website, toll-free telephone number, and mailing address through which you can order your free annual report. To order, visit http://www.annualcreditreport.com, call 877-322-8228, or complete the Annual Credit Report Request Form and mail it to: Annual Credit Report Request Service, P.O. Box 105281, Atlanta, GA 30348-5281. You can print the form from ftc.gov/credit. Do not contact the three nationwide consumer reporting companies individually.

For more details about obtaining a copy of your credit report, visit the credit area of the Federal Trade Commission's website, online at http://www.ftc.gov/credit.

support your position. In addition to providing your complete name and address, your letter should clearly identify each item in your report you dispute, state the facts, and explain why you dispute the information, and request that it be removed or corrected. You may want to enclose a copy of your report with the items in question circled. Send your letter by certified mail, "return receipt requested," so you can document what the consumer reporting company received. Keep copies of your dispute letter and enclosures.

Consumer reporting companies must investigate the items in question—usually within 30 days—unless they consider your dispute frivolous. They also must forward all the relevant data you provide about the inaccuracy to the organization that provided the information. After the information provider receives notice of a dispute from the consumer reporting company, it must investigate, review the relevant information, and report the results back to the consumer reporting company. If the information provider finds the disputed information is inaccurate, it must notify all three nationwide consumer reporting companies so they can correct the information in your file.

When the investigation is complete, the consumer reporting company must give you the results in writing and a free copy of your report if the dispute results in a change. This free report does not count as your annual free report. If an item is changed or deleted, the consumer reporting company cannot put the disputed information back in your file unless the information provider verifies that it is accurate and complete. The consumer reporting company also must send you written notice that includes the name, address, and phone number of the information provider.

If you ask, the consumer reporting company must send notices of any corrections to anyone who received your report in the past six months. You can have a corrected copy of your report sent to anyone who received a copy during the past two years for employment purposes.

If an investigation doesn't resolve your dispute with the consumer reporting company, you can ask that a statement of the dispute be included in your file and in future reports. You also can ask the consumer reporting company to provide your statement to anyone who received a copy of your report in the recent past. You can expect to pay a fee for this service.

Step Two

Tell the creditor or other information provider, in writing, that you dispute an item. Be sure to include copies (NOT originals) of documents that support your position. Many providers specify an address for disputes. If the provider reports the item to a consumer reporting company, it must include a notice of your dispute. And if you are correct—that is, if the information is found to be inaccurate—the information provider may not report it again.

> ☞ **Remember!!**
> When negative information in your report is accurate, only the passage of time can assure its removal.

Adding Accounts To Your File

Your credit file may not reflect all your credit accounts. Although most national department store and all-purpose bank credit card accounts will be

✔ **Quick Tip**

Here's a sample dispute letter you can use as a guide to help you write your own (include the date and your name and return address at the top):

Complaint Department
Name of Company
Address
City, State, Zip Code

Dear Sir or Madam:

I am writing to dispute the following information in my file. I have circled the items I dispute on the attached copy of the report I received.

This item (identify item(s) disputed by name of source, such as creditors or tax court, and identify type of item, such as credit account, judgment, etc.) is (inaccurate or incomplete) because (describe what is inaccurate or incomplete and why). I am requesting that the item be removed (or request another specific change) to correct the information.

Enclosed are copies of (use this sentence if applicable and describe any enclosed documentation, such as payment records or court documents) supporting my position. Please reinvestigate this (these) matter(s) and (delete or correct) the disputed item(s) as soon as possible.

Sincerely,
Your name
Enclosures: (List what you are enclosing.)

included in your file, not all creditors supply information to consumer reporting companies: some travel, entertainment, gasoline card companies, local retailers, and credit unions are among the creditors that don't.

If you've been told that you were denied credit because of an "insufficient credit file" or "no credit file" and you have accounts with creditors that don't appear in your credit file, ask the consumer reporting companies to add this information to future reports. Although they are not required to do so, many consumer reporting companies will add verifiable accounts for a fee. However, understand that if these creditors do not report to the consumer reporting company on a regular basis, the added items will not be updated in your file.

Chapter 9

What Is Credit Scoring?

Credit Scoring

Credit scoring is a system creditors use to help determine whether to give you credit. Information about you and your credit experiences, such as your bill-paying history, the number and type of accounts you have, late payments, collection actions, outstanding debt, and the age of your accounts, is collected from your credit application and your credit report. Using a statistical program, creditors compare this information to the credit performance of consumers with similar profiles. A credit scoring system awards points for each factor that helps predict who is most likely to repay a debt. A total number of points—a credit score—helps predict how creditworthy you are, that is, how likely it is that you will repay a loan and make the payments when due.

Credit scoring is based on real data and statistics, so it usually is more reliable than subjective or judgmental methods. It treats all applicants objectively. Judgmental methods typically rely on criteria that are not systematically tested and can vary when applied by different individuals.

About This Chapter: This chapter includes excerpts from "Credit Scoring," Federal Trade Commission (www.ftc.gov), May 2006; and "Simple Mistakes That Can Lower Your Credit Score...And Cost You Money," *FDIC Consumer News*, Federal Deposit Insurance Corporation (FDIC), February 2003.

How is a credit scoring model developed?

To develop a model, a creditor selects a random sample of its customers, or a sample of similar customers if their sample is not large enough, and analyzes it statistically to identify characteristics that relate to credit-worthiness. Then, each of these factors is assigned a weight based on how strong a predictor it is of who would be a good credit risk. Each creditor may use its own credit scoring model, different scoring models for different types of credit, or a generic model developed by a credit scoring company.

Under the Equal Credit Opportunity Act (ECOA), a credit scoring system may not use certain characteristics—like race, sex, marital status, national origin, or religion—as factors. However, creditors are allowed to use age in properly designed scoring systems. But any scoring system that includes age must give equal treatment to elderly applicants.

Scoring models may be based on more than just information in your credit report. For example, the model may consider information from your credit application as well: your job or occupation, length of employment, or whether you own a home.

How reliable is the credit scoring system?

Credit scoring systems enable creditors to evaluate millions of applicants consistently and impartially on many different characteristics. But to be statistically valid, credit scoring systems

> ✔ **Quick Tip**
> If you've been denied credit, or didn't get the rate or credit terms you want, ask the creditor if a credit scoring system was used. If so, ask what characteristics or factors were used in that system, and the best ways to improve your application. If you get credit, ask the creditor whether you are getting the best rate and terms available and, if not, why. If you are not offered the best rate available because of inaccuracies in your credit report, be sure to dispute the inaccurate information in your credit report.
>
> Source: Federal Trade Commission, 2006.

must be based on a big enough sample. Remember that these systems generally vary from creditor to creditor.

Although you may think such a system is arbitrary or impersonal, it can help make decisions faster, more accurately, and more impartially than individuals when it is properly designed. And many creditors design their systems so that in marginal cases, applicants whose scores are not high enough to pass easily or are low enough to fail absolutely are referred to a credit manager who decides whether the company or lender will extend credit. This may allow for discussion and negotiation between the credit manager and the consumer.

What happens if I am denied credit or don't get the terms I want?

If you are denied credit, the ECOA requires that the creditor give you a notice that tells you the specific reasons your application was rejected or the fact that you have the right to learn the reasons if you ask within 60 days. Indefinite and vague reasons for denial are illegal, so ask the creditor to be specific. Acceptable reasons include: "Your income was low" or "You haven't been employed long enough." Unacceptable reasons include: "You didn't meet our minimum standards" or "You didn't receive enough points on our credit scoring system."

If a creditor says you were denied credit because you are too near your credit limits on your charge cards or you have too many credit card accounts, you may want to reapply after paying down your balances or closing some accounts. Credit scoring systems consider updated information and change over time.

Sometimes you can be denied credit because of information from a credit report. If so, the Fair Credit Reporting Act (FCRA) requires the creditor to give you the name, address, and phone number of the consumer reporting company that supplied the information. You should contact that company to find out what your report said. This information is free if you request it within 60 days of being turned down for credit. The consumer reporting company can tell you what's in your report, but only the creditor can tell you why your application was denied.

♣ It's A Fact!!

Bad Checks: Bad News For Your Record

While credit bureaus keep track of how you handle credit, there are other companies that monitor and report how you manage—or mismanage—your checking account. And, as some consumers have learned, even a single bounced check reported by one of these services may be enough to make it difficult for you to open a new transaction account or get a merchant to accept your check as payment.

Check reporting protects financial institutions and merchants (such as retailers and grocery stores) from losses associated with bounced or fraudulent checks. Under the Fair Credit Reporting Act (FCRA), a bounced check or other wrongdoing reported to a check reporting service may stay on your record for as many as seven years.

How can you avoid getting into this predicament? "Frequently balance and monitor your checking account to avoid bounced checks," says Bret Morgan, an FDIC Examiner. "Don't close one checking account before you have established another one. And before closing your account, make sure any outstanding checks have cleared and account fees have been paid."

Source: From *FDIC Consumer News*, Federal Deposit Insurance Corporation (FDIC), February 2003.

Simple Mistakes That Can Lower Your Credit Score... And Cost You Money

Because so much depends on your credit record and credit score, you should be aware of the pitfalls that can tarnish your financial reputation. This list of common mistakes that can significantly affect your credit history and credit score was compiled by the Federal Deposit Insurance Corporation (FDIC):

Paying Bills Late: One of the biggest factors in the determination of your credit score is your past payment history. While one or two late payments on your mortgage, credit card, or other important obligations over a long period of time may not significantly damage your credit record, if at all, making a habit of this can count against you.

Consistently pay your bills on time because this indicates you're a responsible money manager and likely to take your future commitments (such as a loan) seriously. Be especially careful with payments in the months before you apply for a loan, because lenders put more emphasis on your recent payment history.

Not Paying The Minimum Amount Required: "If you don't make at least the minimum payment on your credit card or other bills, your creditors will eventually report your account as past due, and that's a bad mark on your credit history," says Janet Kincaid, a Senior Consumer Affairs Officer with the FDIC. "Not only that, but paying less than the minimum can result in late fees and additional interest charges, which can add up quickly." Consistently pay your bills on time because this indicates you're a responsible money manager and likely to take your future commitments (such as a loan) seriously.

✔ Quick Tip

Different lenders and credit scoring services may use different calculations when evaluating you—for example, some may include a monthly mortgage payment in their debt-to-income ratio, others may not. So, in general, try to keep your debt level low. How? Don't spend more than you can afford. Don't max out or charge near the limit on your credit card. Also, if possible, try to pay off that credit card balance each month. Follow this strategy and you'll build a good credit history, reduce debts and save on interest payments, too.

Source: From *FDIC Consumer News*, Federal Deposit Insurance Corporation (FDIC), February 2003.

Keeping Debt Levels Too High: Potential creditors will be concerned if there are indications you already owe a lot of money on credit cards and other obligations because additional debt could stretch your ability to repay. One way creditors evaluate whether to approve a loan or charge a higher interest rate (which is done to compensate for higher risk) is to look at how much you owe compared to your income. Creditors also consider how much of your credit card limit you typically use. If you are "maxing out" your credit cards or otherwise keeping a high balance in relation to your credit limit, a lender could question your ability to make payments on additional debt.

Owning Too Many Credit Cards: You may not think twice about offers to "sign up today" for a credit card to receive a percentage off your first purchase, get a free T-shirt, or to have no payments for six months. Depending on your personal situation, these promotions may be good deals. But beware. "If you open a number of credit accounts with retailers just to get the discounts or freebies, these seemingly harmless accounts may linger in your credit file and end up costing you money the next time you get a loan or insurance," warns David Lafleur, an FDIC Policy Analyst on consumer matters. Here's why.

If you have a stack of credit cards and department store cards—even if you rarely use them or don't carry a balance on them—each card represents money that you could borrow. According to the Kincaid, "A potential creditor will look at each card and its $10,000 or $20,000 credit limit and say, 'We don't know when or if you'll access this amount, but if you do, that means you'll have less money available to repay any new obligation.'" The result could be that, if you apply for a mortgage, a car loan, or some other important loan, you may qualify for only a smaller loan amount or perhaps face increased costs or fees.

Also, when you apply to a bank for a credit card or a loan, it will look at the "inquiries" section of your credit report to find out if you've recently applied for loans elsewhere. Several such inquiries on your credit report could indicate to a lender that you may be having financial troubles or that you could be on the verge of getting too deeply in debt. These inquiries remain on your credit report for two years and can be a factor in your credit score.

Not Periodically Checking On Your Credit Report: Many people never or rarely look at their credit report until they apply for a loan or they have been denied a loan or other request based on information in their report. Among the concerns: Inaccurate or missing information in your credit report could raise your borrowing costs or cause delays when you're in a rush to make a major purchase, such as a home. [See Chapters 7 and 8 for more information about credit reports and disputing credit report errors.]

Not Using Your Full Legal Name: Credit bureaus obtain data from a variety of sources, not all of which include a person's full name, Social Security number, or other identifying factors. As a result, aspects of someone else's credit history—perhaps late payments, loan defaults, or other serious

♣ It's A Fact!!

Under some credit scoring systems, canceling credit cards can lower your credit score, not raise it. For example, canceling cards you've owned for many years could lower your credit score because those older cards can establish a long history of responsible credit use. Even so, the Federal Deposit Insurance Corporation (FDIC) still generally favors the idea of canceling cards you rarely or never use. As one possible strategy, Janet Kincaid, a Senior Consumer Affairs Officer with the FDIC suggests this: "Review all the cards you have. Keep only the cards you've had for a long time and handled well by always paying on time."

Source: From *FDIC Consumer News*, Federal Deposit Insurance Corporation (FDIC), February 2003.

problems—could be reported on your credit report and could reduce your credit score.

Always use your full legal name when opening a bank account or applying for a loan or other benefit, such as a job or lease. Never leave off a Junior, Senior, or similar designation, and never use a nickname. Or, at the very least, be consistent by always using the same name when you fill out these kinds of applications or documents. Following this advice doesn't guarantee that someone else's credit history won't appear on your credit report, but it will reduce the potential for a mistake.

Not Alerting Current Or Potential Creditors If You've Moved Or Changed Names: Suppose you move and don't notify your existing creditors. If your monthly credit card statement and other bills don't reach you at your new address, you may miss a payment or two, and that tardiness can be reported on your credit report (not to mention the penalties or interest charges from your card issuer). Or, if you change names because of a marriage or divorce, and you apply for a loan without informing the potential creditor about your previous name, the credit bureau's report may show only your recent financial record under your current name. "If you don't inform your creditors of your name change, your credit record may not reflect your previous hard work at maintaining a good credit history," says Kincaid. Kincaid also says that if your name or address doesn't match what's being reported by the credit bureau or other creditors, "this can prompt a red flag about a potential fraudulent account, and if nothing else, it can slow down your loan application."

Chapter 10

Credit And Your Consumer Rights

The Federal Trade Commission (FTC) enforces the credit laws that protect your right to get, use, and maintain credit. These laws do not guarantee that everyone will receive credit. Instead, the credit laws protect your rights by requiring businesses to give all consumers a fair and equal opportunity to get credit and to resolve disputes over credit errors. This chapter explains your rights under these laws.

Fair Credit Reporting Act

The federal Fair Credit Reporting Act (FCRA) promotes the accuracy and privacy of information in the files of the nation's consumer reporting companies. Under the Fair Credit Reporting Act you have these rights:

- You have the right to receive a copy of your credit report. The copy of your report must contain all the information in your file at the time of your request. Each of the nationwide consumer reporting companies—Equifax, Experian, and TransUnion—is required to

About This Chapter: This chapter includes text excerpted from the following publications of the Federal Trade Commission (FTC): "Credit and Your Consumer Rights," March 2005; "The Credit Practices Rule," November 1992; and "Fair Credit Billing" an undated document reviewed for currency in February 2006. To view the complete text of these documents, or for additional information from the FTC, visit their website at http://www.ftc.gov.

provide you with a free copy of your credit report, at your request, once every 12 months. Under federal law, you're also entitled to a free report if a company takes adverse action against you, like denying your application for credit, insurance, or employment, and you ask for your report within 60 days of receiving notice of the action. Otherwise, a consumer reporting company may charge you up to $9.50 for another copy of your report within a 12-month period. [For more information about obtaining a copy of your credit report, see Chapter 7.]

• You have the right to know who asked for your report within the past year—two years for employment related requests.

♣ It's A Fact!!
Some Federal Laws Protecting Consumers

• **The Electronic Fund Transfer Act** limits a consumer's liability if there's been an unauthorized use of an ATM card, debit card or other electronic banking device.

• **The Equal Credit Opportunity Act** prohibits discrimination against loan applicants based on race, sex, age (provided that the applicant is eligible to enter into a binding contract), marital status, religion, national origin or receipt of various types of government assistance.

• **The Fair Credit Billing Act** establishes procedures for correcting errors on credit card bills. This law also allows a card user to dispute a purchase made with a card.

• **The Truth In Lending Act** requires creditors to give consumers information about the Annual Percentage Rates and other costs of a credit card or loan. This law also protects consumers if a credit card is lost or stolen.

• **The Truth In Savings Act** requires disclosures about interest rates and fees and prohibits misleading or inaccurate advertising for checking and savings accounts.

Source: *FDIC Consumer News*, Federal Deposit Insurance Corporation, Spring 2005.

- If a company denies your application, you have the right to the name and address of the consumer reporting company they contacted, provided the denial was based on information given by the consumer reporting company.

- If you question the accuracy or completeness of information in your report, you have the right to file a dispute with the consumer reporting company and the information provider (that is, the person, company, or organization that provided information about you to the consumer reporting company). Both the consumer reporting company and the information provider are obligated to investigate your claim and are responsible for correcting inaccurate or incomplete information in your report. [For more information about disputing information in your credit report, see Chapter 8.]

- You have a right to add a summary explanation to your credit report if your dispute is not resolved to your satisfaction. You also can ask the consumer reporting company to provide your statement to anyone who received a copy of your report in the recent past. You can expect to pay a fee for this service.

The Credit Practices Rule

The Federal Trade Commission's Credit Practices Rule, which became effective March 1, 1985, prohibits many creditors from including certain provisions in consumer credit contracts. It also requires creditors to provide a written notice to consumers before they cosign obligations for others about their potential liability if the other person fails to pay. [For more information about co-signing a loan, see Chapter 12.] Finally, it prohibits one method of assessing late charges.

What contracts are covered?

The Rule applies to consumer credit contracts offered by finance companies, retailers (such as auto dealers and furniture and department stores), and credit unions for any personal purpose except to buy real estate. It does not apply to banks or bank credit cards, to savings and loan associations, or to some non-profit organizations. (However, similar rules for banks—under the Federal Reserve Board—and for savings and loans—under the Office of Thrift Supervision—went into effect January 1, 1986.) The Rule does not apply to business credit.

What contract provisions are prohibited?

The Rule prohibits creditors from including certain provisions in their consumer credit contracts. Specifically, credit contracts cannot include provisions that make the following stipulations:

- Require you to agree in advance, should the creditor sue you for non-payment of a debt, to give up your right to be notified of a court hearing to present your side of the case or to hire an attorney to represent you. (These clauses were often called "confessions of judgment" or "cognovits.")

- Require you to give up your state-law protections that allow you to keep certain personal belongings even if you do not pay your debt as agreed. (These clauses were called "waivers of exemption.") State law generally allows you to keep your home, clothing, dishes, and other belongings of a fixed minimum value. However, when the debt incurred is to purchase an item and that item is used as security for the debt, it is permissible under the Rule for a creditor to repossess that item.

- Permit you to agree in advance to wage deductions that would pay the creditor directly if you default on the debt, unless you can cancel that permission at any time. (These clauses were called "wage assignments.") However, a wage or payroll deduction plan, through which you arrange to repay a loan, is a common payment method and is permissible under the Rule.

- Require you to use as collateral certain household and uniquely personal items that are of significant value to you but are of little economic value to a creditor. Such items include appliances, linens, china, crockery, kitchenware, wedding rings, family photographs, personal papers, the family Bible, and household pets. (These were called "household goods security" clauses.) However, if you borrowed money to buy any of these household or personal items, and use the items as collateral, the creditor can repossess the purchased item if you do not repay the loan.

How can late charges be assessed?

A creditor can charge a late fee if you do not make your loan payment on time. However, it is illegal under the Rule for a creditor to charge you late fees or payments simply because you have not yet paid a late fee you owe. This practice is called "pyramiding late fees." Under the Rule, this means that if you do not include the late fee you owe with your next regular payment, it is illegal for a creditor to subtract the late fee from your payment and then charge you a second late fee because the current payment is insufficient. For example, your loan contract may state that your monthly payments are $100 and that you will be assessed a $10 late fee if you pay after the grace period. If you make your $100 loan payment after that time and you do not include the $10 late fee with your next $100 payment, a creditor cannot first deduct the missing $10 late fee from the $100 payment, claim you have now paid $90, and then charge you an additional late fee. But, if you skip one month's payment entirely, the creditor can charge late fees on all subsequent payments until you bring your account up to date.

✔ Quick Tip

It is important to check credit billing and electronic fund transfer account statements regularly because these documents may contain mistakes that could damage your credit status or reflect improper charges or transfers. If you find an error or discrepancy, notify the company and dispute the error immediately.

Source: Federal Trade Commission (http://www.ftc.gov), March 2005.

Equal Credit Opportunity Act

The Equal Credit Opportunity Act (ECOA) prohibits credit discrimination on the basis of sex, race, marital status, religion, national origin, age, or receipt of public assistance. Creditors may ask for this information (except religion) in certain situations, but they may not use it to discriminate against you when deciding whether to grant you credit. Here is a summary of your rights under the Equal Credit Opportunity Act:

- You cannot be denied credit based on your race, sex, marital status, religion, age, national origin, or receipt of public assistance.

- You have the right to have reliable public assistance considered in the same manner as other income.

- If you are denied credit, you have a legal right to know why.

Fair Credit Billing Act

The Fair Credit Billing Act (FCBA) applies to "open end" credit accounts, such as credit cards, and revolving charge accounts—such as department store accounts. It does not cover installment contracts—loans or extensions of credit you repay on a fixed schedule. Consumers often buy cars, furniture and major appliances on an installment basis, and repay personal loans in installments as well.

The FCBA settlement procedures apply only to disputes about "billing errors." Here are some examples:

- Unauthorized charges (Federal law limits your responsibility for unauthorized charges to $50.)

- Charges that list the wrong date or amount

- Charges for goods and services you didn't accept or weren't delivered as agreed

- Math errors

- Failure to post payments and other credits, such as returns

- Failure to send bills to your current address—provided the creditor receives your change of address, in writing, at least 20 days before the billing period ends; and

- Charges for which you ask for an explanation or written proof of purchase along with a claimed error or request for clarification.

To take advantage of the law's consumer protections, you must take these steps:

- Write to the creditor at the address given for "billing inquiries," not the address for sending your payments, and include your name, address, account number and a description of the billing error.

- Send your letter so that it reaches the creditor within 60 days after the first bill containing the error was mailed to you.

- Send your letter by certified mail, return receipt requested, so you have proof of what the creditor received. Include copies (not originals) of sales slips or other documents that support your position. Keep a copy of your dispute letter.

The creditor must acknowledge your complaint in writing within 30 days after receiving it, unless the problem has been resolved. The creditor must resolve the dispute within two billing cycles (but not more than 90 days) after receiving your letter.

Here's an important caveat: Disputes about the quality of goods and services are not "billing errors," so the dispute procedure does not apply. However, if you buy unsatisfactory goods or services with a credit or charge card, you can take the same legal actions against the card issuer as you can take under state law against the seller.

To take advantage of this protection regarding the quality of goods or services, you must meet these criteria:

- Have made the purchase (it must be for more than $50) in your home state or within 100 miles of your current billing address

- Make a good faith effort to resolve the dispute with the seller first

The dollar and distance limitations don't apply if the seller also is the card issuer or if a special business relationship exists between the seller and the card issuer.

Fair Debt Collection Practices Act

You are responsible for your debts. If you fall behind in paying your creditors, or if an error is made on your account, you may be contacted by a "debt collector." A debt collector is any person, other than the creditor, who regularly collects debts owed to others, including lawyers who collect debts on a regular basis. You have the right to be treated fairly by debt collectors.

The Fair Debt Collection Practices Act (FDCPA) applies to personal, family, and household debts. This includes money you owe for the purchase of a car, for medical care, or for charge accounts. The FDCPA prohibits debt collectors from engaging in unfair, deceptive, or abusive practices while collecting these debts. Here is a summary of your rights under the Fair Debt Collection Practices Act:

- Debt collectors may contact you only between 8 A.M. and 9 P.M.

- Debt collectors may not contact you at work if they know your employer disapproves.

- Debt collectors may not harass, oppress, or abuse you.

- Debt collectors may not lie when collecting debts, such as falsely implying that you have committed a crime.

- Debt collectors must identify themselves to you on the phone.

- Debt collectors must stop contacting you if you ask them to do so in writing.

✔ **Quick Tip**

Here are some tips for solving credit problems:

- If you want to dispute a credit report, bill or credit denial, write to the appropriate company and send your letter "return receipt requested."

- When you dispute a billing error, include your name, account number, the dollar amount in question, and the reason you believe the bill is wrong.

- If in doubt, request written verification of a debt.

- Keep all your original documents, especially receipts, sales slips, and billing statements. You will need them if you dispute a credit bill or report. Send copies only. It may take more than one letter to correct a problem.

- Be skeptical of businesses that offer instant solutions to credit problems: There aren't any.

- Be persistent. Resolving credit problems can take time and patience.

- There is nothing that a credit repair company can charge you for that you cannot do for yourself for little or no cost.

Source: Federal Trade Commission (http://www.ftc.gov), March 2005.

Chapter 11

Getting A Loan: Shopping For Credit

The marketplace offers goods and services at competitive prices. Many people are good comparison shoppers when it comes to food or gas but ignore the shopping opportunities for credit.

For example, if you are in the market for a washer and dryer, how many sources of credit might finance the purchase for you? Would they all charge the same rates of interest or have the same terms? Before answering these questions, read the following information that describes the three basic types of credit and the major sources offering credit.

Types Of Credit

Consumer Loans: A consumer borrows an amount of money from a person or company regularly in the business of making loans, such as a credit union, bank, or savings and loan institution. A consumer loan may be either secured by a product such as an automobile or furniture or unsecured based solely on the borrower's signature. The loan may be repaid in installment payments or as one lump sum—principal and interest. Consumer loans, however, are generally paid in regular installments.

About This Chapter: Text in this chapter is from "Credit: What Are Your Choices?" by J. McKenna and C. Makela, Colorado State University Cooperative Extension, updated June 2006. Reprinted with permission. J. McKenna is a Colorado State University Cooperative Extension family resource management specialist and professor of design and merchandising; C. Makela is professor in school of education at Colorado State University.

When property is pledged for a secured loan, the property may be repossessed if payments are not made. Auto loans are examples of secured loans. Unsecured loans have no security and are made to people who have good credit ratings, often customers of the lending institution where they do business. Rates may be higher on unsecured loans because there is no property to be claimed if the loan is not repaid.

Credit Sales: The consumer buys goods or services and credit is arranged by the seller of the product. In most cases, the merchandise is used as security for the loan. Credit sales are frequently arranged for furniture and auto purchases and paid in regular installments.

♣ **It's A Fact!!**

Getting A Loan:
A Responsibility To Be Taken Seriously

Borrowing money can be a great way to buy something now and pay for it over time. And yes, there are ways for a teen to borrow money. But there are some important things to remember if you borrow money. One is that borrowing usually involves a cost called "interest," which is the fee to compensate the bank or other lender when you use their money. This is the reverse of what happens when the bank pays you interest to put your money in the bank.

Also, when you borrow money you are promising to repay the loan on a schedule. If you don't keep that promise, the results can be very costly—either in late payments you'll owe or in damage to your reputation, which means you could have a tougher time borrowing money in the future.

Here are some of your options...and important considerations.

For many teens, their first lenders are their parents. If your parents are willing to lend you money, they probably will set repayment terms (how much to pay back and when). They also may require you to pay more money than you borrowed, as a bank would do when it lends people money and charges interest.

You may be able to get access to a credit card or bank loan. Under most state laws, for example, you must be at least 18 years old to obtain your own credit

Credit Cards: Credit cards are offered by retail stores, credit unions, and banks. Finance charges are added each month whenever there is an outstanding account balance.

Sources Of Credit

Credit unions lend only to members, however, most people in a geographical area can become members. Credit unions offer consumer loans, credit cards, debit cards, and sometimes even mortgage loans. Rates are usually lower than other lenders because credit unions loan members' money, are eligible for federal tax exemptions, and generally take fewer credit risks.

card and be held responsible for repaying the debt. If you're under 18, though, you can qualify for a credit card along with a parent or other adult.

If you and your parents are comfortable with you having access to a credit card, there are cards designed just for teens. One is a credit card with a low credit limit (maximum amount you can borrow), which can keep you from getting deeply in debt.

An alternative to buying with a credit card is to use a debit card, but this also comes with costs and risks. A debit card allows you to make purchases without paying interest or getting into debt because the money is automatically deducted from an existing savings or checking account. Again, if you're under 18, you may qualify for this card with a parent or other adult.

One example of a debit card that may be appropriate for teens 13 and older is a pre-paid card that carries a certain value from which purchases are deducted. This kind of debit card isn't linked to your bank account. Instead, just like with a pre-paid telephone plan, there is a limit on how much you may spend.

Keep in mind that many debit cards have fees that can add up quickly, so make sure you ask about fees before using a debit card. Also, because a debit card can provide a thief easy access to an account, you need to protect your card and any PINs (personal identification numbers) that go with it.

Source: From *FDIC Consumer News*, Federal Deposit Insurance Corporation (FDIC), Summer 2006.

Commercial banks mainly cater to customers with established credit histories. They offer consumer loans, credit cards, debit cards, and mortgage loans. They may make short term loans to good customers. Banks often require items for security, and vary interest rates according to the type of loan. Their rates may be lower than other lenders because they take fewer risks and have money from customers' savings to lend.

Savings and loan associations select credit-worthy individuals and often require security for loans. Similar to credit unions and commercial banks, savings and loan rates are often lower because they loan depositors' money. Savings and loan associations offer consumer loans, credit cards, and mortgage loans.

Consumer finance companies will lend to some individuals who do not meet credit standards of other lenders. Rates are often higher because they take greater risks and must borrow money to lend to customers. They mainly finance consumer loans.

Retail stores charge interest on monthly revolving accounts. Rates may be higher than lending institutions. Sometimes major purchases may be made on 90-day contracts at lower rates of interest. Retail establishments may offer a store credit card and/or accept most bank credit cards.

Some retail stores that sell merchandise such as furniture, appliances, and automobiles may offer credit sale contracts at their places of business. These contracts frequently are sold to a financial institution such as a bank or consumer finance company. Because the interest rates may be higher than other credit sources, before agreeing to these loan terms consumers should investigate the credit terms they can arrange on their own from another source.

✔ **Quick Tip**

- Shopping for credit can save you hundreds of dollars.

- If you have good credit and shop for the best loans, you have the most choices for how much you want to pay for interest.

- Interest rates for payday loans may exceed 500 percent.

Source: McKenna and Makela, Colorado State University Cooperative Extension, 2006.

❖ It's A Fact!!

Payday loans are a growing market for financial services. These small, short term, very high-rate loans go by a variety of names: "payday loans," "cash advance loans," "check advance loans," "post-dated check loans," or "delayed deposit check loans." Typically, a borrower writes a personal check payable to the lender for the amount he wishes to borrow, plus the fee. The loan must be repaid within 40 days. Colorado law limits the lender from renewing the loan (at high interest rates) more than once [although other states may permit this practice]. [In Colorado] if the loan is refinanced a second time, the interest rate can not exceed 36 percent [but rules differ in other states]. Fees for payday loans are most often a percentage of the face value of the check or a fee per $100 loaned. In total, Colorado consumers can be charged over 520 percent on payday loans [and consumers in other states may pay even more].

Source: McKenna and Makela, Colorado State University Cooperative Extension, 2006.

Life insurance companies lend the cash value of life insurance policies to policy holders. The rates are less because they take no risk and have no collection costs. Outstanding loans against life insurance policies will be deducted from survivor benefits.

Pawnbrokers loan money on items that are left for security. Interest rates generally are close to the maximum allowed by law. If you can't repay the loan within the specified time period, the pawnshop will sell your items.

Friends and relatives may be willing to make loans. Rates will vary. It is essential to have a written agreement that is considered as binding as any other credit obligation.

Check-cashing stores and payday loans are short-term loans (cash advance) based on your paycheck. Effective annual interest rates may be more than 250 percent.

Rent-to-own is a special situation where people pay little or no down payment to rent furniture, appliances, and electronics. When they make the last payment, they own the item. Instead of stating interest rates for people who pay until they own the merchandise, a total purchase price is given. It is up to the consumer to compute the interest rate. Rent-to-own contracts usually offer low payments plus fees for repair and delivery services. In Colorado, rent-to-own agreements are considered rental agreements and interest rates are not capped at consumer loan or credit sale maximums. The rent-to-own business in Colorado is regulated by the Colorado Attorney

Table 11.1. Interest Costs

This information does not apply to [only] payday or rent-to-own loans. It is a general statement comparing interest rates of all loans. The total interest cost varies greatly according to the interest charges. Here is an example of a $1,000 loan borrowed for one year [assuming monthly payments are made regularly and on time].

APR	Total Interest
9%	$49.42
18%	$100.16
27%	$152.21
250%	$1,787.75

Source: McKenna and Makela, Colorado State University Cooperative Extension, 2006.

✔ Quick Tip

For the latest information about credit cards and rates, visit these websites:

- http://www.cardtrak.com
- http://www.bankrate.com
- http://www.lendingtree.com
- http://www.credit-search.com

Remember that websites that end in .com are commercial sites and will usually have something to sell. You should also check the Colorado State University Cooperative Extension Financial Web Resources listing of current websites that address financial topics: www.ext.colostate.edu/pubs/finance/general.html.

Source: McKenna and Makela, Colorado State University Cooperative Extension, 2006.

General's UCCC Administrator www.ago.state.co.us/uccc/uccchome.htm and the federal Uniform Consumer Credit Code. [Although the federal laws will apply in all states, different state regulations will apply in other states.]

A rent-to-own customer could end up paying a total that would include annual interest rates of 100 percent on average and possibly as high as 275 percent. If someone used a rent-to-own contract on a 19" television, they could pay $9.99 per week for 78 weeks, a total of $780. They could purchase the same television for $218 at a retail store. Because the rent-to-own contract is not considered credit, the merchandise can be picked up any time a payment is missed—even if there are only three payments remaining on a 78-week contract.

Colorado does provide some protection [and state laws in other states offer varying amounts of protection]. Late charge payments cannot be more than $5.00 for the month after the payment is 5 days late. Late charges for

Table 11.2. Types of credit offered by different credit sources.

Credit Source	Consumer Loans	Credit Sales	Credit Cards
Credit unions	X		X
Banks	X		X
Savings & loan associations	X		X
Consumer finance companies	X		
Retail stores	X	X	
Life insurance companies	X		
Pawnbrokers	X		
Friends and relatives	X		
Check-cashing stores	X		
Payday loans	X		
Rent-to-own stores	X[1]		

[1]Technically, rent-to-own financing is not a loan.

Source: McKenna and Makela, Colorado State University Cooperative Extension, 2006.

weekly payments cannot be more than $3.00 for the week after the payment is three days late. There is no penalty for ending the lease agreement, and the lender is not to sell insurance.

Credit Choices

Now back to the question about the washer and dryer purchase—how many sources of credit could be tapped for the credit needed? The correct answer is that most of the sources of credit might be used to purchase a washer and dryer. Table 11.2 shows the types of credit offered by different credit sources. The interest rates can vary from 0 percent from a friend to more than 250 percent per year from a rent-to-own store.

The federal Truth-in-Lending Act requires lenders to state their interest charges as an annual percentage rate (APR) so that consumers can compare true costs of borrowing. The APR is based on finance charges, amount borrowed, and the repayment schedule. For example, if you borrow $600 with a finance charge of $60 and pay the entire $660 at the end of twelve months, you will be paying an APR of 10 percent. If, on the other hand,

♣ **It's A Fact!!**
Consumer Loans/
Credit Sales

[In Colorado] lenders can charge 21 percent of the total financed or:

- 36 percent per year on amounts from $0 to $1,000; plus

- 21 percent per year on amounts over $1,000 to $3,000; plus

- 15 percent per year on amounts over $3,000.

This doesn't mean, however, that a lender will only charge 15 percent on a $3,500 loan. When the stairstep rates are computed, the maximum rate could end up being 26.82 percent. For example:

36 percent on the first $1,000

+ 21 percent on the next $2,000

+ 15 percent on the remaining $500

=26.82 percent average interest rate

In addition, a lender may charge a maximum finance charge of $25.00. [Laws in other states may vary.]

Source: McKenna and Makela, Colorado State University Cooperative Extension, 2006.

you borrow $600 with a $60 finance charge and agree to repay in twelve monthly payments, you do not have the use of the $600 for the entire year. The APR on this loan would be 18.5 percent.

The APR and total finance charges must be clearly stated on all credit contracts. Compare APRs when shopping for credit to determine the most favorable rate of credit.

Interest Rates Differ

The maximum amount of interest that can be charged for financing a product or service depends on the type of credit used. The Colorado Uniform Consumer Credit Code (UCCC) sets the maximum rates for credit cards, consumer loans, and credit sales. [In other places rates are governed by local state laws; information from Colorado is used here as an example].

Consumer Loans: [In Colorado], the maximum rate that a lending institution can charge for a consumer loan is set by Colorado statute [rates in other states are regulated by local state laws]. Maximum interest rates allowable are the same whether the loan is secured or unsecured, set up on an installment plan or repayable in one lump sum, or the interest is deducted at the beginning of the loan or added to monthly payments.

Credit Sales: Rates for credit sales are also set by Colorado [and other state] law and are the same as consumer loans.

Credit Cards: For credit cards the maximum allowable interest charge is 1.75 percent per month or 21 percent per year for credit granted from Colorado-based lenders. Lenders charging the maximum amount must allow consumers to pay for goods and service without interest in 25 days. [Laws in other states vary.]

Payday Loans: These are also known as post-dated check loans and paycheck advance loans. [In Colorado] the top amount that can be borrowed at one time is $500. Lenders may charge 20 percent on the first $300 borrowed and 7.5 percent on amounts from $301 to $500. [Laws in other states vary.]

Interest Rebates: If you want to pay a loan off early, how would the final interest charge be computed? The amount of interest reduction you would be entitled to is computed by using the Rule of 78. This rule is based on the idea that the creditor is entitled to earn more interest in the early months of the loan when you owe more money. The creditor earns less interest in subsequent months when you owe less money.

☞ Remember!!

Lenders sell credit just as department stores sell clothing. In order to buy the product, which in the case of credit is money, the consumer must pay a fee. Be aware of the cost of credit. By comparing the cost from one lending institution to another you can save yourself hundreds and sometimes thousands of dollars. A credit shopping expedition can be well worth the effort.

Chapter 12

Cosigning A Loan

A friend or relative has asked you to cosign a loan, perhaps to buy a car or home, or for some other worthy purpose. You're told your signature is needed because he or she has no established credit record, or maybe there have been credit problems in the past. "Honest, all you've got to do is sign a piece of paper. I'll pay everything back. You won't owe a thing."

The Federal Deposit Insurance Corporation (FDIC) can't tell you if cosigning a particular loan is a good or bad idea—that's a personal decision. But they will tell you that cosigning a loan can be risky. It means you are guaranteeing to pay the money back if the other person doesn't. And even though you may have great trust in your friend or relative, the odds say you may indeed be called upon to pay money.

The Federal Trade Commission (FTC) says that as many as three out of four cosigners are requested to make payments on a loan. "When you're asked to cosign, you're being asked to take a risk that a professional lender won't take," explains the FTC. "If the borrower met the (basic lending) criteria, the lender wouldn't require a cosigner" in the first place. In addition, the borrower may become unemployed or ill and no longer be able to repay the loan.

About This Chapter: Text in this chapter is from "Co-Signing a Loan Can Be Costly," *FDIC Consumer News*, Federal Deposit Insurance Corporation (FDIC), Summer 2002.

Unfortunately for the cosigner, the lender often looks to him or her soon after troubles start with a loan. "In many states, if the borrower misses just one payment, the lender can immediately try to collect from the cosigner without first trying to collect from the borrower," says Robert Patrick, an FDIC attorney.

And what could happen if you, as a cosigner, refuse to make the loan payments? You could get a bad mark on your credit record, and that could make it

> **Remember!!**
> Even though you may trust your friend or relative, the odds say you may be called upon to pay money.

tougher to get a loan, a job, an insurance policy, or something else you might apply for in the future. The lender can sue you and attempt to "garnish" wages (withhold a percentage of your paycheck until the loan is paid). You may be responsible for late fees or legal fees. And, if you offered collateral (such as furniture) as security for the loan, the lender may seize the property and sell it to cover the debt.

If you decide to cosign a loan after all, the FDIC offers the following suggestions:

Before you sign on the dotted line: The borrower may not realize that when he or she is late with payments or misses a payment, that could tarnish your credit record. So, it's best to have an understanding (if not a written agreement) with the borrower that you will get early notice of any troubles, including late payments, so you can keep on top of the loan and work out problems with the lender before your credit record is damaged. Also, be sure you can afford to pay the loan, if you have to.

Be sure that the lender gives you a notice required by federal law before you agree to cosign a loan. It explains your risks and responsibilities. (The fact that a lender didn't provide the required notice doesn't automatically excuse your debt as a cosigner, but it may help you in the long run. In some instances, for example, juries have decided that cosigners weren't liable for loan payments because they weren't advised of their responsibilities.) Ask the lender to estimate the amount of money you might owe if the borrower defaults. And, while a lender isn't obligated to do so, perhaps it would agree to limit what you'd owe in the event of a default. Such as, maybe you'd be expected to pay back the loan amount but not certain additional fees or costs. Be sure to include any limitations on your liability in the loan contract.

After you cosign the loan: "Keep copies of all loan documents," says FDIC attorney Susan van den Toorn. "These records could protect you from excessive fees or penalties if the borrower defaults on the loan."

If you have questions or complaints: Try to resolve the matter with the lender directly. If you can't, a government agency may be able to help. In the case of a loan from a banking institution, call or write the appropriate federal agency. For nonbank lenders, such as a consumer finance company or automobile dealer, contact the Federal Trade Commission (call toll-free 877-382-4357, use the

---

♣ It's A Fact!!
Notice To Cosigners

Under federal law, creditors are required to give you a notice that explains your obligations. The cosigner's notice states these facts:

- You are being asked to guarantee this debt. Think carefully before you do. If the borrower does not pay the debt, you will have to. Be sure you can afford to pay if you have to, and that you want to accept this responsibility.

- You may have to pay up to the full amount of the debt if the borrower does not pay. You may also have to pay late fees or collection costs, which increase this amount.

- The creditor can collect this debt from you without first trying to collect from the borrower. (Depending on your state, this may not apply. If state law forbids a creditor from collecting from a cosigner without first trying to collect from the primary debtor, this sentence may be crossed out or omitted altogether.) The creditor can use the same collection methods against you that can be used against the borrower, such as suing you, garnishing your wages, etc. If this debt is ever in default, that fact may become a part of your credit record.

- This notice is not the contract that makes you liable for the debt.

Source: Excerpted from "Cosigning a Loan," Federal Trade Commission, March 1997.

online complaint form accessible through their website at http://www.ftc.gov or write to the FTC, Consumer Response Center, 600 Pennsylvania Avenue, NW, Room 130, Washington, DC 20580).

Finally, if you have questions or concerns about the collection methods used by a lender or a collection agency, start with your state government's consumer protection office, division of financial regulation or Attorney General, which should be listed in your local phone book.

Chapter 13

Understanding Vehicle Financing

Most consumers need financing or leasing to acquire a vehicle. In some cases, buyers use "direct lending:" they obtain a loan directly from a finance company, bank, or credit union. In direct lending, a buyer agrees to pay the amount financed, plus an agreed-upon finance charge, over a period of time. Once a buyer and a vehicle dealership enter into a contract and the buyer agrees to a vehicle price, the buyer uses the loan proceeds from the direct lender to pay the dealership for the vehicle.

The most common type of vehicle financing, however, is "dealership financing." In this arrangement, a buyer and a dealership enter into a contract where the buyer agrees to pay the amount financed, plus an agreed-upon finance charge, over a period of time. The dealership may retain the contract, but usually sells it to an assignee (such as a bank, finance company, or credit union), which services the account and collects the payments.

About This Chapter: This chapter includes "Understanding Vehicle Financing," February 2003, "Buying a New Car," April 2006, "Buying a Used Car," April 1998, "Car Ads: Reading Between the Lines," March 1997, Federal Trade Commission (http://www.ftc.gov); "Kicking the Tires on an Auto Loan: Don't Kick Yourself for Paying Too Much," Federal Deposit Insurance Corporation (http://www.fdic.gov), 2004; and "Vehicle Leasing: Quick Consumer Guide," The Federal Reserve Board (http://www.federalreserve.gov), February 7, 2005.

What Happens When You Apply For Dealership Financing

Most dealerships have a Finance and Insurance (F&I) Department. The F&I Department manager will ask you to complete a credit application. Information on this application may include: your name; Social Security number; date of birth; current and previous addresses and length of stay; current and previous employers and length of employment; occupation; sources of income; total gross monthly income; and financial information on existing credit accounts.

The dealership will obtain a copy of your credit report, which contains information about current and past credit obligations, your payment record, and data from public records (for example, a bankruptcy filing obtained from court documents). For each account, the credit report shows your account number, the type and terms of the account, the credit limit, the most recent balance, and the most recent payment. The comments section describes the current status of your account, including the creditor's summary of past due information and any legal steps that may have been taken to collect.

Dealers typically sell your contract to an assignee, such as a bank, finance company, or credit union. The dealership submits your credit application to one or more of these potential assignees to determine their willingness to purchase your contract from the dealer.

These finance companies or other potential assignees will usually evaluate your credit application using automated techniques such as credit scoring, where a variety of factors, like your credit history, length of employment, income, and expenses may be weighted and scored.

Since the bank, finance company, or credit union does not deal directly with the prospective vehicle purchaser, it bases its evaluation upon what appears on the individual's credit report and score,

> **☞ Remember!!**
>
> *What Influences Your APR?*
>
> Your credit history, current finance rates, competition, market conditions, and special offers are among the factors that influence your APR.
>
> Source: Federal Trade Commission, 2003.

the completed credit application, and the terms of the sale, such as the amount of the down payment. Each finance company or other potential assignee decides whether it is willing to buy the contract, notifies the dealership of its decision and, if applicable, offers the dealership a wholesale rate at which the assignee will buy the contract, often called the "buy rate."

Your dealer may be able to offer manufacturer incentives, such as reduced finance rates or cash back on certain models. You may see these specials advertised in your area. Make sure you ask your dealer if the model you are interested in has any special financing offers or rebates. Generally, these discounted rates are not negotiable, may be limited by a consumer's credit history, and are available only for certain models, makes, or model-year vehicles.

When there are no special financing offers available, you can negotiate the annual percentage rate (APR) and the terms for payment with the dealership, just as you negotiate the price of the vehicle. The APR that you negotiate with the dealer is usually higher than the wholesale rate described earlier. This negotiation can occur before or after the dealership accepts and processes your credit application.

Before Visiting The Dealership

• Evaluate your financial situation and determine how much you can afford to pay each month. A longer-term finance contract may mean smaller monthly payments than a shorter-term finance contract (if all other terms are the same)—but will result in more money paid over time on your contract.

What's It Mean?

Know The Terms Of Financing Before You Sign

<u>Assignee:</u> The bank, finance company, or credit union that purchases the contract from the dealer.

<u>Amount Financed:</u> The dollar amount of the credit that is provided to you.

<u>Annual Percentage Rate Or "APR":</u> The cost of credit for one year expressed as a percentage.

<u>Credit Insurance:</u> Optional insurance that pays the scheduled unpaid balance if you die or scheduled monthly payments if you become disabled. As with most contract terms, the cost of optional credit insurance must be disclosed in writing, and, if you want it, you must agree to it and sign for it.

<u>Down Payment:</u> An initial amount paid to reduce the amount financed.

<u>Extended Service Contract:</u> Optional protection on specified mechanical and electrical components of the vehicle available for purchase to supplement the warranty coverage provided with the new or used vehicle.

<u>Finance Charge:</u> The total dollar amount you pay to use credit.

<u>Fixed Rate Financing:</u> The finance rate remains the same over the life of the contract.

<u>Guaranteed Auto Protection (GAP):</u> Optional protection that pays the difference between the amount you owe on your vehicle and the amount you receive from your insurance company if the vehicle is stolen or destroyed before you have satisfied your credit obligation.

<u>Monthly Payment Amount:</u> The dollar amount due each month to repay the credit agreement.

<u>Negotiated Price Of The Vehicle:</u> The purchase price of the vehicle agreed upon by the buyer and the dealer.

<u>Variable Rate Financing:</u> The finance rate varies and the amount you must pay changes over the life of the contract.

Source: Federal Trade Commission, 2003.

- Determine the price range of the vehicle you're thinking of buying. Check newspaper ads, the internet, and other publications.

- Understand the value and cost of optional credit insurance if you agree to purchase.

- Know the difference between buying and leasing a vehicle.

- Be aware that your credit history may affect the finance rate you are able to negotiate. Generally, you'll be able to get a lower rate if you've paid your monthly credit obligations on time.

- Compare annual percentage rates and financing terms from multiple finance sources such as a bank, finance company, and credit union. This information may also be available from the finance sources' and vehicle manufacturers' websites.

When Visiting The Dealership

- Stay within the price range that you can afford.

- Negotiate your finance or lease arrangements and terms.

- Consider carefully whether the transaction is best for your budget and transportation needs.

- Understand the value and cost of optional products, such as an extended service contract, credit insurance, or guaranteed auto protection, if you agree to purchase. If you don't want these products, don't sign for them.

- Read the contract carefully before you sign. You are obligated once you have signed a contract.

After Completing The Vehicle Purchase Or Lease

- Be aware that if you financed the vehicle, the assignee (bank, finance company, or credit union that purchases the contract) holds a lien on the vehicle's title (and in some cases the actual title) until you have paid the contract in full.

- Make your payments on time. Late or missed payments incur late fees, appear on your credit report and impact your ability to get credit in the future.

• Be aware that repossession can occur if you fail to make timely payments. It does not relieve you of your obligation to pay for the vehicle. The law in some states allows the creditor or assignee to repossess your vehicle without going to court.

Kicking The Tires On An Auto Loan: Don't Kick Yourself For Paying Too Much

Buying a new vehicle is stressful enough without having to make a decision about how to pay for it. Zero-percent financing, rebate offers of thousands of dollars, small down payments, bank financing, dealer financing—so many choices are enough to make your head spin even before you've taken your dream purchase out for a spin. The Federal Deposit Insurance Corporation (FDIC) offers these tips to help you save time and money when it comes to shopping for an auto loan.

Review your credit report long before you intend to apply for a loan.

Why should you see your credit report before applying for a car loan? To correct any error before it slows down your credit approval or prevents you from getting the best possible loan terms. "Erroneous information can cost you hundreds of dollars because you could be disqualified from the best financing terms available," says Joni Creamean, a Senior Consumer Affairs Specialist with the FDIC. "You will be considered a riskier borrower and charged higher rates or be required to provide a larger down payment." Creamean adds that it could take months to correct errors in your credit history.

✎ **What's It Mean?**

Credit Report: A summary of your financial reliability—for the most part, your history of paying debts and other bills—as compiled by a company called a credit bureau. You are entitled to one free credit report annually from each of the three national credit bureaus. You can order your free annual report online at http://www.annualcreditreport.com or by calling 877-322-8228.

Source: Federal Deposit Insurance Corporation, 2004.

Shop for a loan before you visit a dealership or bid for a car over the internet.

Contact your bank and several other local lenders. Ask about the loans they offer—the number of months for which you can borrow, the interest rates being offered, whether there are penalties if you pay the loan off early, and so on. Ask about other options for financing the car.

Janet Kincaid, FDIC Senior Consumer Affairs Officer, points to yet another reason to shop for a loan before you shop for a car: "Knowing what your spending limit is and sticking to it permits you to focus only on the vehicles within that range," she says. "This also helps you avoid taking on more debt than you are comfortable with in the long run."

Also consider getting pre-approved for a loan, meaning a lender evaluates your creditworthiness and explains your loan options and likely costs before you buy a car. "Getting pre-approved doesn't mean you have a loan in hand but it does give you the benefit of knowing what you can afford and what it will cost you in the way of a loan," Kincaid explains. "You'll also know you won't be surprised with news that you've been denied credit or charged a higher rate due to your credit record." (Consumer advocates also suggest that you not tell the dealer if you've been pre-approved elsewhere for a loan until after you've negotiated the best price on a car. Some dealers may be less flexible on the price of the vehicle if it's clear that the dealership won't be earning money on a loan.)

After you know what's available in the marketplace, including the interest rates, consider learning what the dealers are offering by reading their advertisements, making phone calls, or checking the internet. Find out if only certain models are eligible for zero-percent financing from the dealer or if a manufacturer's rebate isn't available if you opt for zero-percent financing. Having this information helps you make a good decision about financing when you're face-to-face with a sales person or finance officer at the dealership. For example, "In some situations, it may be best to accept the dealer's rebate and pass up the zero-percent financing in favor of a loan from a bank that does charge interest," says Creamean. "You'll have to do the math and decide what is best for you."

Be careful figuring out how much to borrow and for how long.

Of course, the dollar amount of your loan largely will be determined by the sale price of the vehicle minus your down payment, any rebates, and the value of any trade-in. But there are other costs that you should consider when deciding how much of a car you can afford and how much of a loan you need. Those costs include auto insurance, sales taxes, annual property taxes on the car (if any), and options you may be inclined to buy, such as an extended warranty. Also remember that every item you add to your loan instead of paying up-front will add to the total cost of the loan because you will be paying interest on the amount financed.

After you determine how big a loan you need, try to pick a repayment period that makes sense for you. For example, a $15,000 loan at 4 percent interest for 36 months equals a monthly payment of $443. Stretch the same loan out to 48 months and the monthly payment drops to $339. While it's tempting to go with a longer loan to reduce your payment, be careful. "Don't make the common mistake of thinking only in terms of monthly payments rather than the total cost of the loan," warns Creamean. "In the end, extending a loan term will cost you more since you will be paying interest on the loan another year or more."

Creamean says to be especially cautious before taking an auto loan term of five years or more. "First," she says, "if you have little cash for a down payment and you have to take on a loan of five or seven years, you might be trying to buy more car than you can really afford. Also, in the later years of the loan, you'll still be making payments on what is an older vehicle that may have a lot of repair and maintenance costs."

Creamean also cautions that, in five or seven years, you may still owe more on the loan than the trade-in value of the car, and that puts you in a difficult financial position. "Just when you need or want

> ✔ **Quick Tip**
> And for more information about how to get a good auto loan, visit the FTC (Federal Trade Commission) website at http://www.ftc.gov/bcp/conline/edcams/automobiles/index.html.
>
> Source: Federal Deposit Insurance Corporation, 2004.

Remember!!

The bottom line: By being better informed about auto loans, you're more likely to drive away happy with extra savings in your bank account that can be used for other things, such as gas money... or fuzzy dice.

Source: Federal Deposit Insurance Corporation, 2004.

a new vehicle," she says, "problems with your old car may require you to come up with extra cash to pay off the old loan or you might have to roll the old loan into a new loan, which may push up your interest rate. It can become a vicious cycle."

Know what you are signing and speak up if you think there's a problem.

A variety of laws provide consumer protections in the context of auto loans. Among them: the federal Truth in Lending Act, which requires lenders to disclose to borrowers the terms of a loan (including the Annual Percentage Rate and the total cost of the loan), and federal and state laws that prohibit unfair or deceptive business practices. However, you have a responsibility for protecting yourself, too.

"One of the most important things a borrower can do is to carefully review the loan document before signing it, because this is a contract legally binding you to repay according to the terms of the document," says FDIC attorney Mark Mellon. While the Truth in Lending Act gives consumers the right to cancel certain mortgage contracts up to three business days after signing the contract, Mellon says, "there may or may not be a similar protection for your auto loan depending on your circumstances and state law, so it's best to be comfortable with your decision before you sign on the dotted line."

Leasing Is Different From Buying

Under the federal Consumer Leasing Act, you, the consumer, have a right to information about the costs and terms of a vehicle lease. This information will help you compare lease offers and negotiate a lease that best fits your needs, budget, and driving patterns.

This information is for a closed-end lease, the most common type of vehicle lease. With a closed-end lease, you may return the vehicle at the end of the lease term, pay any end-of-lease costs, and walk away.

Ownership

- **Leasing:** You do not own the vehicle. You get to use it but must return it at the end of the lease unless you choose to buy it.

- **Buying:** You own the vehicle and get to keep it at the end of the financing term.

Up-Front Costs

- **Leasing:** Up-front costs may include the first month's payment, a refundable security deposit, a capitalized cost reduction (like a down payment), taxes, registration and other fees, and other charges.

- **Buying:** Up-front costs include the cash price or a down payment, taxes, registration and other fees, and other charges.

Monthly Payments

- **Leasing:** Monthly lease payments are usually lower than monthly loan payments because you are paying only for the vehicle's depreciation during the lease term, plus rent charges (like interest), taxes, and fees.

- **Buying:** Monthly loan payments are usually higher than monthly lease payments because you are paying for the entire purchase price of the vehicle, plus interest and other finance charges, taxes, and fees.

Early Termination

- **Leasing:** You are responsible for any early termination charges if you end the lease early.

- **Buying:** You are responsible for any pay-off amount if you end the loan early.

Vehicle Return

- **Leasing:** You may return the vehicle at lease-end, pay any end-of-lease costs, and "walk away."

- **Buying:** You may have to sell or trade the vehicle when you decide you want a different vehicle.

Future Value

- **Leasing:** The lessor has the risk of the future market value of the vehicle.

- **Buying:** You have the risk of the vehicle's market value when you trade or sell it.

Mileage

- **Leasing:** Most leases limit the number of miles you may drive (often 12,000–15,000 per year). You can negotiate a higher mileage limit and pay a higher monthly payment. You will likely have to pay charges for exceeding those limits if you return the vehicle.

- **Buying:** You may drive as many miles as you want, but higher mileage will lower the vehicle's trade-in or resale value.

Excessive Wear

- **Leasing:** Most leases limit wear to the vehicle during the lease term. You will likely have to pay extra charges for exceeding those limits if you return the vehicle.

- **Buying:** There are no limits or charges for excessive wear to the vehicle, but excessive wear will lower the vehicle's trade-in or resale value.

End Of Term

- **Leasing:** At the end of the lease (typically 2–4 years), you may have a new payment either to finance the purchase of the existing vehicle or to lease another vehicle.

- **Buying:** At the end of the loan term (typically 4–6 years), you have no further loan payments.

Consider Beginning, Middle, And End-Of-Lease Costs

At the beginning of the lease, you may have to pay your first monthly payment; a refundable security deposit or your last monthly payment; other fees for licenses, registration, and title; a capitalized cost reduction (like a down payment); an acquisition fee (also called a processing or assignment fee); freight or destination charges; and state or local taxes.

During the lease, you will have to pay your monthly payment; any additional taxes not included in the payment such as sales, use, and personal property taxes; insurance premiums; ongoing maintenance costs; and any fees for late payment. You'll also have to pay for safety and emissions inspections and any traffic tickets. If you end your lease early, you may have to pay substantial early termination charges.

At the end of the lease, if you don't buy the vehicle, you may have to pay a disposition fee and charges for excess miles and excessive wear.

Know Your Rights And Responsibilities

When you lease a vehicle, you have the right to:

- Use it for an agreed-upon number of months and miles.

- Turn it in at lease-end, pay any end-of-lease fees and charges, and "walk away."

- Buy the vehicle if you have a purchase option.

- Take advantage of any warranties, recalls, or other services that apply to the vehicle.

You may be responsible for:

- Excess mileage charges when you return the vehicle. Your lease agreement will tell you how many miles you can drive before you must pay for extra miles and how much the per-mile charge will be.

✔ **Quick Tip**

You can compare different lease offers and negotiate some terms. Consider:

- The agreed-upon value of the vehicle—a lower value can reduce your monthly payment.

- Up-front payments, including the capitalized cost reduction.

- The length of the lease.

- The monthly lease payment.

- Any end-of-lease fees and charges.

- The mileage allowed and per-mile charges for excess miles.

- The option to purchase either at lease-end or earlier.

- Whether your lease includes "gap" coverage, which protects you if the vehicle is stolen or totaled in an accident.

Ask for alternatives to advertised specials and other lease offerings.

Source: Federal Reserve Board, 2005.

- Excessive wear charges when you return the vehicle. The standards for excessive wear, such as for body damage or worn tires, are in your lease agreement.

- Substantial payments if you end the lease early. The earlier you end the lease, the greater these charges are likely to be.

Buying A New Car

A new car is second only to a home as the most expensive purchase many consumers make. According to the National Automobile Dealers Association, the average price of a new car sold in the United States is $28,400. That's why it's important to know how to make a smart deal.

Buying Your New Car

Think about what car model and options you want and how much you're willing to spend. Do some research. You'll be less likely to feel pressured into making a hasty or expensive decision at the showroom and more likely to get a better deal.

Consider these suggestions:

- Check publications at a library or bookstore, or on the internet, that discuss new car features and prices. These may provide information on the dealer's costs for specific models and options.

- Shop around to get the best possible price by comparing models and prices in ads and at dealer showrooms. You also may want to contact car-buying services and broker-buying services to make comparisons.

- Plan to negotiate on price. Dealers may be willing to bargain on their profit margin, often between 10 and 20 percent. Usually, this is the difference between the manufacturer's suggested retail price (MSRP) and the invoice price.

- Because the price is a factor in the dealer's calculations regardless of whether you pay cash or finance your car—and also affects your monthly payments—negotiating the price can save you money.

- Consider ordering your new car if you don't see what you want on the dealer's lot. This may involve a delay, but cars on the lot may have options you don't want—and that can raise the price. However, dealers often want to sell their current inventory quickly, so you may be able to negotiate a good deal if an in-stock car meets your needs.

✎ **What's It Mean?**

Learning The Terms

Negotiations often have a vocabulary of their own. Here are some terms you may hear when you're talking price.

Base Price: The cost of the car without options, but includes standard equipment and factory warranty. This price is printed on the Monroney sticker.

Dealer Sticker Price: Usually on a supplemental sticker, is the Monroney sticker price plus the suggested retail price of dealer-installed options, such as additional dealer markup (ADM) or additional dealer profit (ADP), dealer preparation, and undercoating.

Invoice Price: The manufacturer's initial charge to the dealer. This usually is higher than the dealer's final cost because dealers receive rebates, allowances, discounts, and incentive awards. Generally, the invoice price should include freight (also known as destination and delivery). If you're buying a car based on the invoice price (for example, "at invoice," "$100 below invoice," "two percent above invoice") and if freight is already included, make sure freight isn't added again to the sales contract.

Monroney Sticker Price (MSRP): Shows the base price, the manufacturer's installed options with the manufacturer's suggested retail price, the manufacturer's transportation charge, and the fuel economy (mileage). Affixed to the car window, this label is required by federal law, and may be removed only by the purchaser.

Source: Federal Trade Commission, 2006.

♣ It's A Fact!!

Some dealers and lenders may ask you to buy credit insurance to pay off your loan if you should die or become disabled. Before you buy credit insurance, consider the cost, and whether it's worthwhile. Check your existing policies to avoid duplicating benefits. Credit insurance is not required by federal law. If your dealer requires you to buy credit insurance for car financing, it must be included in the cost of credit. That is, it must be reflected in the APR. Your state Attorney General also may have requirements about credit insurance. Check with your state Insurance Commissioner or state consumer protection agency.

Source: Federal Trade Commission, 2006.

Trading In Your Old Car

Discuss the possibility of a trade-in only after you've negotiated the best possible price for your new car and after you've researched the value of your old car. Check the library for reference books or magazines that can tell you how much it is worth. This information may help you get a better price from the dealer. Though it may take longer to sell your car yourself, you generally will get more money than if you trade it in.

Considering A Service Contract

Service contracts that you may buy with a new car provide for the repair of certain parts or problems. These contracts are offered by manufacturers, dealers, or independent companies and may or may not provide coverage beyond the manufacturer's warranty. Remember that a warranty is included in the price of the car while a service contract costs extra.

Before deciding to purchase a service contract, read it carefully, and consider these questions:

- What's the difference between the coverage under the warranty and the coverage under the service contract?

- What repairs are covered?

- Is routine maintenance covered?

- Who pays for the labor? The parts?

- Who performs the repairs? Can repairs be made elsewhere?

- How long does the service contract last?

- What are the cancellation and refund policies?

Buying A Used Car

"I can't wait to get my own car." Sound familiar? Before you start shopping for a used car as a teenager, do some homework. It may save you serious money. Consider driving habits, what the car will be used for, and your budget. Research models, options, costs, repair records, safety tests, and mileage through libraries, book stores, and websites.

Cash Or Credit?

Once you've settled on a particular car, you have two payment options: paying in full or financing over time. Financing increases the total cost of the car because you're also paying for the cost of credit, including interest and other loan costs. You also must consider how much money you can put down, the monthly payment, the loan term, and the Annual Percentage Rate (APR). Rates usually are higher and loan periods shorter on used cars than on new ones. Dealers and lenders offer a variety of loan terms. Shop around and let your parents help you negotiate the best possible deal. Be cautious about financing offers for first-time buyers. They can require a big down payment and a high APR. To get a lower rate, you may decide to have a parent or guardian cosign on the loan. If money is tight, you might consider paying cash for a less expensive car than you first had in mind.

Dealer Or Private Sale?

The Federal Trade Commission's Used Car Rule requires dealers to post a Buyers Guide in every used car they offer for sale. The Buyers Guide gives a great deal of information, including:

- whether the vehicle is being sold "as is" or with a warranty;

- what percentage of the repair costs a dealer will pay under the warranty;

- the fact that spoken promises are difficult to enforce; and

- the major mechanical and electrical systems on the car, including some of the major problems you should look out for.

The Buyers Guide also tells you to:

- get all promises in writing;

- keep the Buyers Guide for reference after the sale; and

- ask to have the car inspected by an independent mechanic before the purchase.

Buying a car from a private individual is different from buying from a dealer. That's because private sales generally aren't covered by the Used Car Rule, or by "implied warranties" of state law. A private sale probably will be "as is"—you'll have to pay for anything that goes wrong after the sale.

Before You Buy

Whether you buy a used car from a dealer or an individual:

- examine the car using an inspection checklist. You can find checklists in magazines and books and on internet sites that deal with used cars;

- test drive the car under varied road conditions—on hills, highways, and in stop-and-go-traffic;

- ask for the car's maintenance record from the owner, dealer, or repair shop; and

- hire a mechanic to inspect the car.

Other Costs To Consider

There's more to buying a car than just paying for it. Other items to budget for include insurance, gas, maintenance, and repairs. Here are some tips to help you save money:

- Compare coverage and premiums with several insurance companies. Buy from a low-price, licensed insurer, or see if you can be added to your parents' policy. Some companies offer discounts to students with good grades.

- Pump your own gas and use the octane level your owner's manual specifies.

- Keep your car in safe driving condition. Following the vehicle's maintenance schedule can help forestall costly repairs.

- Look for a mechanic who is certified, well established, and communicates well about realistic repair options and costs. Find one who has done good work for someone you know.

Car Ads: Reading Between The Lines

Many new car dealers advertise unusually low interest rates and other special promotions. Ads promising high trade-in allowances and free or low-cost options may help you shop, but finding the best deal requires careful comparisons.

Many factors determine whether a special offer provides genuine savings. The interest rate, for example, is only part of the car dealer's financing package. Terms like the size of the down payment also affect the total financing cost.

Questions About Low Interest Loans

A call or visit to a dealer should help clarify details about low interest loans. Consider asking these questions:

- Will you be charged a higher price for the car to qualify for the low-rate financing? Would the price be lower if you paid cash, or supplied your own financing from your bank or credit union?

- Does the financing require a larger-than-usual down payment? Perhaps 25 or 30 percent?

- Are there limits on the length of the loan? Are you required to repay the loan in a condensed period of time, say 24 or 36 months?

☞ Remember!!

Remember that it pays to drive safely and observe speed limits. Traffic violations can cost money in tickets and higher insurance premiums.

Source: Federal Trade Commission, 1998.

- Is there a significant balloon payment—possibly several thousand dollars—due at the end of the loan?

- Do you have to buy special or extra merchandise or services such as rustproofing, an extended warranty, or a service contract to qualify for a low-interest loan?

- Is the financing available for a limited time only? Some merchants limit special deals to a few days or require that you take delivery by a certain date.

- Does the low rate apply to all cars in stock or only to certain models?

- Are you required to give the dealer the manufacturer's rebate to qualify for financing?

Questions About Other Promotions

Other special promotions include high trade-in allowances and free or low-cost options. Some dealers promise to sell the car for a stated amount over the dealer's invoice. Asking questions like these can help you determine whether special promotions offer genuine value.

- Does the advertised trade-in allowance apply to all cars, regardless of their condition? Are there any deductions for high mileage, dents, or rust?

- Does the larger trade-in allowance make the cost of the new car higher than it would be without the trade-in? You might be giving back the big trade-in allowance by paying more for the new car.

- Is the dealer who offers a high trade-in allowance and free or low-cost options giving you a better price on the car than another dealer who doesn't offer promotions?

- Does the "dealer's invoice" reflect the actual amount that the dealer pays the manufacturer? You can consult consumer or automotive publications for information about what the dealer pays.

- Does the "dealer's invoice" include the cost of options, such as rustproofing or waterproofing, that already have been added to the car? Is one dealer charging more for these options than others?

- Does the dealer have cars in stock that have no expensive options? If not, will the dealer order one for you?

- Are the special offers available if you order a car instead of buying one off the lot?

- Can you take advantage of all special offers simultaneously?

Once you decide which dealer offers the car and financing you want, read the invoice and the installment contract carefully. Check to see that all the terms of the contract reflect the agreement you made with the dealer. If they don't, get a written explanation before you sign. Careful shopping will help you decide what car, options, and financing are best for you.

☞ Remember!!

You're not limited to the financing options offered by a particular dealer. Before you commit to a deal, check to see what type of loan you can arrange with your bank or credit union.

Source: Federal Trade Commission, 1997.

Chapter 14

Loans For Education

Student loans, unlike grants and work-study, are borrowed money that must be repaid, with interest, just like car loans and mortgages. You cannot have these loans canceled because you didn't like the education you received, didn't get a job in your field of study, or because you're having financial difficulty. Loans are legal obligations, so before you take out a student loan, think about the amount you'll have to repay over the years.

Types Of Loans

Federal Perkins Loans: Here are facts about Federal Perkins Loans:

• Made through participating schools to undergraduate, graduate, and professional degree students.

• Offered by participating schools to students who demonstrate financial need.

• Made to students enrolled full-time or part-time.

• Repaid by you to your school.

Stafford Loans: These loans are for undergraduate, graduate, and professional degree students. You must be enrolled as at least a half-time student to be eligible for a Stafford Loan. There are two types of Stafford Loans: subsidized

About This Chapter: Excerpted from "Funding Education Beyond High School: The Guide to Federal Student Aid 2007–08," U.S. Department of Education, January 2007.

✎ What's It Mean?

Academic Year: A period of time schools use to measure a quantity of study. For example, a school's academic year may consist of a fall and spring semester during which a full-time undergraduate student must complete 24 semester hours. Academic years vary from school to school and even from educational program to educational program at the same school.

Capitalized: With certain loans, such as subsidized FFEL Loans, the U.S. Department of Education pays the interest that accrues while the student is enrolled at least half-time and during periods of deferment. However, with subsidized loans in forbearance, unsubsidized loans, or PLUS Loans, the student or the student's parents and graduate or professional degree students are responsible for paying interest as it accrues on these loans. When the interest is not paid, it is capitalized or added to the principal balance, which increases the outstanding principal amount due on this loan. Interest that is capitalized and, therefore, has been added to the original amount of the loan subsequently accrues interest, adding an additional expense to the loan.

Cost Of Attendance (COA): The total amount it will cost you to go to school—usually expressed as a yearly figure. It's determined using rules established by law. The COA includes tuition and fees; on-campus room and board (or a housing and food allowance for off-campus students); and allowances for books, supplies, transportation, loan fees, and, if applicable, dependent care. It also includes miscellaneous and personal expenses, including an allowance for the rental or purchase of a personal computer. Costs related to a disability are also covered. The COA includes reasonable costs for eligible study-abroad programs as well. For students attending less than half-time, the COA includes tuition and fees and an allowance for books, supplies, transportation, and dependent care expenses; but can also include room and board for up to three semesters or the equivalent at the institution, but no more than two of those semesters or the equivalent may be consecutive. Talk to the financial aid administrator at the school you're planning to attend if you have any unusual expenses that might affect your cost of attendance.

Default: Failure to repay a loan according to the terms agreed to when you signed a promissory note. For the FFEL and Direct Loan programs, default is more specific—it occurs if you fail to make a payment for 270 days if you repay monthly (or 330 days if your payments are due less frequently). The consequences of default are severe. Your school, the lender or agency that holds your loan, the state and the federal government may all take action to recover the money, including notifying national credit bureaus of your default. This may affect your credit rating for as long as seven years. For example, you might find it difficult to borrow money from a bank to buy a car or a house. In addition, the Internal Revenue Service can withhold your U.S. individual income tax refund and apply it to the amount you owe, or the agency holding your loan might ask your employer to deduct payments from your paycheck. Also, you may be liable for loan collection expenses. If you return to school, you're not entitled to receive additional federal student financial aid. Legal action also might be taken against you. In many cases, default can be avoided by submitting a request for a deferment, forbearance, discharge, or cancellation and by providing the required documentation.

Guaranty Agency: The guaranty agency is an organization that administers the Federal Family Education Loan (FFEL) Program in your state. This agency is the best source of information on FFEL Loans. For the name, address and telephone number of the agency serving your state, you can contact the Federal Student Aid Information Center at 800-4-FED-AID (800 433-3243).

Half-Time: According to federal student aid guidelines, "half-time" is at least six semester hours or quarter hours per term for an undergraduate program at schools measuring progress in credit hours and semesters, trimesters, or quarters. At schools measuring progress by credit hours but not using semesters, trimesters, or quarters, "half-time" is at least 12 semester hours or 18 quarter hours per year. At schools measuring progress by clock hours, "half-time" is at least 12 hours per week. Note that schools may choose to set higher minimums than these. You must be attending school at least half-time to be eligible for a Stafford Loan. Half-time enrollment is not a requirement to receive aid from the Federal Pell Grant, Federal Supplemental Educational Opportunity Grant, Federal Work-Study and Federal Perkins Loan programs.

Promissory Note: A promissory note is a binding legal document you sign when you get a loan. It lists the conditions under which you're borrowing and the terms under which you agree to pay back the loan. It will include information on how interest is calculated and what deferment and cancellation provisions are available to the borrower. It's very important to read and save this document because you'll need to refer to it later when you begin repaying your loan or at other times when you need information about provisions of the loan, such as deferments or forbearances.

Loan Program	Eligibility	Award Amounts	Interest Rates	Lender/Length of Repayment
Federal Perkins Loans	Undergraduate and graduate students	Undergraduate—up to $4,000 a year (maximum of $20,000 as an undergraduate) Graduate—up to $6,000 a year (maximum of $40,000, including undergraduate loans) Amount actually received depends on financial need, amount of other aid, availability of funds at school	5 percent	Lender is your school Repay your school or its agent Up to 10 years to repay, depending on amount owed
FFEL Stafford Loans (subsidized and unsubsidized)	Undergraduate and graduate students; must be enrolled at least half-time	Depends on grade level in school and dependency status Financial need is required for subsidized loans Financial need not necessary for unsubsidized loans	Fixed rate of 6.8 percent for loans first disbursed on or after July 1, 2006 Government pays interest on subsidized loans during school and certain other periods	Lender is a bank, credit union or other participating private lender Repay the loan holder or its agent Between 10 and 25 years to repay, depending on amount owed and type of repayment plan selected
Direct Stafford Loans (subsidized and unsubsidized)	Same as above	Same as above	Same as above	Lender is the U.S. Department of Education; repay Department Between 10 and 25 years to repay, depending on amount owed and type of repayment plan selected
FFEL PLUS Loans	Parents of dependent undergraduate students enrolled at least half-time (see dependency status); and graduate or professional degree students. Must not have negative credit history	Student's Cost of Attendance – Other aid student receives = Maximum loan amount	Fixed rate at 8.5 percent for loans first disbursed on or after July 1, 2006; borrower pays all interest	Same as for FFEL Stafford Loans above
Direct PLUS Loan	Same as above	Same as above	Fixed rate at 7.9 percent for loans first disbursed on or after July 1, 2006; borrower pays all interest	Same as for Direct Stafford Loans above, except that Income Contingent Repayment Plan is not an option

Figure 14.1. Student Loan Comparison Chart.

and unsubsidized. You must have financial need to receive a subsidized Stafford Loan. Financial need is not a requirement to obtain an unsubsidized Stafford Loan. The U.S. Department of Education will pay (subsidize) the interest that accrues on subsidized Stafford Loans during certain periods. These loans are made through one of two U.S. Department of Education programs:

- **William D. Ford Federal Direct Loan (Direct Loan) Program:** Loans made through this program are referred to as Direct Loans. Eligible students and parents borrow directly from the U.S. Department of Education at participating schools. Direct Loans include subsidized and unsubsidized Direct Stafford Loans (also known as Direct Subsidized Loans and Direct Unsubsidized Loans), Direct PLUS Loans, and Direct Consolidation Loans. You repay these loans directly to the U.S. Department of Education.

- **Federal Family Education Loan (FFEL) Program:** Loans made through this program are referred to as FFEL Loans. Private lenders provide funds that are guaranteed by the federal government. FFEL Loans include subsidized and unsubsidized FFEL Stafford Loans, FFEL PLUS Loans and FFEL Consolidation Loans. You repay these loans to the bank or private lender that made you the loan.

PLUS Loans: PLUS loans are loans parents can obtain to help pay the cost of education for their dependent undergraduate children. In addition, graduate and professional degree students may obtain PLUS Loans to help pay for their own education. These loans are made through both the Direct Loan and FFEL programs mentioned above.

♣ It's A Fact!!
Whether you (or your parents) receive a Direct or a FFEL Stafford Loan depends on which program the school you attend participates in. Most schools participate in one or the other, although some schools participate in both.

It's possible for you to receive both Direct and FFEL Stafford Loans but not for the same period of enrollment.

Years	Dependent Undergraduate Student	Independent Undergraduate Student	Graduate and Professional Degree Student
First Year	$3,500	$7,500—No more than $3,500 of this amount may be in subsidized loans.	$20,500—No more than $8,500 of this amount may be in subsidized loans.
Second Year	$4,500	$8,500—No more than $4,500 of this amount may be in subsidized loans.	
Third and beyond (each year)	$5,500	$10,500—No more than $5,500 of this amount may be in subsidized loans.	
Maximum Total Debt from Stafford Loans When You Graduate	$23,000	$46,000—No more than $23,000 of this amount may be in subsidized loans.	$138,500—No more than $65,500 of this amount may be in subsidized loans. The graduate debt limit includes Stafford Loans received for undergraduate study.

Figure 14.2. Maximum Annual Loan Limits Chart—Subsidized and Unsubsidized Direct and FFEL Stafford Loans.

♣ It's A Fact!!

The value of a postsecondary education as a credential for future employment and earnings is expected to rise. About 90 percent of the fastest-growing jobs in the new knowledge-driven market economy require some postsecondary education.

Consolidation Loans: Consolidation loans (Direct or FFEL) allow student or parent borrowers to combine multiple federal education loans into one loan with one monthly payment.

What are the differences in these loan programs?

The chart shown in Figure 14.1 shows basic loan comparisons. The Financial Aid Office at your school can explain which programs are available to you.

How do I apply for a Perkins or Stafford Loan?

As with all federal student financial aid, you apply for a Perkins or Stafford Loan by completing the Free Application for Federal Student Aid (FAFSA). A separate loan application is not required. However, you'll need to sign a promissory note, which is a binding legal contract that says you agree to repay your loan according to the terms of the promissory note. Read this note carefully before signing it and save a copy for your records.

Can I cancel my student loan if I change my mind, even if I have signed the promissory note agreeing to the terms of the loan?

Yes. Before your loan money is disbursed, you may cancel all or part of your loan at any time by notifying your school. After your loan is disbursed, you may cancel all or part of the loan within certain timeframes. Your promissory note and additional information you receive from your school will explain the procedures and timeframes for canceling your loan.

PLUS Loans

The law now allows graduate and professional degree students to borrow from the PLUS program. The terms and conditions applicable to parent PLUS Loans (made to parents of dependent students) also apply to PLUS Loans made to graduate and professional degree students. These terms and conditions include: a requirement that the applicant not have an adverse credit history; a repayment period that begins on the date of the last disbursement of the loan; and a fixed interest rate of 8.5 percent for FFEL PLUS Loans and 7.9 percent for Direct PLUS Loans. As with PLUS Loans made to parent borrowers, eligible graduate and professional degree students may borrow under the PLUS program up to their cost of attendance, minus other financial aid received.

> ☞ **Remember!!**
>
> • Student loans are borrowed money that must be repaid, with interest, just like car loans and mortgages.
>
> • Student loans cannot be canceled because you didn't get—or didn't like—the education you paid for with the loans, didn't get a job in your field of study or because you're having financial difficulty.
>
> • Loans are legal obligations, so think about the amount you'll have to repay before you take out a loan.

Unlike parent PLUS applicants, graduate and professional degree student PLUS applicants must file a FAFSA. In addition, graduate and professional degree students must have their annual loan maximum eligibility under the Stafford Loan program determined by the school before they apply for a PLUS Loan.

Chapter 15

Types Of Loans And Capital For Entrepreneurs

The following is a brief description of the types of capital available for small businesses which will help you understand the options that are most attractive and realistically available for businesses. In no way is this meant to be a comprehensive listing and is designed to get you acquainted with the most common terms and places where businesses can obtain financing.

Debt Financing

Debt financing means borrowing money that is repaid over a period of time, usually with interest. Debt typically carries the burden of monthly payments, whether or not you have positive cash flow. Interest on the loan is deductible and the financing cost is a relatively fixed expense. Debt financing is usually available to all types of businesses and most business owners go to their banks for such loans. In smaller businesses, personal guarantees are likely to be required. Debt financing includes asset-based financing, leasing, trade credit, and various loans that require repayment, with accumulated interest, at some future date. Debt financing does not sacrifice any ownership interests in your business.

About This Chapter: "Types of Capital for Entrepreneurs," © Asian Women in Business. Reprinted with permission. The text of this document can be found online at http://www.awib.org/content_frames/articles/capital.html; accessed January 13, 2007.

Equity Financing

Equity financing is an exchange of money for a share of business ownership. It generally comes from investors who expect little or no return in the early stages, but require much more extensive reporting as to the company's progress. They have invested on the gamble of very high returns and scrutinize how well you have put their money to use. Such investors anticipate that goals and milestones will be met. Equity financing is generally for businesses with fast and high growth potential. The major disadvantage to equity financing is the dilution of your ownership interests and the possible loss of control that may accompany a sharing of ownership.

♣ It's A Fact!!
Debt Versus Equity Financing

Typically, financing is categorized into two basic types: debt financing and equity financing, and under these categories, there are various modes of implementation. Debt and equity financing provide different opportunities for raising funds and a commercially acceptable ratio between debt and equity financing should be maintained. From the lender's perspective, the debt-to-equity ratio measures the amount of available assets or cushion available for repayment of a debt in the case of default. Excessive debt financing may impair your credit rating and your ability to raise more money in the future. If you have too much debt, your business may be considered overextended and risky and an unsafe investment. In addition, you may be unable to weather unanticipated business downturns, credit shortages, or an interest rate increase if your loan's interest rate floats. Conversely, too much equity financing can indicate that you are not making the most productive use of your capital; the capital is not being used advantageously as leverage for obtaining cash. Too little equity may suggest the owners are not committed to their own business.

Lenders will consider the debt-to-equity ratio in assessing whether the company is being operated in a sensible, creditworthy manner. Generally speaking, a local bank will consider an acceptable debt-to-equity ration to be between 1:2 and 1:1.

Angels

Angels are individual private investors who make up a large portion of informal venture capital. These investors tend to invest small amounts, and they can be difficult to locate because they usually don't belong to networks or trade associations.

Angels are found among friends, family, customers, third party professionals, suppliers, brokers, and competitors. There are a few private investor locating services out there. Do your homework, check these people out and negotiate a commission if your request is placed.

The internet is a good place to find out about angels. There is a Small Business Administration (SBA)-sponsored website that shows some promise (though not yet realized) for businesses looking for angels. It is called Access to Capital Electronic Network, better known as ACE-Net. For entrepreneurs, ACE-Net links small companies looking for angel investors to invest between $250,000 to $5 million. The ACE-Net listings use federal securities Regulation D, Rule 504, to raise up to $1 million, or Regulation A to raise up to $5 million, and must meet the corresponding state securities requirements. A majority of the states have adopted new initiatives to permit companies raising less than $1 million on ACE-Net to use a "short-form" listing that significantly reduces the effort. This permits a company to file a simplified single listing along with their business plan.

Venture Capital

Venture capital comes from private individuals, investment bankers, or other private financial syndicates, or, on a small loan scale, the SBA. Venture capitalists offer limited financing opportunities for a small population of companies. There just isn't enough venture capital to go around and the $7.4 billion or so the nation's venture capital partnerships started with in 1998 is just a fraction of the estimated $50 to $60 billion America's high-growth companies need each year. These funding sources get thousands of requests each year and only invest in a small number. In general, 80% of a venture capitalist's portfolio is in technology.

Joint Ventures/Strategic Partnerships

This is where two or more companies with parallel interests get together based on their mutual needs: They have the money, you have the plan. You have the product, they have the distributors. Do your homework. Seek out companies with parallel interests to your own. This requires much more research than simply asking for a loan. Most of these partners will settle for 20% to 40% equity in your company. Be careful to protect your ideas by having any potential partners sign a non-circumvention document.

Small Business Administration (SBA)

A tremendous resource, but the paperwork can be tiring. This is a great place to look. The SBA has many different programs which are implemented through banks. The most common loan program is called the SBA 7(a) loan. This means that the bank will finance the project minus the required injection and the SBA will guarantee up to 75% of the project. The bank sets the rates and the terms of the loan, which can be from 7 years to 25 years. The maximum guarantee is $750,000. There is a SBA guarantee blended fee of 3% on the first $250,000, 3.5% on the next $250,000 and 3.875% on the last $250,000 of the guarantee. To learn more about the SBA, visit their website at http://www.sba.gov.

Also, your local bank should have an SBA loan officer who can explain them to you. SBA loans require a personal guarantee. This program is also used for restructuring existing debt. This is a guarantee from the SBA and not an actual loan.

Small Business Investment Corporation (SBIC)

Hi-bred is a close description. These firms leverage their private capital into government money to form a sort of venture capital fund. Most SBICs are part of commercial banks. They offer both long-term loans and equity participation. They are generally conservative in the placements, investing only in established companies for management buyouts, funds to go public, strategic partnerships and bridge financing.

Commercial Paper

This is a short term debt instrument typically issued from two to 270 days. An issue is normally a promissory note that is unsecured and may either pay interest or be sold at a discount off the face value that is paid at maturity. Commercial paper is considered safe by big investors even though the loans are usually not backed by any specific collateral. They are normally issued only by very solid firms and may also be backed by bank lines of credit, letters of credit, or some other from of credit guarantee. The company may pledge assets to obtain a credit guarantee which is then leveraged into an issue of commercial paper. Usually, only very large banks, corporations, and mutual funds are involved in such transactions.

Letters Of Credit

This is a financial instrument used in international trade but can be used for domestic transactions as well. A letter of credit is essentially a set of instruments from a seller's bank to the buyer's bank. The instructions stipulate the conditions that both parities must meet in order for payment and delivery to take place. There are various types of letters of credit. The bank might issue the L/C based on your pledge of a receivable or other hard asset.

Receivable Factoring

Factoring is an arrangement in which you raise cash against the value of your receivables for a hefty interest charge. This can be a costly means to raise short-term capital. But since it's undeniably an option, especially for those companies that can't raise funds from banks, it makes sense to explore this option. Basically, funds are advanced against goods sold, accepted, and not yet paid for. Normal advances on accounts receivable are 80% to 90%. The lenders are looking for ninety (90) days or less to be paid. Funding is available for older accounts receivable, but the rates take a dramatic turn upwards.

Purchase Order Advances

This involves leveraging your future. If you have purchase orders with your customer base, you may be able to get advances towards their completion. The typical advance is less than 50%, and the rates are very high.

Equipment Leasing

You can think of this as renting assets. You gain the capital equipment you need and agree to pay rent for a specific period of time. There is no interest rate here, but the rates tend to be higher than commercial loans. Some of that is offset by being able to expense 100% the payments (pretax). Check with your tax accountant to be sure.

Asset Sale Lease-Backs

If you are cash poor and asset heavy, this may work for you. Here you are selling your asset for cash to a funding source who leases it back to you (typically with a lease end purchase option). This is most commonly used in commercial real estate transaction but can also apply to various other assets.

The benefits of a leaseback are these: it frees up capital; the rent or payment you make can be deducted as a business expense; if you sell and lease back, you maintain an interest in the property; and it may allow you to buy back the property at the end of the lease period.

Private Placements

Private placement is the general term for several kinds of stocks or bonds that are sold directly to investors; cannot be resold on the public market; and are not required to be registered with the SEC. Even though private placements need not be SEC registered, they are subject to state securities regulations and to U.S. fraud statutes. A private placement is a way to raise capital with a small number of investors (typically less than 35). These are now available in a boilerplate format in most states. Contact your state's Department of Corporations for information on what is required to stay out of trouble.

Initial Public Offerings (IPOs)

IPOs are forms of stock offerings that let you raise more money if you are willing to negotiate the perils of the capital markets. In order to go public, a company must register the IPO with the SEC and become subject to the SEC regulations for a publicly held company. In 1998, there were about 700 initial public offerings compared to about 800,000 new businesses that were formed. The cost for an IPO is quite high and is, thus, not the way most businesses raise money. However, for certain businesses it is often the only way to generate the huge influx of money needed.

Limited Partnerships

In a limited partnership, one or more general partners are responsible for the actual management of the business. One or more limited partners provide investment dollars but normally have no management input. Limited partners have no responsibility for debts or litigation losses the company might incur and the general partners bear all those risks. Limited partnerships usually exist for the purpose of investing. The general partner has all the exposure and management duties, while the limited partners have put up all the money.

There are numerous Limited Partnerships out there that have been formed to invest in businesses. You can search them out or inquire with your State as to the requirements for forming your own.

Convertible Debt

Convertibles are typically corporate bonds or preferred stocks that are issued with provisions allowing the holder to exchange them for (convert them to) a fixed number of shares of common stock at a specified price. These are most common with seed or start-up funding where the lender would like a piece of the rock in the event you become a tremendous success.

👉 Remember!!

There are numerous creative ways to finance a business. If one of those comes your way take a moment to investigate it. You can never know too much about how to capitalize your business.

Lines Of Credit

Lines of credit are revolving accounts that are continuous in nature. The funds are available as draw downs against the total line. These types of accounts are most commonly secured with accounts receivable and inventory as collateral.

Chapter 16

What Is A Mortgage?

A mortgage is a loan of money that enables you to buy a house or other real estate. It's a lot of money that you'll pay back over a long time.

You may not realize it, but there are many different kinds of mortgages. In addition to conventional mortgages, there are other types of mortgages available for people who might not otherwise qualify for a loan, including people with low- and moderate-incomes, U.S. veterans, and first-time home buyers. The Federal Housing Administration (FHA) insures loans made to first-time home buyers and low- and moderate-income people. The Department of Veterans Affairs (VA) partially guarantees loans made to veterans, which is meant to encourage lenders to offer mortgages to veterans. The Rural Housing Service (RHS) is managed by the U.S. Department of Agriculture and offers housing and loan programs that encourage rural development. For more information about these loan programs, please visit the U.S. Department of Housing and Urban Development's website at http://www.hud.gov.

No matter what type of mortgage it is, having one is a big responsibility, but not impossible to achieve.

About This Chapter: This chapter includes "What Is a Mortgage?" "Fixed-Rate vs. Adjustable Rate," "Buydown vs. GPM," © 2007 Government National Mortgage Association (Ginnie Mae). The Home Zone. http://www.ginniemae.gov/homezone/index.html. Reprinted with permission.

✎ What's It Mean?

Adjustable-Rate Loans (also known as variable-rate loans): The interest rate fluctuates over the life of the loan based on market conditions, but the loan agreement generally sets maximum and minimum rates. When interest rates rise, generally so do your loan payments; and when interest rates fall, your monthly payments may be lowered.

Conventional Loans: Mortgage loans other than those insured or guaranteed by a government agency such as the FHA (Federal Housing Administration), the VA (Veterans Administration), or the Rural Development Services (formerly know as Farmers Home Administration, or FmHA).

Fixed-Rate Loans: Both the interest rate and the monthly payments (for principal and interest) stay the same during the life of the loan.

Interest Rate: The cost of borrowing money expressed as a percentage rate. Interest rates can change because of market conditions.

Loan Origination Fees: Fees charged by the lender for processing the loan and are often expressed as a percentage of the loan amount.

Mortgage: A document signed by a borrower when a home loan is made that gives the lender a right to take possession of the property if the borrower fails to pay off on the loan.

Points: Fees paid to the lender for the loan. One point equals 1 percent of the loan amount. Points are usually paid in cash at closing. In some cases, the money needed to pay points can be borrowed, but doing so will increase the loan amount and the total costs.

Transaction, Settlement, Or Closing Costs: May include application fees; title examination, abstract of title, title insurance, and property survey fees; fees for preparing deeds, mortgages, and settlement documents; attorneys' fees; recording fees; and notary, appraisal, and credit report fees. Under the Real Estate Settlement Procedures Act, the borrower receives a good faith estimate of closing costs at the time of application or within three days of application. The good faith estimate lists each expected cost either as an amount or a range.

Source: Excerpted from "Looking for the Best Mortgage," Housing and Urban Development (www.hud.gov), 1999.

A mortgage payment has at least two components: Principal and interest. (You may also be responsible for insurance and other costs that are figured into your monthly payment, which is called a premium.) The principal is the original amount of the loan, and the interest is a fee that the lender charges you in exchange for loaning you money. Payments of principal and interest are broken down into monthly payments over the life of the loan. In the beginning, your monthly payments will go primarily toward paying interest. After a time, bigger percentages of your monthly payments start going toward the principal, and that's when you start building equity.

Determining the payment for a mortgage is a valuable tool in understanding the parts and basis of a mortgage. Using the formula below, the payment for a mortgage can be calculated. First, however, several items are needed. These items are principal (amount of money mortgaged); interest rate (annual charge for lending money); length (the period, usually in years, of the mortgage.)

Payment Calculation

$P = A/D$

Where:

P = Payment per time interval
A = Total amount borrowed
D = Discount factor (see calculation below)

Discount Factor Calculation

$$D = \frac{(1 + j)^n - 1}{j(1 + j)^n}$$

Where:

D = Discount factor amount
j = Quarterly interest rate
n = Number of payment periods

Using The Formula

Using the formulas displayed above, let's work a problem for a home mortgage. Start with a principal amount of $ 10,000 and an annual interest rate of 5 percent. Assume the loan will be paid back on a quarterly basis over two years. How much would your quarterly payments be?

Step 1: First, the annual interest rate (5%) must be adjusted to a periodic rate in decimal form. (In this case, quarterly) This is done because the payment should include only that portion of the annual interest applicable to the period.

To calculate the quarterly rate in decimal form, use the formula:
j (quarterly interest in decimal form) = annual interest rate/(4 × 100)

The annual interest rate is 5 %. Put this value in the formula:

Step 1 Solution: j (Quarterly interest in decimal form) = 5/ (4 × 100) = .0125

Step 2: Calculate the number of quarters the mortgage is to be repaid. To calculate the number of quarters it takes to repay the mortgage, use the formula: n (number of quarters for repayment) = 1 (Length, in years, of the mortgage) × 4

Step 2 Solution: n (Number of quarters for repayment) = 2 × 4= 8

Step 3: Calculate the discount factor. Write the formula

$$D = \frac{(1 + j)^n - 1}{j(1 + j)^n}$$

Step 4: Substitute .0125 for j and 8 for n.

$$D = \frac{(1 + .0125)^8 - 1}{.0125(1 + .0125)^8}$$

Step 5: Solve.

$$D = \frac{(1.0125)(1.0125)(1.0125)(1.0125)(1.0125)(1.0125)(1.0125)(1.0125) - 1}{.0125 (1.0125)(1.0125)(1.0125)(1.0125)(1.0125)(1.0125)(1.0125)(1.0125)}$$

$$D = \frac{.1044861}{.0138060}$$

$$D = 7.56816$$

Step 6: Now calculate the loan payment amount. Write the formula.

$$P = \frac{A}{D}$$

Step 7: Substitute $10,000 for A and 7.56816 for D.

$$P = \frac{\$ 10,000}{7.56816}$$

Step 8: Solve

$$P = \$1,321.33$$

Once the quarterly payment is calculated, the loan can be amortized. Amortization is the liquidation of a debt by regular installments of principal and interest. An amortization schedule is a table showing the payment amount, interest, principal, and unpaid balance for the entire term of the loan. Table 16.1[on the next page] shows the amortization schedule for the mortgage problem just calculated.

Fixed-Rate Vs. Adjustable Rate

Fixed-Rate Mortgage: A fixed-rate mortgage applies the same interest rate toward monthly loan payments for the life of the loan. Fixed-rate mortgages are more straightforward and easier to understand than adjustable rate mortgages (ARMs), are more secure for the buyer, and are popular with first-time home buyers. Since the risk to the lender is higher, fixed-rate mortgages generally have higher interest rates than ARMs.

For example, a lender can offer a 30-year fixed loan to a home buyer at a 7.0% interest rate. The loan is locked in to the 7.0% interest rate, even if the market interest rate rises to 9.0%. Conversely, if the market interest rate decreases to 5.5%, the borrower will continue to pay the 7% interest rate.

Fixed-rate benefits include:

• No change in monthly principal and interest payments regardless of fluctuations in interest rates;

• More stability may give you "peace-of-mind."

Table 16.1. Sample Loan Amortization Schedule

Column #1 Payment #	Column #2 Balance	Column #3 Loan Payment	Column #4 Quarterly Interest [(2) x .0125]	Column #5 Principal Repayment [(3) - (4)]	Column #6 Ending Balance [(2) - (5)]
1	$ 10,000.00	$ 1,321.33	$ 125.00	$ 1,196.33	$ 8,803.67
2	8,803.67	1,321.33	110.05	1,211.28	7,592.39
3	7,592.39	1,321.33	94.90	1,226.43	6,365.96
4	6,365.96	1,321.33	79.57	1,241.76	5,124.20
5	5,124.20	1,321.33	64.05	1,257.28	3,866.92
6	3,866.92	1,321.33	48.33	1,273.00	2,593.92
7	2,593.92	1,321.33	32.42	1,288.91	1,305.01
8	1,305.01	1,321.32	16.31	1,305.01	0.00
Totals:		$ 10,570.63	$ 570.63	$ 10,000.00	

Fixed-rate considerations include:

* Higher initial monthly payments compared to those of adjustable rate mortgages;

* Less flexibility.

Adjustable Rate Mortgage: An adjustable rate mortgage (ARM) does not apply the same interest rate toward monthly payments for the life of the loan. Throughout the life of that loan, the home buyer's principal and interest payment will adjust periodically based on fluctuations in the interest rate.

♣ It's A Fact!!

What is an I-O mortgage payment?

Traditional mortgages require that each month you pay back some of the money you borrowed (the principal) plus the interest on that money. The principal you owe on your mortgage decreases over the term of the loan. In contrast, an I-O payment plan allows you to pay only the interest for a specified number of years. After that, you must repay both the principal and the interest.

Most mortgages that offer an I-O payment plan have adjustable interest rates, which means that the interest rate and monthly payment will change over the term of the loan. The changes may be as often as once a month or as seldom as every 3 to 5 years, depending on the terms of your loan. For example, a 5/1 ARM has a fixed interest rate for the first 5 years; after that, the rate can change once a year (the "1" in 5/1) during the rest of the loan.

The I-O payment period is typically between 3 and 10 years. After that, your monthly payment will increase—even if interest rates stay the same—because you must pay back the principal as well as the interest. For example, if you take out a 30-year mortgage loan with a 5-year I-O payment period, you can pay only interest for 5 years and then both principal and interest over the next 25 years. Because you begin to pay back the principal, your payments increase after year 5.

Source: Excerpted from "Interest-Only Mortgage Payments and Option-Payment ARMS," Federal Deposit Insurance Corporation, October 2006.

For example, a lender could offer a 30-year ARM loan to a home buyer at an initial 6.5% interest rate. During an adjustment period for the ARM loan, the market interest rate could rise to 8.0%, resulting in a significantly larger interest payment. Similarly, the market interest rate could decrease to 6.0%, resulting in lower interest payments.

ARM benefits include:

- Initial payments lower due to lower beginning interest rate, usually about 2 percentage points below the fixed rate;

- Ability to qualify for a higher loan amount due to lower initial interest rates;

- Lower interest payments if the interest rate drops over time;

- Interest rate caps limit the maximum interest payment allowed for the loan.

ARM considerations include:

- Initial lower interest rate and monthly payments are temporary and apply to the first adjustment period. Typically, the interest rate will rise after the initial adjustment period.

✤ It's A Fact!!
What is a payment-option ARM?

A payment-option ARM is an adjustable-rate mortgage that allows you to choose among several payment options each month. The options typically include the following:

- A traditional payment of principal and interest (which reduces the amount you owe on your mortgage). These payments may be based on a set loan term, such as a 15-, 30-, or 40-year payment schedule.

- An interest-only payment (which does not change the amount you owe on your mortgage).

- A minimum (or limited) payment (which may be less than the amount of interest due that month and may not pay down any principal). If you choose this option, the amount of any interest you do not pay will be added to the principal of the loan, increasing the amount you owe and increasing the interest you will pay.

Source: Excerpted from "Interest-Only Mortgage Payments and Option-Payment ARMS," Federal Deposit Insurance Corporation, October 2006.

- Higher interest payments if the interest rate rises over time.

Buydown Vs. Graduated Payment Mortgage (GPM)

While these two mortgage types start the home buyer off at one rate and increase the rate over time, one of these types of mortgages may be right for you.

Buydown

- Type of mortgage loan where the loan rate is reduced by paying more up-front at closing and is increased by one percent each year for the

♣ It's A Fact!!
Rates And Points

The interest rate determines the monthly interest payments over the lifetime of the loan. A "point" or "discount point" is equivalent to 1% of the loan amount and usually reduces or "discounts" the loan rate by an eighth of a percentage point.

For example: You want to get a loan for $100,000 to buy a home. Each "point" would cost you 1% of $100,000 or $1,000 but would reduce your loan's interest rate by .125%. The lender might offer you an 8.0% loan with zero points, a 7.875% loan with one point, or a 7.75% loan with 2 points.

Points, like the down payment, are paid at closing. In some cases, lenders will allow borrowers to finance the points over the term of the loan. Lenders sometimes use points to make their interest rates appear lower. Be aware that lower interest rates offered by a lender may translate into higher points requirements.

Source: © 2007 Government National Mortgage Association (Ginnie Mae). The Home Zone. http://www.ginnie mae.gov/homezone/index.html. Reprinted with permission

period set for the loan product. For example: For a 2-1 buydown at an 8% rate, Year 1 the rate is 6%, Year 2 the rate is 7%. For Year 3 through the life of the loan, the rate is 8%.

- Qualification rules for the loan programs remain the same. Depending on the lender, the buyer may qualify using the reduced rate. (Example: For a 3-2-1 Buydown at a rate of 8%, the buyer could qualify using the 5% rate.)

- The difference between the actual payment schedule and the rate schedule is usually paid "up-front" at closing. This can be paid by the seller, the buyer, the homebuilder, or in some cases, the lender. If the cost is borne by the lender, it is usually offset with increased rates or in points. Generally the funds used to buy down the loan are held in a separate account and are applied with the borrower's payment to equal the true interest rate.

Graduated Payment Mortgage (GPM)

- Type of mortgage loan where the mortgage payments increase gradually for a period established in the loan product, typically five years. This is a negatively amortizing loan, which means that the difference between the interest paid and the interest due is deferred and added to the loan balances. Because of this, your loan amount will increase once you start paying off the loan; it will amortize normally at the end of the loan period. These loan products are more popular when the interest rates are higher, providing a financial incentive for potential buyers.

- Since many lenders will qualify a buyer at a lower rate, a buyer can secure a larger mortgage. These loan types are good for those buyers who expect their incomes to increase to cover the increase in loan amount.

Chapter 17

Credit Protection: What To Consider Before You Buy

Think about the last time you applied for a new loan or a credit card. Did the lender ask if you'd like to buy something called "credit insurance" or a similar credit protection product that would make your loan payments if you die, become ill or unemployed? And after you got the loan or credit card, did your lender continue to offer credit protection programs in mail solicitations or telemarketing calls? Chances are you answered "yes" to these questions. But it's also likely that you have your own questions, such as: Do I really need this insurance? And, how can I tell if this coverage is a good deal?

"We're all prone to focus on the benefits of an offer, written in bold, without evaluating the conditions and exclusions," says Deirdre Foley, an senior policy analyst with the Federal Deposit Insurance Corporation (FDIC). "You should review your financial situation and weigh the costs and benefits before deciding if this type of coverage makes sense for you."

Here's an overview of what credit protection is and what you need to know to protect yourself from high-cost or unnecessary coverage.

About This Chapter: Excerpted from "Credit Protection: What to Consider Before You Buy," *FDIC Consumer News*, Federal Deposit Insurance Corporation (FDIC), Summer 2003.

What are credit insurance, debt cancellation, and debt suspension programs?

Credit insurance is offered with certain kinds of financing, such as some home loans, credit cards, and loans offered by department stores or auto dealers. In general, credit insurance is a type of life, accident, health, disability, or unemployment insurance that will pay off a debt if the borrower dies or make monthly payments if the borrower becomes ill, injured, or unemployed.

For the most part, each state government regulates credit insurance sales in that state, and the insurance department enforces the state laws and regulations governing pricing, disclosures to buyers, minimum insurance benefits, and other consumer protections.

Moreover, most types of credit insurance are voluntary. An important exception is property or hazard insurance. A creditor may require that you maintain this kind of insurance to cover the costs of repairing or replacing property (such as your home or auto) that serves as collateral for a loan. And in those instances in which insurance is required, a bank cannot condition approval of the loan on the purchase of insurance from the bank or an affiliate.

In addition, some depository institutions (such as banks and credit unions) sell "debt cancellation" and "debt suspension" programs under various names. In general, debt cancellation eliminates the debt if the borrower dies or cancels the monthly payment if the borrower becomes disabled, unemployed, or suffers some other specified hardship. Debt suspension is different. It temporarily postpones all or part of the monthly payment while the borrower is facing a specified hardship—the borrower is still expected to make the suspended payments in the future. These programs are similar to credit insurance products in terms of their function, but fees and other features may be significantly different. Debt protection programs are offered by depository institutions directly, not by insurance companies. These programs are subject to regulation by the appropriate federal or state depository institutions supervisor.

How can you protect yourself from costly mistakes?

Here are a few steps you can take to evaluate credit protection plans and decide what's best for you.

♣ It's A Fact!!

Most types of credit insurance are voluntary. And in those instances in which insurance is required, a bank cannot condition approval of the loan on the purchase of insurance from the bank or an affiliate.

Remember that most credit protection is optional: If you are asked to purchase credit protection before your loan closes, find out whether your lender requires that you purchase it, and why. Don't assume that credit protection is required. When in doubt, contact the appropriate state or federal regulator for more information. If you obtain optional credit protection and later decide you don't want it, you may have a right to cancel the coverage and obtain a refund for up-front payments.

Evaluate your insurance costs, coverage, and needs annually: You could be under-insured in certain areas or over-insured in others. Talk with your insurance agent or financial adviser about your situation, including any questions about credit protection. You may, for example, have enough savings to cover your minimum loan payments due, the amount generally covered by these programs, if you become sick or unemployed.

Before purchasing a credit protection product, consider if you already have, or would be better off with, traditional insurance: For many people, especially those in good health, they probably can get traditional insurance that can meet their needs at a more reasonable price than a credit protection plan. But for some people, especially those who are elderly, have a serious health problem, or are concerned about making loan payments if they lose their job, credit protection may be the best or only coverage they can obtain.

If you're considering a credit protection program, understand what is covered, what isn't, and whether the costs and restrictions outweigh the benefits. For example, remember that credit insurance and debt cancellation programs only apply to a specific debt. In many situations, you and your family might be better served with the proceeds from a traditional insurance policy that can be used to pay off any debts and expenses as you see fit, not just that one loan.

"Consumers who do not read the terms and conditions of these programs may be unaware of the limitations and as a result, they might pay more for less coverage than they expect," cautions Tim Burniston, FDIC Associate Director for Compliance Policy and Examination Support.

Pay attention to loan documents and monthly statements from your lender and question any unusual charges or fees: For example, if you fail to maintain the required property or hazard insurance coverage or you forget to give the lender evidence of your coverage, the creditor typically reserves the right to purchase the insurance and charge you for it, perhaps as part of your loan payment. If you're not monitoring your payments, you could be paying for a property insurance policy purchased by the lender that is more expensive and more limited than what you could obtain by shopping around.

Try to resolve problems as soon as possible: First contact the creditor or insurance company. If you're not satisfied with the outcome, contact your state insurance commissioner or, in the case of a debt cancellation/suspension contract, the appropriate federal or state regulator. Also, retain copies of your loan documents and related credit protection policies, terms and conditions. You may need to refer to this information if you have a question, a concern or an insurance claim.

Part Three

Credit And Debit Cards

Chapter 18

Choosing And Using Credit Cards

Chances are you've gotten your share of "pre-approved" credit card offers in the mail, some with low introductory rates and other perks. Many of these solicitations urge you to accept "before the offer expires." Before you accept, shop around to get the best deal.

Credit Card Terms

A credit card is a form of borrowing that often involves charges. Credit terms and conditions affect your overall cost. So it's wise to compare terms and fees before you agree to open a credit or charge card account. The following are some important terms to consider that generally must be disclosed in credit card applications or in solicitations that require no application. You also may want to ask about these terms when you're shopping for a card.

Annual Percentage Rate (APR): The APR is a measure of the cost of credit, expressed as a yearly rate. It also must be disclosed before you become obligated on the account and on your account statements.

The card issuer also must disclose the "periodic rate"—the rate applied to your outstanding balance to figure the finance charge for each billing period.

About This Chapter: "Choosing and Using Credit Cards," Facts for Consumers, Federal Trade Commission, January 1999; available online at http://www.ftc.gov/bcp/conline/pubs/credit/choose.htm, accessed January 13, 2007.

Some credit card plans allow the issuer to change your APR when interest rates or other economic indicators—called indexes—change. Because the rate change is linked to the index's performance, these plans are called "variable rate" programs. Rate changes raise or lower the finance charge on your account. If you're considering a variable rate card, the issuer must also provide various information that discloses to you:

- that the rate may change; and

- how the rate is determined—which index is used and what additional amount, the "margin," is added to determine your new rate.

At the latest, you also must receive information, before you become obligated on the account, about any limitations on how much and how often your rate may change.

Free Period: Also called a "grace period," a free period lets you avoid finance charges by paying your balance in full before the due date. Knowing whether a card gives you a free period is especially important if you plan to pay your account in full each month. Without a free period, the card issuer may impose a finance charge from the date you use your card or from the date each transaction is posted to your account. If your card includes a free period, the issuer must mail your bill at least 14 days before the due date so you'll have enough time to pay.

Annual Fees: Most issuers charge annual membership or participation fees. They often range from $25 to $50, sometimes up to $100; "gold" or "platinum" cards often charge up to $75 and sometimes up to several hundred dollars.

Transaction Fees And Other Charges: A card may include other costs. Some issuers charge a fee if you use the card to get a cash advance, make a late payment, or exceed your credit limit. Some charge a monthly fee whether or not you use the card.

Balance Computation Method For The Finance Charge: If you don't have a free period, or if you expect to pay for purchases over time, it's important to know what method the issuer uses to calculate your finance charge.

This can make a big difference in how much of a finance charge you'll pay—even if the APR and your buying patterns remain relatively constant. Table 18.1 shows examples of how the methods can affect your costs.

♣ It's A Fact!!
Can teens get credit cards?

Yes, teens can get—or get access to—credit cards and debit cards. Under most state laws, for example, you must be at least 18 years old (a young adult) to obtain your own credit card and be held responsible for repaying the debt. And if you're under 18, you can qualify for a credit card if a parent co-signs, but only the parent can be held accountable for the payments.

Credit and debit cards can be good ways for teens to pay without carrying cash or checks, and they can help teach kids about how to manage money. But teens—and their parents—need to be especially careful to avoid serious debt problems or a bad credit record at a young age.

First, make financial education a priority, especially the lessons about borrowing responsibly. "Teens need to be aware that a bad credit record can affect their ability to rent an apartment or even find employment after graduation," says Lynne Gottesburen, a Federal Deposit Insurance Corporation (FDIC) Consumer Affairs Specialist.

Also, understand the alternatives. There are cards with features sometimes described as "training wheels" for young cardholders. One is a credit card with a low credit limit—say, $300 or $500—which can keep a teen from getting too deeply in debt. Another is a pre-paid, re-loadable payment card that parents can get for teens aged 13 or older and that comes with parental controls, including spending limits. A debit card also enables a teen to make purchases without paying interest or getting into debt because the money is automatically deducted from an existing bank account.

Source: "Just for Teens," *FDIC Consumer News*, Federal Deposit Insurance Corporation (FDIC), Fall 2002.

Examples Of Balance Computation Methods

Average Daily Balance: This is the most common calculation method. It credits your account from the day payment is received by the issuer. To figure the balance due, the issuer totals the beginning balance for each day in the billing period and subtracts any credits made to your account that day. While new purchases may or may not be added to the balance, depending on your plan, cash advances typically are included. The resulting daily balances are added for the billing cycle. The total is then divided by the number of days in the billing period to get the "average daily balance."

Adjusted Balance: This is usually the most advantageous method for card holders. Your balance is determined by subtracting payments or credits received during the current billing period from the balance at the end of the previous billing period. Purchases made during the billing period aren't included.

This method gives you until the end of the billing cycle to pay a portion of your balance to avoid the interest charges on that amount. Some creditors exclude prior, unpaid finance charges from the previous balance.

Previous Balance: This is the amount you owed at the end of the previous billing period. Payments, credits and new purchases during the current billing period are not included. Some creditors also exclude unpaid finance charges.

Two-Cycle Balances: Issuers sometimes use various methods to calculate your balance that make use of your last two month's account activity. Read your agreement carefully to find out if your issuer uses this approach and, if so, what specific two-cycle method is used.

> **✔ Quick Tip**
> If you don't understand how your balance is calculated, ask your card issuer. An explanation must also appear on your billing statements.
>
> FTC, 1999.

Other Costs And Features

Credit terms vary among issuers. When shopping for a card, think about how you plan to use it. If you expect to pay your bills in full each month, the annual fee and other charges may be more important than the periodic rate and the APR, if there is a grace period for purchases. However, if you use the cash advance feature, many cards do not permit a grace period for the amounts due—even if they have a grace period for purchases. So, it may still be wise to consider the APR and balance computation method. Also, if you plan to pay for purchases over time, the APR and the balance computation method are definitely major considerations.

You'll probably also want to consider if the credit limit is high enough, how widely the card is accepted, and the plan's services and features. For example, you may be interested in "affinity cards"—all-purpose credit cards sponsored by professional organizations, college alumni associations, and some members of the travel industry. An affinity card issuer often donates a portion of the annual fees or charges to the sponsoring organization, or qualifies you for free travel or other bonuses.

Receiving A Credit Card

Federal law prohibits issuers from sending you a card you didn't ask for. However, an issuer can send you a renewal or substitute card without your request. Issuers also may send you an application or a solicitation, or ask you by phone if you want a card—and, if you say yes, they may send you one.

Cardholder Protections

Federal law protects your use of credit cards.

Prompt Credit For Payment: An issuer must credit your account the day payment is received. The exceptions are if the payment is not made according to the creditor's requirements, or the delay in crediting your account won't result in a charge.

Table 18.1. Here's how some different methods of calculating finance charges affect the cost of credit.

	Average Daily Balance (including new purchases)	Average Daily Balance (excluding new purchases)
Monthly rate	1½%	1½%
APR	18%	18%
Previous Balance	$400	$400
New Purchases	$50 on 18th day	$50 on 18th day
Payments	$300 on 15th day (new balance = $100)	$300 on 15th day (new balance = $100)
Average Daily Balance	$270*	$250**
Finance Charge	$4.05 (1½% x $270)	$3.75 (1½% x $250)

*To figure average daily balance (including new purchases): ($400 x 15 days) + ($100 x 3 days) + ($150 x 12 days)/30 days = $270

**To figure average daily balance (excluding new purchases): ($400 x 15 days) + ($100 x 15 days)/30 days = $250

	Adjusted Balance	Previous Balance
Monthly rate	1½%	1½%
APR	18%	18%
Previous Balance	$400	$400
Payments	$300	$300
Average Daily Balance	N/A	N/A
Finance Charge	$1.50 (1½% x $100)	$6.00 (1½% x $400)

To help avoid finance charges, follow the issuer's mailing instructions. Payments sent to the wrong address could delay crediting your account for up to five days. If you misplace your payment envelope, look for the payment address on your billing statement or call the issuer.

Refunds Of Credit Balances: When you make a return or pay more than the total balance at present, you can keep the credit on your account or write your issuer for a refund—if it's more than a dollar. A refund must be issued within seven business days of receiving your request. If a credit stays on your account for more than six months, the issuer must make a good faith effort to send you a refund.

Errors On Your Bill: Issuers must follow rules for promptly correcting billing errors. You'll get a statement outlining these rules when you open an account and at least once a year. In fact, many issuers include a summary of these rights on your bills.

If you find a mistake on your bill, you can dispute the charge and withhold payment on that amount while the charge is being investigated. The error might be a charge for the wrong amount, for something you didn't accept, or for an item that wasn't delivered as agreed. Of course, you still have to pay any part of the bill that's not in dispute, including finance and other charges.

If you decide to dispute a charge, take these steps:

- Write to the creditor at the address indicated on your statement for "billing inquiries." Include your name, address, account number, and a description of the error.

- Send your letter soon. It must reach the creditor within 60 days after the first bill containing the error was mailed to you.

The creditor must acknowledge your complaint in writing within 30 days of receipt, unless the problem has been resolved. At the latest, the dispute must be resolved within two billing cycles, but not more than 90 days.

Unauthorized Charges: If your card is used without your permission, you can be held responsible for up to $50 per card.

If you report the loss before the card is used, you can't be held responsible for any unauthorized charges. If a thief uses your card before you report it missing, the most you'll owe for unauthorized charges is $50.

To minimize your liability, report the loss as soon as possible. Some issuers have 24-hour toll-free telephone numbers to accept emergency information. It's a good idea to follow-up with a letter to the issuer—include your account number, the date you noticed your card missing, and the date you reported the loss.

Disputes About Merchandise Or Services: You can dispute charges for unsatisfactory goods or services. To do so, you must meet these criteria:

- Have made the purchase in your home state or within 100 miles of your current billing address.

- The charge must be for more than $50. (These limitations don't apply if the seller also is the card issuer or if a special business relationship exists between the seller and the card issuer.)

- First make a good faith effort to resolve the dispute with the seller. No special procedures are required to do so.

If these conditions don't apply, you may want to consider filing an action in small claims court.

✔ Quick Tip

Keep these tips in mind when looking for a credit or charge card.

- Shop around for the plan that best fits your needs.

- Make sure you understand a plan's terms before you accept the card.

- Hold on to receipts to reconcile charges when your bill arrives.

- Protect your cards and account numbers to prevent unauthorized use. Draw a line through blank spaces on charge slips so the amount can't be changed. Tear up carbons.

- Keep a record —in a safe place separate from your cards—of your account numbers, expiration dates and the phone numbers of each issuer to report a loss quickly.

- Carry only the cards you think you'll use.

Source: FTC, 1999.

Chapter 19

How Is A Debit Card Different From A Credit Card?

Debit cards are also known as check cards. Debit cards look like credit cards or ATM (automated teller machine) cards, but operate like cash or a personal check. Debit cards are different from credit cards. While a credit card is a way to "pay later," a debit card is a way to "pay now." When you use a debit card, your money is quickly deducted from your checking or savings account.

Debit cards are accepted at many locations, including grocery stores, retails stores, gasoline stations, and restaurants. You can use your card anywhere merchants display your card's brand name or logo, even on the internet. They offer an alternative to carrying a checkbook or cash.

Use your debit card for:

- Shopping;

- ATM transactions and getting cash;

- Instant banking.

Do You Have A Debit Card?

You may not realize that you have a debit card. Many banks are replacing their standard ATM cards with upgraded ATM cards that have a debit feature. You may also receive in the mail what looks like a credit card when in fact it is a debit card.

What Is The Difference Between A Debit Card And A Credit Card?

It's the difference between "debit" and "credit." Debit means "subtract." When you use a debit card, you are subtracting your money from your own bank account. Debit cards allow you to spend only what is in your bank account. It is a quick transaction between the merchant and your personal bank account.

Credit is money made available to you by the bank or other financial institution, like a loan. The amount the issuer allows you to use is determined by your credit history, income, debts, and ability to pay. You may use the credit with the understanding that you must repay the charges, plus interest, if you do not pay the account in full each month. You will receive a monthly statement detailing your charges and payment requirements.

Two Ways Debit Cards Work

- **With A PIN:** You provide your personal identification number, or PIN, at the time of sale.

- **Without A PIN, Or PIN-less:** You sign a receipt for the purchase, as you would with a credit card.

Some debit cards are designed to work only with a PIN, others can be used with either a PIN or a signature. PIN-only debit cards offer greater security because it's more difficult for unauthorized people to use them. Cards that can work both in the PIN and PIN-less methods offer more flexibility, especially when dealing with merchants who do not have the equipment needed to process PIN transactions. In either case, the funds are automatically deducted from your account within a short time.

Table 19.1. Credit Cards And Debit Cards... At A Glance

	Credit Cards	Debit Cards
Payments	Buy now, pay later.	Buy now, pay now.
Interest Charges	Yes, if you carry a balance or your card offers no "grace period."	No.
Other Potential Benefits	Freebies, such as cash rebates and bonus points good for travel deals. Some purchase protections.	Easier and faster than writing a check. Avoid debt problems. More cards now offering freebies. Some purchase protections.
Other Potential Concerns	Fees and penalties. Also, not all cards offer grace periods (time to repay without incurring interest). Over-spending can cause debt problems.	Fees on certain transactions. You may overdraw your account if you're lax about recording debit card transactions.

Source: *FDIC Consumer News*, Federal Deposit Insurance Corporation (FDIC), Fall 2002.

What You Should Know About Debit Cards

- Obtaining a debit card is often easier than obtaining a credit card.

- Using a debit card instead of writing checks saves you from showing identification or giving out personal information at the time of the transaction.

- Using a debit card frees you from carrying cash or a checkbook.

- Using a debit card means you may no longer have to stock up on traveler's checks or cash when you travel.

- Debit cards may be more readily accepted by merchants than checks, even when you travel.

- The debit card is a quick, "pay now" product, giving you no grace period.

- As with credit cards, you may dispute unauthorized charges or other mistakes within 60 days. You should contact the card issuer if a problem cannot be resolved with the merchant. However, using a debit card may mean you have less protection than with credit card purchase for items which are never delivered, are defective, or were misrepresented.

- Returning goods or canceling services purchased with a debit card is treated as if the purchases were made with cash or a check.

✔ Quick Tip
Seven Tips For Using Debit Cards Responsibly

1. If your card is lost or stolen, report the loss immediately to your financial institution.

2. If you suspect your card is being fraudulently used, report this immediately to your financial institution.

3. Take your receipts. Don't leave them for others to see. Your account number may be all someone needs to order merchandise through the mail or over the phone at your expense, especially if the card can be used without a PIN.

4. If you have a PIN number, memorize it. Do not keep your PIN number with your card. Also, don't choose a PIN number that a smart thief could figure out, such as your phone number or birthday.

5. Never give your PIN number to anyone. Keep your PIN private.

6. Always know how much money you have available in your account. Don't forget to consider money that you have set aside to cover a check that has not yet cleared your bank.

7. Deduct debits and any transaction fees from the balance in your check register immediately. Keep the receipts in one place in case you need them later.

Be Aware

If your debit card works with either a PIN or a signature and the store accepts both, you choose which way to use it at the point of sale. If you choose "debit" on the merchant's terminal and "swipe" your card through, you will be asked for your PIN. If you choose "credit" on the terminal and swipe your card through, you will be asked to sign a receipt. "Credit" does not mean that you will be billed, as with a credit card. The money will be debited from your account automatically.

What You Should Know Before You Use a Debit Card

1. Know if it is a credit card or a debit card. Also, decide whether you want a PIN-only debit card or one that can be used with either a PIN or a signature. Ask the card issuer about your options.

2. Know if there are fees applied to using the card. Some financial institutions charge a monthly fee or a per-transaction fee, others do not. These fees are set by the card issuer and must be disclosed to consumers.

3. Know about your liability for the unauthorized use, theft, or loss of your debit card. Ask if the issuer has any special liability policies and how they work.

4. Know how problems with nondelivery, defective merchandise, or misrepresentation will be handled. This is especially important when you use a debit card to purchase goods or services for future delivery, rather than on a "cash and carry" basis. Ask the issuer about its policies for these types of disputes.

What If My Card Is Lost Or Stolen?

In the event that your card is lost or stolen, you need to know the extent of your protection. Government regulations require debit card issuers to set a maximum liability of $50 if the debit card is reported lost or stolen within two days of discovery. Liability increases to $500 if the lost or stolen debit card is reported within 60 days. Neglect to notify the bank of the theft within 60 days after a bank statement is sent, and you could lose everything in your checking and overdraft accounts.

Check with your financial institution about your liability. Many debit card issuers offer consumers better protection than the government regulations require. Some even offer consumers "zero liability" in cases of fraud, theft, or other unauthorized card use if the cardholder reports the problem within a certain time.

If a problem arises, remember that it is your money that is at stake.

- Under government regulations, financial institutions may have up to 20 days to provide provisional credit to consumers for losses due to debit card theft or unauthorized use of the card.

- In cases where a cardholder's debit card has been used fraudulently, some issuers promise even faster provisional credit for lost funds, in as few as five business days after notification.

- You may not know that your debit card or its number has been stolen until checks you have written have bounced. Be aware that the issuer is not required to waive bounced check charges or cover any fees that may be imposed by the recipients of checks that unintentionally bounced because a debit card was stolen. Many banks do, however, refund these fees as a measure of good customer service.

Debit cards offer the consumer many conveniences. They are more readily accepted by merchants than checks, especially when you are out of your own state or in other countries. You are not required to provide identification or give personal information when using a debit card. This makes the transaction quicker and allows you to keep personal information to yourself.

However, because the money spent using a debit card comes directly from your bank account, you need to be careful in order to prevent fraudulent use of your card number.

☞ Remember!!
Ask for the details of the card issuer's liability policy.

Chapter 20

Advantages And Disadvantages Of Credit Cards

Credit Cards Give You Lots Of Advantages

A Safe Alternative To Cash: When you have your card in your wallet, you don't have to carry cash that can be lost or stolen. If your credit card is lost or stolen, you can report the missing card to the card company. The company will then stop accepting any charges on your card. What's more, you won't be charged for purchases made by someone else.

Builds A Good Credit History: If you use your card responsibly, you can begin to build a good credit rating for yourself. Later in life, when you need a loan, a lender will want proof that you pay your debts. A good credit card history will help you get your loan. A poor credit history will work against you.

Bails You Out Of Emergencies: Got engine trouble miles from home? Need to be towed? The tow truck and the auto repair shop will accept your credit card. Too far from home? Use your card to stay in a motel—any phone calls home to describe your bad luck will be charged to your card, too.

About This Chapter: This chapter includes text from "Credit Cards Give You Lots of Advantages," "The Big Disadvantage," and "Facts about Students and Credit Cards." This information is from www.mint.org, which was conceived, written, and sponsored by the Northwestern Mutual Foundation, the charitable arm of Northwestern Mutual, to help families educate young people about personal money management. © 2007 The Northwestern Mutual Life Insurance Company, Milwaukee WI. Reprinted by permission. All rights reserved.

Gives You Time To Pay: Depending on when you make your purchase and when your monthly bill comes due, you can get extra time to save up and pay for what you just charged. If you can pay off the bill ENTIRELY, you are really making the credit card work for you.

The Big Disadvantage

After all those great advantages, how can credit cards be so dangerous? It has to do with you, not the card itself. You have to know how to control your impulses when it comes to spending.

Way Too Tempting: Whipping out a piece of plastic is so easy. It doesn't even feel like you're spending money. Do that enough times in a month, and SURPRISE! Look at that balance! Where did it come from? It came from all those not-so-big purchases you made over the month. For example:

> ♣ **It's A Fact!!**
> **Carrying A Balance**
>
> You say, I'll always pay my bill in full and on time. That may be what you intend to do, but the plain fact is that about 60% of cardholders carry a balance (owe money) from month to month. Many of these people thought they would pay off their bills each month, too. The convenience of credit can be very hard to resist.

- That pair of shoes you just couldn't pass up. $79
- The night you were dying for pizza after you'd gone rock climbing. $24
- The great sale on baseball stuff. $65
- Those two new CDs that you just couldn't live without. $29

Suddenly you're in debt. And you don't have the $197. So you pay $60, all you can afford. What happens next month? The $60 you paid the credit card company has made you short on cash this month—so you charge more, and your debt grows larger.

Debt In The Real World

So what's it like to be in debt? Let's say that you find the perfect winter jacket. What luck! It's marked down from $220 to $180. That's a $40 savings.

You don't have the $180 right now, but you hate to pass up the sale, so you charge the jacket. You decide to pay for it over time.

Because you work only one day a week, you can't afford large monthly payments. But you can pay $15 every month and still have some money left over for other things. You faithfully pay the $15 each month, but the months seem to drag on forever. Plus, you pay late once, and you're charged a $30 penalty fee for missing the payment date.

Although you've bought the winter jacket in November, it takes you 16 months (that's two winters, a summer, and a spring) to pay off the purchase! At a 17.9% interest rate and with a $30 penalty fee, guess how much you paid for that "sale" jacket? $228.26. That's more than the original price! Those finance charges really add up.

By the time you're done paying for the jacket, you'll be ready to buy a new one.

Facts About Students And Credit Cards

- 78% of college students have credit cards

- 32% of college students have four or more credit cards

- Average credit card debt of these students: $2,748

- Nearly 1 in 4 college students owes more than $3,000

♣ **It's A Fact!!**
According to the National Credit Research Foundation, 55% of high school and college students age 16–22 have a major credit card.

Use of credit is on the rise. The average credit card debt among college students has increased nearly $1,000 from 1999–2001. Student debt is getting worse, not better.

According to the National Credit Research Association, college students owe almost half of the nation's $285 billion credit card debt.

Chapter 21

Understanding Credit Card Offers: What's The Catch?

"I applied for a credit card with a 5.9% interest rate. A few months later, the credit card company changed the rate to 21%! They told me that even though I've never missed a payment to them, they changed my rate because I was one day late paying another company."

"I'm trying to pay down my credit card debt. I got an offer to transfer my balances to another card at zero percent interest. I thought that was great until I got my first statement. There was $178 in fees. They charged a 'balance transfer fee' of $90, an annual fee of $59, and on top of that a $29 fee for exceeding the credit limit—which happened because the first two fees put me over the limit."

The offers fill your mailbox: pre-approved credit cards, low interest rates, 0% interest balance transfer offers, frequent flier miles or rebates, and more. They sound good, but many consumers apply for new credit cards only to find that the low interest rate doesn't last or that the card comes with unexpected fees.

To protect yourself: Read the details of the credit card offer before you apply for the card, and make sure you fully understand the terms being offered. The details are usually in small print. You might be surprised at what you find.

About This Chapter: "Credit Card Offers: What's the Catch?" © 2005 Maryland Office of the Attorney General, Consumer Protection Division. Reprinted with permission.

Below are some things to consider when reviewing a credit card offer:

Low Interest Rate: Many cards offer a low annual percentage rate (APR)—but only for a short time. The introductory rate might only last a few months and then jump to an extremely high rate. If you want to use a new, low-interest rate card to consolidate and pay off your higher interest rate debt, find the card with the longest time period for the low-interest offer. Credit card companies should disclose how long the low-interest offer will last and what the interest rate will be once the low rate ends.

Also, check the offer to see if the low rate will be revoked for any reason. Many cards specify that the interest rate will rise if you make a late payment, if you make a late payment to any other creditor, or if your balance ever exceeds the credit limit. The credit card company will monitor your credit report to see if you miss making a payment to other creditors.

Balance Transfer Fee: Some cards, even if they offer zero-percent interest on balance transfers, charge a fee to transfer the balance from one credit card to another. For example, a 4% balance transfer fee on a $2,000 transfer would cost you $80. And be careful—if you transfer the maximum amount allowed on the new card, and there is a balance transfer fee, you will then be over the credit limit and will probably be charged an over-the-limit fee.

You're Pre-Approved: Don't count on it. Credit card companies get your name from credit reporting agencies by paying the agencies for lists of consumers that meet certain criteria. Once you call to accept the offer or send in the form, the credit card company will seek your full credit report and determine if you qualify. You might not. The company might decline to issue you a card, or send you a card with a lower credit limit, or a higher interest rate than advertised.

Credit Line: The amount of credit offered may not be available to you. If you look closely, you'll probably see the words "up to" before the number. Depending on your credit history, you might receive a card with a lower credit limit than you were expecting.

Cash Advance Fees And Rates: Many cards charge a fee for cash advances, or the interest rate for cash advances is much higher than for credit purchases. If you're likely to use the card to get cash advances, be sure you know what it will cost you.

No Annual Fee: Many promotions promise you won't have to pay an annual fee. But some cards are free only for the first year.

User Bonuses: Some cards offer perks such as frequent flier miles or cash back for using the card. Often, these cards charge annual fees or have a higher interest rate than other cards. If you carry a balance, you might be better off choosing a lower-interest-rate card even if it offers no bonuses.

Over-The-Limit Fee: Some consumers assume that if they make a charge that would put them over their credit limit, the card would simply refuse the charge. Instead, the credit card company will often allow the transaction to go through but charge the consumer a fee, as much as $39, for exceeding the credit limit.

Card Guaranteed In Exchange For A Fee: Never pay a fee in advance for a card. This is a scam. Many people have paid up to $200 for a "major credit card" only to receive nothing, or they received a merchandise catalog and a card that was only good for purchases from that catalog.

When You Receive Your New Card

Once you receive a new credit card, read the accompanying credit card agreement to be sure you understand and accept the terms. If you receive a card that was not what you wanted—for example, it has a lower credit limit or a higher interest rate—you should notify the company that you decline the card. You should read the accompanying card agreement or ask the company for any specific directions on how to refuse the card.

Even if you plan to keep the card, read the agreement carefully. Note what it says about your interest rate and what events might trigger a rate increase; how long the grace period is before interest is charged; when a late charge will be applied and how much the late fee is; and what happens if a charge causes your balance to exceed the credit limit.

✎ What's It Mean?

<u>Annual Fee:</u> Yearly charge for use of the credit card. If you expect to pay your balance in full most months, look for a card with a full grace period and no annual fee. However, if you plan on carrying a balance or you're looking for club perks, then a card with an annual fee and low APR may be a better choice.

<u>Balance Computation Method:</u> How the card company will determine the balance on which you may be charged interest. If you expect to carry a balance most months or if your card offers a short or no grace period, the balance calculation method could be a big factor in your finance charges. Perhaps the most common method is the "average daily balance" approach, where finance charges are calculated on the daily average for the billing period. Other calculation methods may be more costly, including one called the "two-cycle" system where, if you pay in full one month but only pay part of the bill the next month, you'll be charged interest for both months instead of just one.

<u>Grace Period:</u> The number of days before the card company starts charging you interest on purchases. If you plan to avoid interest charges by paying your balance in full most months, make sure your card's terms permit that. It's getting harder to find credit cards that give several weeks of interest-free purchases. Some cards have no grace period, meaning you'd always pay interest from the date of purchase.

<u>Introductory Rates:</u> Also known as "teaser rates," these are very low interest rates offered to entice you to open a new account. But as explained in the fine print, the introductory rate may increase dramatically after six months or so. Low introductory rates may only apply to balances you transfer to your card from other loans or cards you have and not to any new purchases.

<u>Rewards:</u> Incentives for using the card, such as cash back or bonus points toward airline travel or the purchase of a car. Be aware of the rules and restrictions, including limits on how much you can earn or deadlines for taking advantage of a reward. Also, compare the likely value of the bonuses with the potential costs of the card.

Source: Excerpted from "A Reader's Guide to Credit Card Mailings (and the Fine Print)," *FDIC Consumer*, Federal Deposit Insurance Corporation (FDIC), Fall 2002.

Watch Out For Changes In Terms

Even if you shopped carefully for a credit card and are happy with the one you chose, there is no guarantee its terms will stay the same. Most credit cards reserve the right to change their terms, including the interest rate, at any time as long as they give their customers notice. Your credit card company might send you the notice of the change in terms as a separate notice, or with (or on) your monthly statement. Therefore, it's a good idea to look carefully at your statement each month and any inserts that might come with it. You will be given a certain period of time, often 15 or 30 days, in which to tell the company if you do not choose to accept the new terms. If you do nothing, the new terms will go into effect and you will be bound by them.

If you choose not to accept the terms, check your credit card agreement and the notice to see what options you have to pay off your card balance.

Chapter 22

Common Problems With Plastic

Problems With Plastic: Tips For Tackling Your Top Five Concerns

What are the most common problems reported with credit or debit cards, according to staff members at the Federal Deposit Insurance Corporation (FDIC) who respond to consumer inquiries? Here they are, along with guidance on how to prevent and resolve those problems.

1. Billing Errors And Other Disputed Transactions

Billing errors include a charge on your credit card bill that isn't yours or an incorrect dollar amount on a credit or debit card transaction. Other problems might include a payment that didn't show up on your statement or a dispute with a merchant over something you purchased.

Promptly review your monthly statements. With your credit card, the Fair Credit Billing Act (FCBA) protects you from paying for a purchase that wasn't yours or that you didn't agree to. But you must write the creditor

About This Chapter: This chapter includes excerpts from the following articles that originally appeared in *FDIC Consumer News*, Federal Deposit Insurance Corporation (FDIC): "Problems With Plastic: Our Tips for Tackling Your Top Five Concerns," Fall 2002; and "Five Things You Should Know About Credit Cards," Spring 2005. "Credit and Debit Card Blocking" is from the Facts for Consumers series of publications produced by the Federal Trade Commission (FTC), June 2003.

(a call isn't sufficient) using the address given for billing inquiries (not the payment address), and your letter (or any complaint form provided with your bill) must reach the creditor within 60 days after the first bill containing the error was mailed to you. "I recommend that you send your dispute by certified mail, with a return-receipt requested, so that you have proof that the creditor received it on time," says FDIC Senior Consumer Affairs Officer Janet Kincaid. Also include copies—not originals— of any sales slips or other relevant documentation, and keep a copy of your request.

The FCBA also allows you to withhold payment for defective goods or services purchased with a credit card until the problem has been corrected, under certain conditions. In general, the purchase must be for more than $50 from a merchant in your home state or within 100 miles of your home. Your card issuer may offer additional protections.

Even though debit card transaction amounts are deducted from your bank account immediately—or within a few days—you have protections against errors and defective purchases under the Electronic Fund Transfer Act (EFTA) and industry practices. So, notify your financial institution immediately if there is a problem involving your debit card. While the EFTA does not require you to put your complaint in writing, it's a good idea to do so.

2. Application Denied Or Downgraded

Consumers get upset when they apply for a credit card and, because of incorrect information in their credit report, their request is denied or they are offered less favorable credit terms than they expected. Credit report errors can happen, so periodically get a copy of your credit report to make sure everything is correct. It's especially smart to review your credit report before applying for a mortgage, credit card, or other important loan, so that an error doesn't slow down your credit approval. And if you do find an error in your credit record, write to the credit bureau that prepared the report and provide copies of relevant documentation. [You can find more information about credit reports and correcting credit report errors in Chapters 7 and 8.]

3. Late Payment Fees

You say you mailed your credit card payment on time or you paid through your bank's electronic bill payment service... and you still got hit with a $30 late fee. Why? Financial institutions mark credit card payments as "paid" on the day they are received, not the day you mailed it. While the federal Truth in Lending Act (TILA) says a card issuer must credit your payment as of the date of receipt, most card issuers suggest that consumers allow seven to 10 days for payments to be received and credited. Find out your bank's cutoff time for card payments. Some have a 10:00 A.M. deadline for payments to be credited that day. Also, send your payment to the address indicated by your card company. Mailing to the wrong address can cause late or even missed payments. And if you know your "late" payment arrived on time, contact your card issuer to resolve the matter.

> ✔ **Quick Tip**
>
> Consumers using their bank's electronic bill payment service also should recognize that it still may take two or more days for their credit card company to receive the funds. To be safe, pay a few days in advance.
>
> Source: FDIC, Fall 2002.

4. Changes In Terms

Credit card companies have the right to change interest rates or terms, as outlined in the cardmember agreement. A notice must be mailed or delivered to you at least 15 days prior to the effective date. If you don't want to accept a rate increase or other change, you can contact the card issuer and try to negotiate a better deal, but there's no guarantee it will agree. If you decide to close the account, do so in writing and know the rules for canceling the card under the existing terms.

With debit cards, federal rules generally require that a notice of changes in fees or terms be mailed or delivered at least 21 days before the effective date. Again, read the information that is sent to you and, if you disagree, try to negotiate or shop around for a better deal.

5. Confusion Over Promotional Offers

You're probably familiar with deals like "zero percent interest" on a credit card or "no payment on merchandise until next year" if you put your purchase on your charge card. These offers usually are for limited purposes and time periods, something many consumers don't focus on until they run up unexpected charges. "These offers can be good, but you've got to read the fine print and do the math," adds Kincaid. Example: Some offers may require you to pay the balance in full by the due date or you'll be charged interest on the entire balance, starting with the date of purchase, even if you have been making payments throughout the term of the promotion.

Five Things You Should Know About Credit Cards

1. Use Them Carefully: Credit cards offer great benefits, especially the ability to buy now and pay later. But you've got to keep the debt levels manageable. If you don't, the costs in terms of fees and interest, or the damage to your credit record, could be significant.

2. Choose Them Carefully: Don't choose a credit card just to get freebies (T-shirts or sports items) or because there's no annual fee. Look for a card that's best for your borrowing habits.

> ♣ **It's A Fact!!**
> **Watch Your Backside...**
> **On Your Credit Card**
>
> You're about to use your credit card to purchase something over the internet or the telephone and you're asked to provide the three or four numbers printed on the back of the card. Is it a valid question and is it safe to respond? It depends on who's asking. A merchant has a legitimate purpose for obtaining those numbers, but an ID thief can use them to commit fraud.
>
> The numbers on the back of your credit card, often printed on the strip provided for your signature, are part of a new security code. The purpose is to verify that the person making a purchase online or over the phone—when the merchant cannot see the card—actually has the card in hand and is not someone else who simply knows the card number and expiration date.
>
> Source: *FDIC Consumer News*, Federal Deposit Insurance Corporation (FDIC), Fall 2004.

✔ **Quick Tip**

If you expect to carry a balance on your card from month to month, which means you'll be charged interest, it's more important to look for a card with a low interest rate or a generous "grace period" (more time before your payments are due).

Source: FDIC, Spring 2005.

3. Pay As Much As You Can: Pay as much as you can to avoid or minimize interest charges. If possible, pay your bill in full each month. Remember, paying only the minimum due each month means you'll be paying a lot of interest for many years, and those costs could far exceed the amount of your original purchase.

4. Pay On Time: You'll avoid a late fee of about $35 or more. But more importantly, continued late payments on your credit card may be reported to the major credit bureaus as a sign that you have problems handling your finances.

And if your credit rating gets downgraded, your card company could raise the interest rate on your credit card, reduce your credit limit (the maximum amount you can borrow), or even cancel your card.

Late payment on your credit card also can be a mark against you the next time you apply for an apartment or a job.

5. Protect Your Credit Card Numbers From Thieves: Never provide your credit card numbers—both the account numbers and expiration date on the front and the security code on the back—in response to an unsolicited phone call, e-mail, or other communication you didn't originate.

When using your credit card online make sure you're dealing with a legitimate website and that your information will be encrypted (scrambled for security purposes) during transmission.

Major credit card companies also are offering more protection by providing "zero-liability" programs that protect consumers from the unauthorized use of their card.

In general, only give your credit card or card numbers to reputable merchants or other organizations.

Credit And Debit Card Blocking

Have you ever been told you were over your credit card limit, or had your debit card declined, even though you knew you had available credit, or money in your bank account? If this happened shortly after you used your card for another transaction, the problem could have been card "blocking."

What's Blocking?

When you use a credit or debit card for some transactions—such as to check into a hotel or rent a car—the clerk usually contacts the company that issued your card to give an estimated total. If the transaction is approved, your available credit (credit card) or the balance in your bank account (debit card) is reduced by this amount. That's a "block." Some companies also call this placing a "hold" on those amounts.

Blocking is used to make sure you don't exceed your credit line (credit card) or overdraw your bank account (debit card) before checking out of a hotel or returning a rental car, leaving the merchant unpaid. If you're nowhere near your credit limit or don't have a low balance in your bank account, blocking probably won't be a problem. But if you're reaching that point, be careful. Exceeding your credit line or overdrawing your account as a result of blocking can lead to embarrassment, inconvenience, and hefty fees.

Chapter 23

Understanding Credit Card Finance Charges And Penalties

How Finance Charges Are Figured

Sure, you pay the finance charge on your bill, but do you understand how the credit card company arrives at the number?

Check out four of the most common calculation methods. But be warned: the method alone only tells part of the story. To make sure you're getting the best deal on a card, ask how the company calculates the charges and whether interest is calculated on a daily or monthly basis. Find out if there is a grace period for new purchases. And have the company rep explain when and how your monthly payments are applied.

Calculation Methods

Type Of Balance: How it's calculated.

Average Daily Balance: The company averages your daily balance. For instance, if you charged $100 on the first day of June and $200 on the 16th, your average daily balance would be $150. That number times roughly one-twelfth your annual percentage rate (APR) equals your monthly finance charge. Interest may be calculated on a daily or monthly basis.

Daily Balance: The company calculates the actual balance you carried each day of your billing cycle and multiplies it by roughly 1/365th of your APR and adds it together.

Two-Cycle Balance: Similar to an average daily balance except that the daily average is based on your last two billing months, not just one. With this method, if you don't pay off your card in full one month, you'll be hit with retroactive interest on your next bill.

Previous Balance: The bill will show beginning balance and ending balance for your account. The finance charge is based on the outstanding balance at the beginning of the billing cycle.

FAQ On Fees

Understanding how your credit card company assesses finance charges and penalties can save you hundreds of dollars. Bankrate expert Dr. Don Taylor answers some of the more frequently asked questions on these charges.

My credit card interest rate was jacked up to 29.99 percent when I was late paying the bill. What is the maximum allowable annual percentage rate (APR) on credit cards?

It's a popular misconception that state usury laws protect borrowers from high interest rates on their credit card debt.

Credit card issuers scored a sweeping victory in 1978 when the Supreme Court ruled in Marquette vs. First Omaha Services that it was legal for nationally chartered banks to export the more costly terms of their cards to states where the laws regarding interest rates restricted such practices. The credit card issuer need only follow the law of the state in which its credit card operations are located, not the laws of the cardholder's state of residency.

After this Supreme Court ruling, credit card issuers migrated to states with permissive credit policies like South Dakota and Delaware.

That's why it's so important to make timely payments, even if it is just the required minimum payment. Besides avoiding late charges, you keep your payment history intact and avoid giving your credit card company an excuse to raise your interest rate.

By the way, many credit card agreements are now written so the company can raise your rate if you are late on any of your bills, not just their credit card.

✔ Quick Tip

Get a copy of your credit report and your credit score and see for yourself how bad things really are. You can order your credit report online and get the results in minutes. Correct any mistakes on your report, and start the rebuilding process. Although late payments stay on your credit report for seven years, the negative effect of these items lessens with time as you rebuild your credit history.

Getting A Lower-Rate Card: You need to get out from under this 30-percent albatross. After reviewing your credit report for mistakes and making any needed corrections, you're ready to look for replacement credit.

First, talk with your current lender and ask them to reduce your rate. Make it clear that you plan to vote with your feet and find a new lender if they aren't willing to reduce your rate. It's not likely to work, but it's worth asking. If they say no, then it's time to do some shopping.

If you belong to a credit union, or are eligible to join a credit union, talk to them about transferring this balance to their credit card. Or look at taking out a personal loan for the amount needed to pay off the card.

Just don't apply for debt all over town. Multiple credit applications make you look desperate, and lenders don't like to lend to desperate people.

If none of this works, make every effort to pay down as much as you can each month on this card until you pay it off.

I usually pay on time, but occasionally I miss the due date by a day or two. Are these exorbitant $35 late fees fair practice?

I'm going to start out on the bank's side on this one. A credit card is a line of credit. The bank commits to loaning you money up to your credit line, and you commit to paying them back. When you don't pay your bill on time, the bank starts to wonder if you're going to pay it at all. By penalizing cardholders for late payment, the bank both trains you to make timely payments and gets periodic affirmation of your commitment to repay them.

OK, so nobody likes negative reinforcement, and $35 is a pretty expensive reminder. Especially when a couple of late payments are then used as an excuse to raise the interest rate on your credit card.

What to do? First, call the credit card company. Tell them that you plan to move the account if they don't rescind the late fee. That should work the first time, and it won't the second time. Then ask yourself why you're late with these bills. You may need to organize the due dates to fit your monthly budget flow.

Can a credit card company continue to charge over-the-limit fees on an outstanding balance of a closed account?

First off, you can't close an account that has an outstanding balance. You can, however, notify the credit card company that you want the account closed to new purchases. Interest charges and fees aren't purchases and can continue to increase the outstanding balance.

Credit card companies have the ability to not authorize purchases that would put your account over its credit limit. So anything that is above your credit limit was either done with their authorization or by interest and fees taking the balance over your limit. Regardless of how the fees got there, they aren't illegal.

The credit card company isn't likely to help you with your problem. You've closed the account to new purchases, so they know they don't have you as a long-term customer. Now, they're just making what money they can off the account before you pay it off or it goes into default.

Considering Transferring Balances: You can't afford to not pay down this debt. I'd hate to see you go in to credit counseling for this one debt because of the negative effect it has on your credit report, but you need to find some way to make this stop. I'm going to suggest that you apply for a new credit card and, if successful, transfer the balances away from your current credit card.

First check your credit report. Dispute any erroneous items. Then search for a new credit card on Bankrate (www.bankrate.com). Apply for only one card. All credit applications will show up on your credit report, and multiple applications and denials will hurt your ability to get credit in the future.

You're actually more concerned about the new card's credit line than the interest rate because you need a line big enough to be able to transfer the balance and close the old account, so don't chase a low introductory rate that you won't qualify for. Just being able to put the $35 a month you were paying in fees toward paying down the balance will help out a lot.

✔ Quick Tip

The National Foundation for Credit Counseling can help you find a credit counselor in your area or even counsel you online. The Federal Trade Commission (FTC) has a list of questions to ask when meeting with a credit counselor (http://www.ftc.gov/bcp/conline/pubs/credit/fiscal.htm). If you choose to go this route, you should interview two or three credit counseling agencies before signing with one.

Credit Counseling: If you can't qualify for a new card, then credit counseling may be your best solution. A credit counselor can negotiate a repayment plan with your creditors and may be able to reduce the interest rate on your debt. They will definitely be able to stop the over-the-limit fees.

Most agencies are nonprofit, but that doesn't mean that they won't charge you a fee to put together a budget and repayment plan.

A company has offered to help me get a low-rate card for a high fee. Is this my only option for a low-rate card?

No, you don't have to pay to get a low-rate credit card. You don't need a middleman to get your foot in the door with a national bank.

Your credit history is what it is. You can correct errors in your credit report and rebuild your credit over time, but paying someone a high fee for the privilege of having them find you a credit card is wasted money. Put that money toward your credit card bills.

People who are choking on their credit card interest rates should review their credit reports, and correct any errors in the report by using the dispute process established under the Fair Credit Reporting Act. Do that first, so you know that you're putting your best foot forward when applying for a new credit card.

Then you can go shopping for a new card using Bankrate's credit card search feature. Apply for only one card, and see what happens. Multiple credit card applications make you look desperate, and firms hate to lend to desperate people.

I did a balance transfer from one credit card to another. My new credit card company sent me a check to pay off my old account but started charging me interest immediately. Is it fair to pay interest on money I've not received yet?

Balance transfers are typically treated as cash advances, and interest will accrue from the day the check was issued. There's nothing improper about the credit card company charging you interest from the time they cut the check.

If there was a several-day delay between the time you made the request and the date they cut the check, and they charged you interest from the day you made the request, then you have a reason to be upset, and you should talk to a customer service manager.

If that doesn't get results, you could file a complaint with the Federal Reserve Board or the Office of the Comptroller of the Currency if the credit card company is a national bank.

Credit card companies aren't above earning interest on the float from the delay between when the check was cut and when the check clears. It's their float to invest.

I don't understand why they weren't able to wire the funds to your bank or send the check via overnight delivery, but the cost to you for those services would likely outstrip what you paid in interest on the money.

Make sure you're not making a mountain out of a molehill. If you are transferring a balance of $10,000 at 5 percent, a week's worth of interest is about $10. Think about the money you'll be saving in interest expense during the introductory period, and how you're going to use that interest rate break as an opportunity to pay down your outstanding balances.

Worry more about making the payments on time to avoid late charges; making late payments gives the credit card company an excuse to end the introductory period and raise your interest rate.

I'm looking for a credit card that I plan to use on special occasions and pay off the balance monthly. What card is the best choice for avoiding hidden fees and clauses?

If you're planning to pay off the balance every month, you should be less concerned about the interest rate and more concerned about the grace period before they start charging you interest on your purchases.

Credit card agreements aren't written in stone. Variable rates fluctuate with changes in the Fed Funds rate, but so can rates on a fixed-rate card. The card companies will change terms as needed to remain competitive with other credit card issuers. If you don't like how a credit card issuer has changed the terms on your card, vote with your feet and find a new card to carry.

How does two-cycle credit card billing affect the cost of credit?

With two-cycle billing, the average daily balance used to calculate interest charges is calculated from two billing cycles rather than one. This approach to calculating interest effectively wipes out the grace period for customers who carry a balance. Two-cycle billing is expensive for people who only sometimes carry balances. You'll be paying interest on the average of the two cycles.

Example: Let's say you transfer $5,000 to the two-cycle card and plan to pay down your outstanding balance by $500 a month. Your average balance for the first cycle is $5,000 and you owe $15.95 in interest, so you pay $515.95 and have a $4,500 outstanding balance.

At the end of the second billing cycle, the credit card issuer calculates interest due based on the average balance for the two periods, or $4,750, and your interest payment is $15.15. You've paid $31.10 in interest.

With a one-cycle card at 4.9 percent APR, you pay $19.95 in interest the first month and $17.96 in the second month, for a total of $37.91. The two-cycle card has saved you $6.81 over the two periods.

How To Avoid Late Fees

Being late is going to cost you, big time. With credit card late fees at $39, this is no time to be the least bit tardy with your card payment.

Avoid late fees. These payment tips and strategies from Bankrate.com will show you how to steer clear of those monster late fees.

Seven Ways To Avoid Late Fees

1. Mind Those Payment Rules: One of the most important things you can do is follow your card issuer's payment guidelines precisely. These guidelines are outlined on the back of each credit card bill.

When it comes to processing credit card payments, all these little details are incredibly important.

Payment guidelines may include everything from a specific payment address to the time of day by which the payment must be received to be credited that day. Many issuers also stipulate that payments must arrive in the preprinted envelope sent to the customer.

While the Fair Credit Billing Act requires issuers to credit payments the day they are received, each issuer is allowed to set specific payment guidelines. If any of the guidelines are not met, the issuer can take as many as five days to credit the payment.

An on-time payment could easily become "late" during that five-day period, so follow those payment guidelines carefully.

To ensure your payment gets credited immediately:

- Use the preprinted envelope provided by the credit card company.

- Include the billing coupon, and be sure to write the amount being paid in the box provided.

- Make sure checks are legible and the payment amount is correct. Sign the check. Write the credit card account number on the check.

> ✔ **Quick Tip**
> **To Avoid Late Fees**
>
> - Follow payment guidelines.
> - Pay minimum immediately.
> - Change your due date.
> - Set up automatic online, on-time payments.
> - Pay by phone.
> - Express mail or wire payment.
> - Good payers can ask for waiver.

- Send payment with proper postage to the payment address requested by the issuer. It's a good idea to mail your payment at least one week in advance of the due date. Ten days to two weeks prior to a due date is even better.

2. Pay Minimum Immediately: The safest strategy for anyone sending a card payment by snail mail is to pay the bill as soon as it arrives, even if you can only make the minimum payment. Giving your issuer the 2 percent minimum payment it wants ASAP is a great way to guard against late fees. And you can always send a bigger payment when you've got more cash.

3. Move Your Due Date: Are your credit card bills due at a time of the month when you're running low on cash? Many card issuers will let you set your own due date—if you ask. Why not time it so your credit card bill arrives right after a paycheck? That way you'll have plenty of cash to pay your bill each month.

4. Automatic Online, On-Time Payments: Paying bills online can be a great buffer against late fees. Most major issuers, including Citibank, MBNA, Discover, and American Express accept online payments. You can sign up for these services on issuer websites. Choose an online payment amount that automatically covers the minimum amount due on a credit card each month. Next, choose an automatic payment date well in advance of your credit card due date. This is a great way to pay credit card bills while traveling. To keep your interest costs down, you'll want to make additional card payments online or by snail mail as soon as you can.

5. Pay By Phone: Paying by phone is a quick and easy way to make a last-minute card payment. Just grab your checkbook and call the toll-free number on the back of your credit card. You'll be asked for a check number and the bank routing number, which is printed at the bottom of every check. After you're done with the call, rip up the check because you won't be able to use it again. Many credit card companies accept payments by phone. Some issuers charge fees, ranging from $7.50 to $25 for this service. Be sure to ask.

6. More Express Options: If the due date is looming, consider sending a credit card payment by express mail or wiring the payment with Western Union. The U.S. Postal Service charges $16.25 for an express mail flat rate envelope, which guarantees next-day delivery by noon to most destinations. Wiring your payment will cost you as well. Western Union's fees for money-wiring service vary depending upon the amount of payment. These express services, while costly, are still cheaper than most credit card late fees. Make sure you send your express payment to the proper address. Many issuers have separate payment addresses for express payments. The last thing you want to do is slow the processing of an express payment by sending it to the wrong address.

7. No Fee If You're "Good": Zapped with a late fee even though you mailed your payment well before the due date? Call and ask your issuer to waive the fee. Many issuers will waive late fees as a courtesy to customers with good payment records.

Smaller Card Issuers

If all these fee-dodging strategies are too much for you, you may want to consider getting a card from a credit union or a local community bank. Smaller card issuers are much more lenient when it comes to penalty fees.

Late fees at community banks range from $15 to $30. Community banks are more likely than conventional banks to waive late fees for their customers under special circumstances, such as job loss.

Credit unions give card customers some leeway as well. Generally, a credit union will accept a card payment 14 days after a due date without penalty. And if a credit union should charge you a late fee, it will only be $15 on average.

Why Your Rates Go Up

Want to know when your credit card issuer can raise your rates? Read your contract, says Kevin Mukri, spokesman for the Comptroller of the Currency, which regulates national banks.

Any reason for raising your APR has to be in the contract. "Banks can't willy-nilly change the terms," says Mukri. "Banks are required to fulfill the contract."

The initial contract should be in plain, readable language, he says. And if the issuer is changing your rates, they have to tell you when and why, says Mukri. "What we require is that people receive notification," he says.

If your APR has gone up, here are some likely culprits:

• You were late with a payment.

- You were late with another debt. (But your contract has to disclose that the issuer can penalize you for your record with other creditors.)

- Your issuer merged with another entity. "The receiving bank has the option of changing the conditions (of the contract)," says Mukri. "But they have to spell it out to the consumer."

- The bank's cost of borrowing money has increased. (Has to be in the contract.)

- Any other reason spelled out in the contract.

If your creditor hikes the rate, don't give up. Ask for an explanation, and try to negotiate a better deal.

Hefty Cost Of Going Over The Limit

What happens when I charge my credit card over the limit?

You will be socked with a hefty penalty fee. Over-the-limit fees of $29 and $35 are common.

Norm Tapper, a Bankrate.com reader in Indiana, was charged a $25 late fee and $25 over-the-limit fee on a Capital One card with a $300 limit.

Issuers point out that fees are spelled out in the credit-card agreement and monthly statements list credit limit, balance information, and due dates. But a lot of people are shocked by over-the-limit fees. In fact, most people learn about a card's over-the-limit penalty after they get charged one.

When You're Charged: Credit card issuers have two basic choices when a customer makes a purchase that exceeds a credit limit. They can decline the transaction or approve the transaction and charge a fee.

✔ Quick Tip

Convinced that the company has raised the rates without cause? The Comptroller of the Currency will investigate. The hotline is: 800-613-6743.

A third option, approve the transaction and automatically lift the credit line, is reserved for the best customers.

Today's issuers are adept at targeting card offers to a customer's specific credit profile and that includes the handling of over-the-limit charges. Issuers decide which customers can go over credit limits and by how much. The last thing an issuer wants to do is decline a card purchase.

Credit Card Limit

So it looks like issuers will continue to charge bigger and bigger fees to customers who outgrow their credit limits. Don't let it happen to you. Here's how:

> ✔ Quick Tip
> **Five Ways To Avoid Exceeding Your Limit**
>
> 1. Monitor spending closely.
> 2. Sign up for free e-mail alerts.
> 3. Make the limit your limit.
> 4. Call ahead and get that limit raised.
> 5. Check out cards from local banks and credit unions.

1. **Monitor Spending Closely:** Keep track of credit card purchases and stay well within your limit. Leave a big enough cushion on your card for large, unexpected expenses. Some consumer experts recommend keeping one credit card cleared for emergencies.

2. **Sign Up For Free E-mail Alerts:** Some issuers send e-mail reminders to customers who are nearing credit limits.

3. **Make The Limit Your Limit:** Card holders at Capital One can request that any limit-busting purchase be declined at the point-of-sale. However, most companies refuse to provide this service.

4. **Call Ahead And Get That Limit Raised:** If you know you're going to go over a credit limit with a purchase, call ahead and request a line increase. Issuers grant increases on a case-by-case basis. It's worth a shot and it could save you $30.

5. **Check Out Cards From Local Banks And Credit Unions:** Penalty fees are much lower, typically $5 to $15, and smaller institutions are much more lenient when it comes to charging them. For example, at Suncoast Schools Federal Credit Union in Tampa, Florida, the $15 over-the-limit fee is not imposed until you exceed the credit line by 8 percent.

Chapter 24

A Guide To Reading Your Monthly Credit Card Statement

Credit card statements are the ultimate math-class word problem. Get one wrong and the bad mark will stay with you a while—on your credit report.

Requirements

To make it even more challenging, nearly every credit card has a slightly different set of requirements and a slightly different statement. So here's a cheat sheet—in plain English—to help you sort through that next bill and save a little money in the process:

Purchases/New Charges: This is where the statement should spell out what you purchased and how much you borrowed. It's also the first thing you want to check, says Mark Oleson, director of the Financial Counseling Clinic at Iowa State University.

His smart credit trick: Save all charge receipts for the month and match them with the bill when it comes in. "I want to make sure that when I pay my bill, I'm paying the amount I charged," Oleson says.

That way if you're double billed or charged for something you didn't buy, you can take action immediately. If you have a problem, quickly contact the credit card company by phone and follow up with a letter.

In addition, you want to look at what rates are applied to what charges. If you took out a cash advance, chances are you might pay that at a higher rate, which probably started the day you received the money. If you have a balance transfer at a special rate, you want to make sure that's noted correctly on your statement.

Previous Balance: Does the number track with your last bill? And is it going down or are you just treading water?

> ♣ **It's A Fact!!**
> **What's On The Statement**
> - Purchases/new charges
> - Previous balance
> - payments and credits
> - Cash advances
> - APR (annual percentage rate)
> - Finance charges
> - Grace period
> - Minimum payment
> - Due/Pay-by date
> - Credit limit
> - Late fee
> - Over-the-limit fee
> - Name, address, account number
> - Miscellaneous fees

Payments And Credits: Did you get credit for that return on December 26? Or for the last check you sent?

"Look to make sure they applied the last payment as they should have," says Rus Halsey, group manager and counselor for GreenPath Debt Solutions, a nonprofit credit counseling service based in Farmington Hills, Michigan.

And if you sent in a check to pay off last month's cash advance, did the company apply the credit correctly?

Cash Advances: This will tell you how much you've borrowed. Many cards charge a higher interest rate on a cash advance than on purchases. They may not offer a grace period. And some don't automatically apply your repayment to the cash-advance debt.

If you have to take a cash advance, find out the rules for borrowing and repaying ahead of time. And track this balance until it's paid off in full.

APR: It stands for annual percentage rate, and it's the "industry standard" for measuring finance charges, says Halsey.

"I don't have to get hung up on how it's calculated daily, monthly, or whatever. I look at the APR."

But credit companies can change the APR, which is one reason to check it when the bill comes in each month. You want to make sure it's "steady and consistent" with what the company has charged you in the past, he says.

Finance Charges: If you carry a balance, and sometimes even if you don't, finance charges are the penalty for using plastic. Some cards won't levy finance charges as long as you pay off your bills in full each month. Others start charging interest from the moment you use the card.

The company will use one of several formulas to calculate your finance charges. Basically, they look at your average balance over the billing period and multiply it times one-twelfth of your annual percentage rate (APR), says Halsey.

But you may have several different finance rates on one card—one for balance transfers, one for cash advances, etc.

"Obviously, [you] want to make sure [the right totals] are in the right baskets," says Oleson.

Grace Period: How long can something stay on your bill before you are charged interest? While some cards have grace periods, others don't. Find out if you have a grace period, whether it applies to purchases or cash advances and what the length of time is.

Minimum Payment: This is the least amount you can pay on your bill. It's usually 2 percent to 2.5 percent of the balance, though some could be as high as 3 percent to 4 percent, says Halsey.

Due/Pay-By Date: This is the date that your payment has to be recorded in the credit card company's computer. Remember, it's not the date your bill has to be postmarked, or even the date it arrives at the company's office. The typical bill cycle is 29 to 31 days, and the payment is usually due 20 to 30 days from when the bill was printed, says Halsey.

Find out the requirements of your credit cards so that you know the rules of engagement. To play it safe, mail payments 10 days to two weeks before they are due. Since it already took the company a week to get the bill to you, it means that when the bill hits your mailbox, you've got to pay it pronto.

Another option is to pay the bill online. "You can make the payment immediately and avoid the whole mailing system," says Oleson.

Credit Limit: What's the maximum the card allows you to borrow?

"Something I'm concerned about is my credit limit," says Oleson. "If I'm in a situation where I'll be pushing that and the finance rates could bump me over, I'm going to call and request an increase."

But the best long-term strategy for consumers and their credit ratings is to have lower limits, he says. "Because [you] have less potential debt."

Late Fee: Remember when you were late to class and got slapped with detention? With a credit card, the late penalty averages from $29 to $35 per month, Oleson says.

Over-The-Limit Fee: If you charge beyond your limit, or if late fees take you over the limit, you get hit with this charge each month until you bring your balance down to your allowed amount. Generally it ranges from $29 to $39, says Oleson.

Name, Address, Account Number: Self-explanatory, yes. But check them over to make sure all the information is right. Addresses and ZIP codes change, and it's easy to transpose account numbers.

Remember!!

Bottom Line: If you see an item you don't recognize, whether it's a charge or a fee, call the company and ask for an explanation.

Miscellaneous Fees: Sometimes there are fees on the bill for things consumers don't recognize, like credit insurance, says Halsey.

"There have been some creditors who have had these on statements, and clients are not aware they are being charged for that," he says.

Chapter 25

Small Payments Can Mean Big Costs

One of the great things about using a credit card is that you can buy now and pay later. But some consumers take the pay-later concept to an extreme—they pay only the minimum amount due on their card's outstanding balance each month and end up paying the maximum costs. (The minimum payment is set by each card issuer—typically it's about two percent of your outstanding balance—and it is shown on your monthly bill.) While it might appear to be a good deal to pay only $20 a month to buy a $1,000 computer, the Federal Deposit Insurance Corporation (FDIC) wants you to know just how much that computer will really cost when you add in the interest charges.

"Many people think if they only make the minimum payment shown on the statement they can keep their account current, keep charging, and have extra cash for other bills," says Janet Kincaid, a Senior Consumer Affairs Officer with the FDIC. "This is generally true, but what people also need to think about is the long-term cost of this alternative." She adds that if you pay only the minimum amount, "it will take you a very long time to pay off the balance, and the interest costs can be shocking."

About This Chapter: Text in this chapter is from "Small Payments Can Mean Big Costs When Borrowing," *FDIC Consumer News*, Federal Deposit Insurance Corporation (FDIC), Summer 2006; and "Minimum Payments, Maximum Costs on Credit Cards," *FDIC Consumer News*, FDIC, Summer 2003.

Table 25.1. Making Only the Minimum Payment Adds To Costs

Starting Balance	Interest Rate (APR)	Monthly Payment	Total Years to Pay Off	Interest Paid	Total Cost
$5,000	18%	The minimum ($100 the first month, then gradually declines)	46	$13,926	$18,926
$5,000	18%	$100	8	$4,311	$9,311
$5,000	18%	$250	2	$986	$5,986

Note: The minimum payment is assumed to be two percent of the outstanding balance or $10, whichever is greater. Years are rounded to the nearest whole year.

How shocking? Take a look at Table 25.1. It shows what would happen if you have a $5,000 outstanding balance on your credit card (to keep things simple, it assumes you make no additional purchases), an annual percentage rate (APR) of 18 percent, and you make only the minimum payment due ($100 initially but gradually declining each month because minimum payments usually are based on a percentage of the balance, which will decrease.) Using this example, it will take 46 years and cost $13,926 in interest charges before you've paid the $5,000, putting the total cost at $18,926. If instead you pay $100 the first month and every month—which would be more than the minimum due—the balance would be paid off in eight years and the interest charges would be cut from $13,926 to $4,311.

How can you protect yourself?

Pay as much as you can on your charge card each month—pay the entire balance, if possible—in order to avoid interest charges. The FDIC and other bank regulators have taken steps to ensure that minimum card payments are reasonable, "but because there is no law or regulation requiring that minimum payments be a certain dollar amount or percentage, card issuers have a lot of flexibility in setting low minimum payments," says FDIC Consumer

♣ It's A Fact!!

Here's an example that shows what a purchase will really cost you if you charge it and only pay back the minimum amount due each month. In this example, a $500 stereo would end up costing you about $900, and a $1,000 computer would set you back more than $2,100. If you instead pay back as much as you can each month—the entire balance, if possible—you can really limit interest charges.

Stereo

- Purchase Price: $500
- Years to Pay Off With Minimum Monthly Payments: 7 (yes, years)
- Total Interest Paid: $367
- Total Cost: $867

Computer

- Purchase Price: $1,000
- Years to Pay Off With Minimum Monthly Payments: 13 (again, this is years)
- Total Interest Paid: $1,129
- Total Cost: $2,129

Note: Years are rounded to the nearest whole year. These examples assume an interest rate (annual percentage rate [APR]) of 18 percent and a minimum monthly payment of the interest due plus one percent of the outstanding balance owed.

Source: FDIC, 2006.

Affairs Specialist Howard Herman. "As credit card interest rates are often quite high, consumers need to take charge of the situation and pay as much of their card balance as they can afford. The amount you pay toward your credit card bill each month can have greater long-term consequences for your finances than how much money you save or invest each month."

And if you can't pay most or all of your credit card bill, try to pay as much above the minimum as possible. "Depending on your balance," Kincaid says, "even stretching to pay an extra $50 a month can make a big difference in reducing your total interest costs."

If you plan to carry a balance each month, look for a card that has a low interest rate and a grace period. The grace period is the number of days before the card company starts charging interest on new purchases. Remember that grace periods can vary. With most cards, if you don't pay your bill in full you can be charged interest immediately on new purchases. Many cards have no grace period, which means you always pay interest on new purchases from the day you make the purchase.

✔ **Quick Tip**

If all you can afford is the minimum amount, pay that... and pay it on time. "Many consumers are not aware that if they pay less than the minimum, the bank may still assess a late fee of $35 or more and could report the account to the credit bureaus as delinquent," says FDIC Supervisory Consumer Affairs Specialist Lynne Gottesburen. This kind of negative information in your credit file could result in your card issuer increasing the interest rate or even canceling your card.

Source: FDIC, 2003.

Kincaid and Herman agree that one of the worst financial moves a consumer can make is to pay only the minimum due on credit card balances. They and other FDIC officials say that while it takes discipline to pay most or all of your credit card bill each month, the sooner you pay off your balance, the less you pay in interest and the more you have available to save for a home, college education, retirement, or something else that truly benefits you.

Chapter 26

Credit And Debit Card Fraud: Protect Yourself

State-of-the-art thieves are concentrating on plastic cards. In the past, this type of fraud was not very common. Today, it is a big business for criminals. Plastic cards bring new convenience to your shopping and banking, but they can turn into nightmares in the wrong hands. This chapter describes credit and debit cards and some common schemes involving card fraud with tips to help you avoid them.

Credit And Debit Cards

Although they may look the same, all plastic cards do not work the same. In fact, there are two very different kinds of cards in use today: credit cards and debit cards.

As the names imply, credit cards allow the extension of credit and the delay of payment while debit cards charge or debit your account at the moment of the transaction.

Credit Cards

Many credit cards work as follows: You charge goods or services and the merchant who accepts your credit card sends the transaction information to

About This Chapter: "Plastic Fraud: Getting a Handle on Debit and Credit Cards," reprinted with permission from the Federal Reserve Bank of San Francisco, http://www.frbsf.org, April 2006.

the card-issuing institution. The institution then bills you, usually on a monthly basis. In many cases, payment may be made by the due date with no interest assessed. If the total bill is not paid by the due date, you often can pay off your debt in monthly payments that include finance charges.

Debit Cards

Debit cards, unlike credit cards, automatically withdraw funds from your account at the time you make a transaction.

Debit cards are used most commonly at automated teller machines (ATMs) and for purchasing goods directly in stores.

The machine-readable plastic card contains a magnetic strip indicating your account number, bank number, and type of account. Debit card users gain access to the issuing institution's computer by using a secret code, their personal identification number (PIN). The PIN should only be known to the card holder.

Avoiding Card Fraud

Although credit and debit card fraud can take many forms, the following examples explain some situations to watch for.

✔ Quick Tip
Guarding Against Fraud

- Sign your cards as soon as they arrive.

- Carry your cards separately from your wallet, in a zippered compartment, a business card holder, or another small pouch.

- Keep a record of your account numbers, their expiration dates, and the phone number and address of each company in a secure place.

- Keep an eye on your card during the transaction, and get it back as quickly as possible.

- Void incorrect receipts.

- Destroy carbons.

- Save receipts to compare with billing statements.

- Open bills promptly and reconcile accounts monthly, just as you would your checking account.

- Report any questionable charges promptly and in writing to the card issuer.

- Notify card companies in advance of a change in address.

Source: Excerpted from "Avoiding Credit and Charge Card Fraud," Federal Trade Commission, August 1997.

Stolen Cards At The Office

Over the lunch hour when you leave your office for lunch, you could be the target of a credit card thief. Credit card thieves often gain illegal access to the offices of employees who are away in order to search unattended. Most times, they leave the offices and immediately go on a shopping spree, charge credit cards to their limits, and withdraw cash on debit cards.

Protect your credit cards as you would cash. Never write your PIN on your debit card. Instead, always commit your PIN to memory.

Extra Copies Of Charge Slips

When processing your credit card, a dishonest merchant may decide to imprint a few extra copies of the charge slip. Later, the merchant can submit these copies to the issuing institution for payment on phony charges.

Keep your eye on your credit card whenever it is in use. Watch clerks process your credit payments. Open your credit card bills promptly each month. Make sure that you made the listed purchases. Also, report any charges that you did not make to the credit card company.

Discarded Charge Slips

Sometimes, people may collect copies of your discarded charge slips from the wastebasket. Dishonest people could use the information from the copies to order merchandise by mail and ship it to a phony address. In addition, they could also sell the copies to counterfeiters who would take the account numbers and use them to alter cards or make new ones.

After signing a credit card slip, ask for your receipt or duplicates. After you have compared them to the charges listed on your monthly credit card statement, tear them up and throw them away.

Unsigned Credit Cards

Stealing and using credit cards that have not been signed is another potential fraud. In other words, credit card thieves could steal your unsigned credit cards and then sign your name on the card in their handwriting. By doing so, they take your name as an alias and they will never have a problem writing and verifying their own signature.

Protect your credit cards. When you receive a new or replacement card, sign the back of it as soon as it is activated. Always be sure to store it in a safe place. Cut up expired cards before disposing of them.

Loss Of Multiple Cards

While shopping, you can easily be targeted by pickpockets. If your purse or wallet is stolen, you may lose all your credit cards at one time.

Separate your cards. Only carry those cards with you that you plan to use. Also, check your cards from time to time and put aside those cards you don't use very often.

Strange Requests For Your PIN

This form of fraud involves thieves who find creative ways to steal your credit or debit cards when you don't know about it. For example, sometimes people crawl behind rows in movie theaters and steal pocketbooks while you are watching a movie. When you return home they call you, identify themselves as bank security agents, and ask for your PIN. If you hesitate, they simply ask you to phone their supervisor and give you an accomplice's phone number to call. By doing so, they are able to get your PIN and use the stolen debit cards to withdraw cash and make purchases.

Again, never reveal your PIN to anyone. Also, never keep your PIN in your purse or wallet. Don't write your PIN on your card either. Always try to memorize it.

Recognizing Counterfeit Cards

Legitimate Cards

Legitimate cards follow standard specifications as to color, tint, quality, and style. Stamped letters and numbers are spaced evenly and sized equally. The signature panel is uniform in size and is almost impossible to scrape off.

Altered Cards

Altered cards are made from actual cards. The original stamped data is melted down or pressed out. Then, the card is re-stamped with legitimate account numbers, names, and expiration dates, which have been illegally obtained. On altered cards, the letters do not line up well and are usually irregular in size. Some credit card companies help merchants identify altered cards by making an authenticator machine available to merchants. The machine authenticates or verifies certain information that is encoded on the back stripe on the back of the card.

Counterfeit Cards

Counterfeiters make most counterfeit cards by silkscreening or painting the card logo and issuing institution's name onto a blank piece of card plastic. Because they are silkscreened, the cards don't look exactly like the real thing. Real credit cards are printed. Also, the signature panel on silkscreened cards may be glued or painted on and can be easily lifted or chipped. This panel may also appear uneven in size or placement.

New Technology

New technology is making it more difficult for criminals to use, alter, or counterfeit credit and debit cards. Some of the innovations are already in use.

These security features have been added to major credit cards:

- **Holograph:** A three-dimensional, laser produced optical device that changes its color and image as the card is tilted.

- **Fine-Line Printing:** A repeated pattern of the card company name positioned as background for the company logo.

- **Ultraviolet Ink:** Special ink that is visible only under ultraviolet light, which will display the credit card company's logo.

"Smart Cards" may be the credit cards of the future. Each card has a built-in computer microprocessor. Signatures have been replaced with personal identification numbers and verification is handled only by computers. Eventually these cards may provide information on investments, charge accounts, and money market accounts. We may someday think of the credit card as a pocket-sized computer memory bank.

Improved verification methods are also being developed and tested. These include fingerprinting, retinal eye scanners, and computerized signature cards.

On The Internet

While using the internet, you can learn about any number of topics and buy almost anything. Be aware, though, that internet shopping, like traditional shopping, may carry some risk. Software to protect you and your privacy is often a part of most websites. In fact, when ordering online, it would be wise to check if you are on a secure server by looking for a security symbol such as an unbroken key or padlock symbol at the bottom of your internet browser window. These symbols indicate that any information you may send to the website, including your credit card numbers, is encrypted or put into computer code prior to transmission.

♣ **It's A Fact!!**
**Credit Card Loss Protection Offers:
They're The Real Steal**

"I got a call from a woman who said I need credit card loss protection insurance. I thought there was a law that limited my liability to $50 for unauthorized charges. But she said the law had changed and that now, people are liable for all unauthorized charges on their account. Is that true?"

Don't buy the pitch—and don't buy the "loss protection" insurance. Telephone scam artists are lying to get people to buy worthless credit card loss protection and insurance programs. If you didn't authorize a charge, don't pay it. Follow your credit card issuer's procedures for disputing charges you haven't authorized. According to the Federal Trade Commission (FTC), your liability for unauthorized charges is limited to $50.

Source: Consumer Alert, Federal Trade Commission, October 2000.

> **✔ Quick Tip**
> **Reporting Losses And Fraud**
>
> If you lose your credit or charge cards or if you realize they've been lost or stolen, immediately call the issuer(s). Many companies have toll-free numbers and 24-hour service to deal with such emergencies. By law, once you report the loss or theft, you have no further responsibility for unauthorized charges. In any event, your maximum liability under federal law is $50 per card.
>
> Source: Excerpted from "Avoiding Credit and Charge Card Fraud," Federal Trade Commission, August 1997.

Consumer Liability

It is important to keep a personal list of your credit and debit card numbers, the issuing banks, and their phone numbers so that you can contact them in case of loss or theft.

Credit Cards

If your credit card is lost or stolen, contact your bank or issuing institution immediately. Your monthly statement should list the phone number of whom to contact.

You do not have to pay for any unauthorized charges made after you have notified the issuing bank or institution. The most you will have to pay for unauthorized charges is $50 on each account. But this can add up if several cards are lost or stolen at the same time.

If you think that you did not make some or all of the purchases listed on your statement, you can take action. The Fair Credit Billing Act, an addition to the Truth-in-Lending law, requires prompt correction of billing mistakes. Within 60 days after the bill was mailed, you must notify the creditor in writing. You do not have to pay the amount in question while you are waiting for an answer.

Debit Cards

If your debit card is lost or stolen, notify the issuing bank or institution immediately. According to the Electronic Funds Transfer Act, if notification is given within two business days of discovery of the loss or theft, you may only be liable for $50. If you do not notify them within the two-day limit, you could lose up to $500. Finally, if notification is not given within 60 days after receiving a statement showing unauthorized withdrawals, you could be liable for everything.

What Is The Law?

The Credit Card Fraud Act imposes prison sentences and stiff fines on persons convicted of unauthorized or counterfeit use of credit cards and debit cards. Also, the law makes it a federal crime to use any unauthorized card, plate, code, or account number to obtain money, goods, or services. The Secret Service is authorized to investigate violations under this act.

Chapter 27

If Your Credit Or Debit Card
Is Lost Or Stolen

Many people find it easy and convenient to use credit cards and ATM or debit cards. The Fair Credit Billing Act (FCBA) and the Electronic Fund Transfer Act (EFTA) offer procedures for you to use if your cards are lost or stolen.

Limiting Your Financial Loss

Report the loss or theft of your credit cards and your ATM or debit cards to the card issuers as quickly as possible. Many companies have toll-free numbers and 24-hour service to deal with such emergencies. It's a good idea to follow up your phone calls with a letter. Include your account number, when you noticed your card was missing, and the date you first reported the loss.

You also may want to check your homeowner's insurance policy to see if it covers your liability for card thefts. If not, some insurance companies will allow you to change your policy to include this protection.

Credit Card Loss Or Fraudulent Charges: Your maximum liability under federal law for unauthorized use of your credit card is $50. If you report the loss before your credit cards are used, the FCBA says the card issuer cannot hold you responsible for any unauthorized charges. If a thief uses

About This Chapter: "Credit, ATM, and Debit Cards: What to do if They're Lost or Stolen," Federal Trade Commission (FTC), June 2002.

your cards before you report them missing, the most you will owe for unauthorized charges is $50 per card. Also, if the loss involves your credit card
number, but not the card itself, you have no liability for unauthorized use.

After the loss, review your billing statements carefully. If they show any
unauthorized charges, it's best to send a letter to the card issuer describing
each questionable charge. Again, tell the card issuer the date your card was
lost or stolen, or when you first noticed unauthorized charges, and when you
first reported the problem to them. Be sure to send the letter to the address
provided for billing errors. Do not send it with a payment or to the address
where you send your payments unless you are directed to do so.

ATM Or Debit Card Loss Or Fraudulent Transfers: Your liability under
federal law for unauthorized use of your ATM or debit card depends on how
quickly you report the loss. If you report an ATM or debit card missing before
it's used without your permission, the EFTA says the card issuer cannot hold
you responsible for any unauthorized transfers. If unauthorized use occurs before you report it, your liability under federal law
depends on how quickly you report the loss.

For example, if you report the loss within
two business days after you realize your
card is missing, you will not be responsible for more than $50 for unauthorized
use. However, if you don't report the loss
within two business days after you discover the loss, you could lose up to $500
because of an unauthorized transfer. You
also risk unlimited loss if you fail to report an
unauthorized transfer within 60 days after your
bank statement containing unauthorized use is
mailed to you. That means you could lose all the money in your bank account
and the unused portion of your line of credit established for overdrafts. However, for unauthorized transfers involving only your debit card number (not the
loss of the card), you are liable only for transfers that occur after 60 days following the mailing of your bank statement containing the unauthorized use and
before you report the loss.

> ✔ **Quick Tip**
> If unauthorized transfers
> show up on your bank state-
> ment, report them to the card is-
> suer as quickly as possible. Once
> you've reported the loss of your
> ATM or debit card, you cannot
> be held liable for additional
> unauthorized transfers that
> occur after that time.

Protecting Your Cards

The best protections against card fraud are to know where your cards are at all times and to keep them secure. For protection of ATM and debit cards that involve a Personal Identification Number (PIN), keep your PIN a secret. Don't use your address, birth date, phone or Social Security number as the PIN and do memorize the number.

The following suggestions may help you protect your credit card and your ATM or debit card accounts.

For Credit And ATM Or Debit Cards

- Be cautious about disclosing your account number over the phone unless you know you're dealing with a reputable company.

- Never put your account number on the outside of an envelope or on a postcard.

- Draw a line through blank spaces on charge or debit slips above the total so the amount cannot be changed.

- Don't sign a blank charge or debit slip.

- Tear up carbons and save your receipts to check against your monthly statements.

- Cut up old cards—cutting through the account number—before disposing of them.

- Open monthly statements promptly and compare them with your receipts. Report mistakes or discrepancies as soon as possible to the special address listed on your statement for inquiries. Under the FCBA (credit cards) and the EFTA (ATM or debit cards), the card issuer must investigate errors reported to them within 60 days of the date your statement was mailed to you.

- Keep a record in a safe place separate from your cards of your account numbers, expiration dates, and the telephone numbers of each card issuer so you can report a loss quickly.

- Carry only those cards that you anticipate you'll need.

For ATM Or Debit Cards

- Don't carry your PIN in your wallet or purse or write it on your ATM or debit card.

- Never write your PIN on the outside of a deposit slip, an envelope, or other papers that could be easily lost or seen.

- Carefully check ATM or debit card transactions before you enter the PIN or before you sign the receipt; the funds for this item will be fairly quickly transferred out of your checking or other deposit account.

- Periodically check your account activity. This is particularly important if you bank online. Compare the current balance and recent withdrawals or transfers to those you've recorded, including your current ATM and debit card withdrawals and purchases and your recent checks. If you notice transactions you didn't make, or if your balance has dropped suddenly without activity by you, immediately report the problem to your card issuer. Someone may have co-opted your account information to commit fraud.

♣ It's A Fact!!
Buying A Registration Service

For an annual fee, companies will notify the issuers of your credit card and your ATM or debit card accounts if your card is lost or stolen. This service allows you to make only one phone call to report all card losses rather than calling individual issuers. Most services also will request replacement cards on your behalf.

Purchasing a card registration service may be convenient, but it's not required. The FCBA and the EFTA give you the right to contact your card issuers directly in the event of a loss or suspected unauthorized use.

If you decide to buy a registration service, compare offers. Carefully read the contract to determine the company's obligations and your liability. For example, will the company reimburse you if it fails to notify card issuers promptly once you've called in the loss to the service? If not, you could be liable for unauthorized charges or transfers.

Part Four

Predatory And Problematic Lending Practives

Chapter 28

Alternative Financial Services: A Helping Hand Or Loan Sharking?

Every industry battles image problems. But imagine the public relations headache when even those in the industry admit that not everyone is playing by the same rules or ethics.

So it is with the alternative financial services industry—payday and title lenders, check cashers, and even pawnshops, part of the so-called "fringe banking" market. Aside from pawnbrokering, a form of pledge literally centuries old, the rest of this market has largely sprung up only in the last decade or so, give or take a few years depending on which business and what state you're talking about.

Following in lock step with that growth is a public perception of the industry—particularly payday and title loan businesses—as nothing but a bunch of shady, fly-by-night operations.

"They have an image problem," said John Caskey, a Swarthmore College economics professor and leading expert on the industry. The image stems

About This Chapter: Text in this chapter is from "A Helping Hand, Or New Age Loan Sharking?" by Ronald A. Wirtz, *fedgazette*, October 2000. Reprinted with permission from the Federal Reserve Bank of Minneapolis, www.minneapolisfed.org. The statistics on the number of outlets described in this chapter have not been updated since 2000, but the principles behind the industry's growth and the criticisms made by industry critics are still of concern.

from too many anecdotes about high fees, poor disclosure, and "particularly aggressive actions on collections," Caskey said.

Even those in the industry acknowledge the stereotypes and public relations conundrum. "People's perception of the industry is that someone is getting cheated ... [and] we're here to prey on the poor," said Cary Geller, owner of four Money Center stores offering check cashing and payday loans in the Twin Cities. "I would have trouble coming to work if that were the case."

"They [the public] think we're out to rip somebody off," said Steven Busse, manager of Advantage Loans of Rapid City, South Dakota, which does payday and title loans in two locations. "I'm sure some of [the criticism] is justified. ... If you were that type of [abusive] person, it could be done."

While pawn and check cashing businesses have their critics, neither tends to receive much attention from consumer advocates, or at least as much as they once did. Pawnbrokering, for one, has gained a certain amount of acceptance from its longevity as an industry. Check cashing (also known as currency exchange) is a single transaction that establishes no binding, future commitments.

Payday and title loans, whose high fees and term structure can tend to snowball on unsuspecting and financially naive applicants, shoulder most of the criticism of the fringe banking industry. Title loans are "so unconscionable they should be prohibited," while payday loans are "designed so consumers get in trouble," according to Jean Ann Fox, director of consumer protection for the Consumer Federation of America, one of the industry's strongest critics.

"We think there needs to be small consumer loans without loan terms that are harmful" to consumers already facing financial hardship, Fox said. "You don't get out of a hole by digging it deeper."

While emotional hard-luck stories about industry abuses are not hard to find, the industry has in some ways received a bum rap for doing legitimate business in subprime markets and providing a service where other financial entities have been unwilling. Few industries are critic-free; while there is evidence of unlawfulness, it doesn't illegitimatize the entire industry or the market it serves.

The Developing Fringe

One thing about this market is crystal clear: It is booming, particularly in states that do not regulate or otherwise cap the fees these businesses are allowed to charge. A state official in South Dakota, where fees are not capped, said the industry "has mushroomed" there, estimating there were at least 95 fringe banking outlets, not including pawnshops.

In the last two years, the number of check cashing stores in Minnesota has roughly doubled to almost 70, according to Terry Meyer of the state Department of Commerce. The number of such outlets nationwide has more than doubled in the last five years to 6,000, many of whom are also beginning to offer payday loans, according to an industry association.

Title lending also appears to be growing. Wisconsin started licensing title lenders last year, and there are now 26 such locations in the state. (In general, however, comparatively little is known about the title lending industry. For one, Wisconsin is among few states to directly license or regulate title loans as a separate lending entity. Compounded by the fact that the industry has no affiliated association, general records of the industry are poor. State trends in the pawn industry are similarly difficult to determine because these businesses are typically licensed at the municipal level.)

The leader of the fringe banking pack—in both number and controversy— is payday lending, which has seen dramatic growth nationwide and in the Ninth [Federal Reserve] District. An industry association estimates there are 9,000 outlets across the country; an investment banking firm put the number at 10,000—this for an industry that hasn't even reached double digits in age, and is nonexistent in 18 states.

The number of licensed payday lenders in Wisconsin went from just one in 1993, to 17 in 1995, to 195 as of August 2000, according to the state Department of Financial Institutions. In the last four full years, the number of loans has increased tenfold to 840,000, and their value has increased almost 20-fold to $200 million.

Franchised chains are driving much of the growth. Cash N' Go is the largest payday lender in Wisconsin with 39 outlets, including eight in the 26 northwestern counties located in the Ninth District, all started since 1996. Advantage Title Loans has 17 offices in South Dakota. Pawn America has 11 stores in Minnesota and is planning four new ones.

Such fast growth has sparked interest among consumer groups and legis- lators to control or otherwise regulate an industry believed to take advantage of those who can least afford it. Not all of the stereotypes heaped on the fringe banking industry fit exactly right, however.

Many believe the industry caters to the very poor; while it is a segment of the market, it's a small one. The average customer for a payday loan, for example, has a full-time job and an income between $25,000 and $35,000 annually. A third-party analysis of Title Loans of America, one of the largest title loan companies in the nation, found that 20 percent of its customers earned less than $20,000 annually, while close to half made more than $40,000.

✎ What's It Mean?

The alternative financial services industry—a.k.a. fringe banking—is a loose term for nonbank entities providing some bank-like service. Sometimes in- cluded in this group (but not discussed in this chapter) are rent-to-own busi- nesses and specialty auto and mortgage lenders. Below is a basic description of the bank-like services and businesses that are the focus of this chapter.

Payday Loans: Payday loans are typically very small consumer loans—usually $150 to $300—backed by postdated checks or authorization to make an elec- tronic debit against an existing financial account. The check or debit is held for an agreed-upon term, usually about two weeks or until an applicant's next payday, and then cashed unless the customer repays the loan reclaims his or her check.

If the customer does not have funds for the check to clear, the same pro- cess is followed to obtain an additional loan or extend the existing loan, com- monly referred to as a rollover or renewal.

Title Loans: Title loans are also small consumer loans that leverage the eq- uity value of a car as collateral. The car title must be owned free and clear by the loan applicant; any existing liens on the car cancel the application. Loan

Check cashers are mistakenly thought to hone in on welfare recipients. But earlier this year, the Department of the Treasury contracted a survey of 130 nonbank financial service centers. Among those doing check cashing, 80 percent of all checks cashed were payroll, and just 16 percent were government checks.

"I'm not interested in [customers on] welfare," said Geller about the check cashing side of his business, because it would subject him to the "ebbs and flows of a whimsical federal government. ... I would starve to death."

If The Shoe Fits ...

A more accurate characterization of the industry—particularly title and payday loans—is that it serves lower-middle income working folks experiencing some financial crisis. "There is a percentage of the population who sometimes has a need for a small amount of money for a short period of time, and banks are not going to provide that loan," Geller said.

---

terms are often for 30 days, and failure to repay the loan or make interest payments to extend the loan allows the lender to take possession of the car.

Check Cashing: Check cashing outlets, also called currency exchanges, cash payroll, government, and personal checks for a set fee, often ranging from about 3 percent to 10 percent of the face value of the check, or $1, whichever is greater. These stores typically offer additional services and products, like money orders, wire transfers, bill paying, and prepaid phone cards. A growing number are also offering payday loans.

Pawnbrokering: Pawnbrokers provide financing on the basis of the value of tangible property brought to a store. Typically a flat fee is charged for the transaction, and the merchandise is held for an agreed-upon period of time for repayment and reclaiming of property. Upon contract expiration, if the loan is not repaid or extended by an interest payment, the broker assumes ownership of the merchandise and can put it up for resale.

Source: Federal Reserve Bank of Minneapolis, www.minneapolisfed.org.

The industry says such loans are intended to be a financial bridge until a person's next paycheck. Consumer groups argue that such loans—given the high fees, short terms, and the cash-strapped nature of the applicant—are rarely paid off. When this happens, the loan is renewed or "rolled over" by simply taking out another loan to pay off the first one, or an interest payment is required to extend the loan. As a result, when a loan comes due many customers face a lose-lose choice, Fox said. "Do I bounce a check ... or do I just pay the fee [for a rollover or extension]?" Fox said. "It's a 'gotcha' kind of transaction."

Once the loan is paid off—even on time—the consumer ends up paying an annual percentage rate (APR) often ranging from 200 percent to 2000 percent. (APR comparisons are themselves a matter of considerable debate. The industry points out, for example, that a payday loan is designed as a two-week loan with an appropriately scaled fee for the risk involved. Other common fees—like late fees on movie rentals or credit card payments and bounced checks—carry similarly high rates if converted to annual percentages.) The industry argues that rollovers happen less than anecdotes might suggest, pointing to some states like Minnesota that restrict rollovers. But in states that do not restrict rollovers, available evidence is not flattering to the industry.

A state of Illinois study on short-term loans found that almost half of title loan customers were repeat customers, and the average duration of loans (including extensions) was about four months. The study also found that payday loan customers average 13 loans (including renewals on original loans) at an APR of 533 percent. While the industry is quick to note it helps those in dire financial straits, that strain "is rarely short-lived," the report pointed out. "Customers playing catch-up with their expenses do not have the ability to overcome unexpected financial hardships because their budgets are usually limited. The high expense of a short-term loan depletes the customer's ability to catch up, therefore making the customer 'captive' to the lender."

In one of the few comprehensive studies to date on the habits of payday loan customers, the state of Indiana examined 47 licensed lenders with 123 stores, looking at the loan history of the most recent 25 to 50 accounts at each store over the previous year. Mark Tarpey, supervisor of the consumer credit division in the Indiana Department of Financial Institutions, said there were "a lot of claims of isolated abuses. We thought it would be useful to have some statistical data" to shed some light on the industry.

The study found that these 5,350 different accounts took out over 54,000 loans during the year. The study looked closer at a random subsection of about 1,400 customers at 36 locations. It found that three of four loans were renewed or rolled over, and fewer than one in 10 customers had no loan rollovers.

"The numbers surprised us," Tarpey said, particularly given that the industry was only about five years old at the time of the study. "It kind of confirmed some of our worst concerns" of keeping people in "perpetual debt."

But not everyone in the business is ready to bleed an unsuspecting customer dry. "I try to help people out who have no where else to turn," said Busse of Advantage Loans in Rapid City. Title loans at his company run from 8.34 percent to 20 percent monthly (100 percent to 240 percent APR), although with no usury laws in South Dakota, the sky's the limit. People often take out loans and "they are just paying the interest, interest, interest and not paying any principal," Busse said. If after six months, a person has only paid interest on the loan, Busse automatically converts the loan—even those at 20 percent—to the lowest 8.34 percent rate and puts them on a six-month installment payment to pay the loan off.

The difference in payment is not dramatic, but the outcome is. A $500 loan at 20 percent monthly makes for a $100 monthly payment in interest alone, and pays off none of the principal. Shifting the loan to 8.34 percent, and requiring the loan to be paid in six months ups the payment to $125, cuts total interest charges by 60 percent, and ultimately closes the loan.

"We need to make some money ... and I want to keep customers coming back," Busse said. If he can help customers get the loan paid off, "they're happy, and I've made some money."

If Abuse Is Rife, Where Are The Squeaky Wheels?

Critics also point to abusive collection tactics, such as the threat of criminal prosecution for trying to pass bad checks for a payday loan, even though this is generally a matter for civil court.

"I've seen threats used on letterhead of some of the major payday lenders," Fox said.

But given alleged abuses and consumer-unfriendly tactics, one might think complaint hotlines would be ringing off the hook as the number of such outlets and their transactions expand annually. That doesn't appear to be the case. None of the Ninth District states registered more than a very small handful of complaints against the industry in the last year or two, despite the fact that total transactions numbered in the millions.

Meyer said Minnesota has had just a single complaint against the payday industry to his knowledge, and that lender was forced out of business in the state. Montana and North and South Dakota officials said their state received very few complaints on the industry. The number of complaints against all nonbank lenders in Wisconsin (which includes title and payday, but also other specialty lenders) was just 17 in all of 1998 and 1999.

But Fox said the "volume of complaints doesn't match the abuse" doled out by these businesses. "If consumers knew they were being abused, they might complain."

And in fact, there is some evidence to suggest this could be a factor. There were very few complaints in Montana before the passage of its payday licensing law last year. Since its passage, complaints "are starting to trickle in," said Kris Leitheiser of the Montana Department of Commerce. "We have several complaints in review right now."

Complaints in Wisconsin are also increasing, if still small. There were three complaints against all nonbank loan companies from 1993 to 1997, but 12 through August of 2000. North Dakota saw an increase in complaints following a publicized warning to pawnbrokers in the state to stop doing payday and title loans, according to Gary Preszler, North Dakota banking commissioner. He added that it's not surprising the state received few prior complaints. "[Payday loan users] aren't going to complain" because they often feel they have nowhere else to turn, he said. "They find a friend in a payday loan."

Critics have also said that bankruptcies and consumer credit agencies would provide better measures of the industry's abusive tendencies. Tracy

Nave, education marketing director for Montana Consumer Credit Counseling, said there were "a lot more clients who have those types of [payday] loans," and these lenders are not always cooperative in restructuring personal finances to get someone out of debt. Nonetheless, she acknowledged, "We haven't heard a lot of complaints."

Bankruptcies, on the other hand, have actually been falling nationwide and in Ninth District states for the last couple of years, according to the American Bankruptcy Institute. Two bankruptcy lawyers said that fringe banking outlets are showing up as creditors in bankruptcy court somewhat more frequently, but are still a small presence.

Greg Waldz, a Minneapolis bankruptcy lawyer, said he's only had a few bankruptcy cases where payday or title loans were part of the debt. "I definitely think they are on the increase. ... [but] numerically, it's not a huge thing."

Lindy Voss, a bankruptcy lawyer for 20 years and currently at Prescott and Pearson, Minnesota's largest personal bankruptcy firm, said there was "not really" any correlation between the increase in fringe banking activities and bankruptcies, adding the firm "very seldom" saw payday or title loans as part of a bankruptcy filing. In fact, personal bankruptcies have been on the decline since 1997 in Minnesota—"we're down probably 30 percent," Voss said—the very period in which the industry has seen strong growth.

Sic The State On 'Em

Lawmakers and advocacy groups have turned to the state to protect consumers from what they believe is fraudulent, or at least unethical, industry practices. In most cases, this has meant passing state laws capping various fees charged by these businesses, which has created a fragmented array of regulations governing each segment of the industry in different states.

Among Ninth District states, North Dakota has all but outlawed the fringe banking industry, save for pawnshops. Payday and title loans are allowed under small consumer loan licenses, but have a maximum interest rate of 30 percent a year for the first $1,000. Preszler said payday and title loan companies inquire often about fee caps in the state. "Because of usury, it's not economic for them so they don't bother with the license," he said.

♣ It's A Fact!!
What are check-cashing stores and what services do they offer?

The concept of check cashing originated in the 1930s as a way for employees who didn't have bank accounts to cash their payroll checks at local bars and stores.

Today check cashing stores provide services for people who are reluctant to, or unaware of how to, use a bank. Unlike banks, however, check cashing stores are not regulated or insured. Often these stores are located in low-income, minority, or economically vulnerable communities, where these stores can seem like an easy solution to the all-too-common fear or confusion about working with a bank.

Customers at check-cashing stores most commonly cash their paychecks, but these stores also typically offer to cash:

- personal checks (checks made out to you from someone else, or your own check made out to "cash"),

- money orders,

- federal benefit payment checks (that is, unemployment, welfare, Social Security benefits, Veterans Affairs benefits, etc.),

- federal and state tax refund checks, and

- insurance checks or drafts.

Check cashing stores also offer "convenience" services like the ability to pay telephone and utility bills as well as to purchase lottery tickets and money orders. However, the convenience these stores offer comes at a steep price.

Check-cashing stores are known for charging high fees to cash checks. The fees vary greatly. Stores will either list fees as a percentage of the amount of the check being cashed or a flat dollar amount per each $50 or $100 being cashed. Because most stores are franchises (meaning that they are owned by individual owners), fees can vary by store, and even by time of day or employee.

For example, a store may advertise that they charge 8% of the amount of the check to cash it. Another store may advertise that they charge $4 for every $100 cashed.

Individuals and families who use check-cashing stores as their primary financial services institution (instead of a bank or credit union), can lose a significant amount of income through the fees charged at these stores. A Consumer Federation Association (CFA) study estimated that a typical family earning $20,000 a year can expect to spend between $86 and $500 a year for check-cashing services. In contrast, a bank would offer the same services for approximately $30–60 annually.

The fees that check cashing stores have charged to cash checks have increased over time. Another CFA report found that the average fees check cashers charged on Social Security checks rose 37 percent between 1987 and 1997. It also reported that fees to cash paychecks went up 44 percent, and personal check fees increased by more than 100 percent in that time. Only 12 states have passed laws to cap fees levied by check cashers.

Knowing how hard you work to earn your paycheck, why might you willingly choose to pay such exorbitant fees to access your cash? People who most often use check-cashing stores would say that they use those stores because:

- They don't think they have enough money to open a bank account,

- They don't speak English,

- They don't have identification needed to open a bank account,

- There aren't any banks or credit unions near where they live or work, or

- They are generally distrusting of large institutions.

According to CFA, 12 million American households are considered "unbanked." And approximately 25 percent of low-income households do not have a relationship with a traditional financial services company (bank, credit union, savings and loan, etc.) (ACORN report, March 2003.) For many "unbanked" U.S. residents, check-cashing stores can seem to offer an easier, less-threatening alternative to the formal environment of a bank.

Source: "Check-Cashing Stores and Sending Money Abroad" is reprinted with permission from www.tomorrowsmoney.org, an educational website produced by the non-profit Bond Market Foundation. © 2007 The Bond Market Foundation. All rights reserved.

The state has about 25 businesses doing title or payday loans through pawnshops, according to Preszler. After receiving the state's warning letter to cease such transactions, one merchant told Preszler that he would discontinue payday lending, but would continue doing check cashing.

"I told him, 'The bad news for you is you better contact a lawyer because you don't have the authority to cash checks,'" Preszler said. North Dakota allows no check cashing outlets because the state considers it a core banking function that requires a charter.

South Dakota and Wisconsin require licensing for these check cashing, payday, and title loans operations, but do not cap fees that vendors can charge. Check cashing is unregulated in Montana, and payday fees are "capped" at 25 percent of a check's face value, which in annual terms calculates to 650 percent for a two-week loan.

The presence of fee caps and other regulation on the industry is both dramatic and somewhat unknown. Caskey of Swarthmore College, for example, said that his research has showed there are a "far greater number of lenders" where there are no fee caps (South Dakota, Wisconsin and, until recently, Montana) compared with regulated states like Minnesota and North Dakota.

Any state fee cap "puts us out of business," said Bob Reich, president and chief executive officer of Title Loans of America, which has 30 offices in the Ninth District. When the state of Kentucky passed interest rate caps, "We shut down every store ... because [the legislated rates] wouldn't even cover our costs," Reich said.

But many other outcomes regarding regulation are unknown. For example, no data or research could be found about the net effect that regulation has on the target population's access to credit and long-term financial well-being.

Also unknown is the simple matter of whether fringe banking businesses are compliant with existing regulations like usury and fee disclosure. Critics arm-wrestle with the industry over whose anecdotes are more representative. In truth, neither side has very good estimates on how compliant the average vendor is, because few are checking regularly.

In Minnesota, examinations are done by the state on a complaint basis only. In Montana, the new deferred deposit law will provide funding (through license fee revenue) for the state to do annual compliance examinations on all licensed payday lenders, according to Leitheiser.

But the law will not cover title lenders in the state. According to one high-ranking Montana official, "many" title lenders choose to stay unlicensed, which subjects such loans to state usury laws—a rough maximum of 15 percent APR. "[I]t is fairly certain that most, if not all, of these [unlicensed title] lenders are charging rates far in excess of what is allowed. Some of these businesses may be ignorant of state law. Others claim to be operating under pawnshop laws. The rest seem to believe that the law doesn't apply to them, or are unconcerned about whether it does."

A report by the state of Tennessee found more than half of all payday lenders were noncompliant with existing laws. However, the report attributed the high rate to new legislation "imposed on a newly regulated industry." It added that the industry "has been very responsive" to correcting violations which decreased significantly upon re-examination.

Increased state regulation is also causing the industry to adapt to survive. For example, many stores are commingling different services and products. The National Check Cashers Association recently changed its name to the Financial Service Centers of America (FSCA) to reflect the fact that 40 percent of its membership now also offer payday loans, according to Henry Shyne, the group's executive director.

Despite stringent caps on payday lending, the number of payday licenses in Minnesota through August 2000 has almost doubled to 34, according to Meyer of the Department of Commerce. Most of the new licenses went to existing check cashing outlets looking to expand their product line.

Geller is one of them. "In this state, it's impossible for a [payday] stand-alone to exist at these rates," Geller said. "The fees are not great enough."

More ominous to some is a practice called "charter renting," whereby a payday lender partners with a nationally chartered bank. Through the interest rate exportation authority of banks, the partnership allows payday lenders in any state—regardless of existing regulations there—to import the more lenient usury laws of the state where the bank is located.

Said Caskey, "State usury laws won't matter any more, or not much."

So far, only a small handful of such partnerships exist, but they could have a quick impact. ACE Cash Express is the nation's largest check-cashing chain with a network of more than 1,000 stores in 32 states. Taking advantage of the trend in complementary services, ACE brought payday lending to roughly 30 percent of its stores in 18 states, according to the company's annual report.

Stephens Inc., an investment banking firm, called ACE's entry into payday lending "potentially the most important event of the past couple of years for the company." One reason is the growth potential, thanks to what ACE called a "strategic relationship" with Goleta National Bank of California, which will allow Goleta "to offer small consumer loans in stores throughout the ACE network," regardless of existing state regulations.

"It is legal, but I don't like it," said Donna Tanoue, chairman of the Federal Deposit Insurance Corporation, during a June 2000 speech to bankers.

The Consumer Catch-22: Choice *Vs.* Protection

Ultimately, who's "right" as it relates to this industry depends on whether consumer protection trumps consumer choice and credit access, or vice versa. Clearly, there have been and continue to be abuses in this industry—people in the industry admit as much. Equally obvious, however, is a market demand for these financial services and products that would otherwise go largely unmet among a population that both critics and the industry agree has few other resources. Where and how to draw the regulatory line is a hotly debated gray area.

"You have to be somewhat paternalistic, or [otherwise] I don't see the need for any usury laws," Caskey said. The average fringe bank customer is "low or middle income with little or no political clout," Caskey said, and as such, consumer protection "ought to be disproportionately directed" to these people.

Preszler agreed. "The problem with it is some of this is absolutely predatory and government needs to do something" to protect citizens, he said. "We don't need to regulate it so that you make it uneconomical, but controlled so it doesn't create social costs."

Many in the industry even agree on the notion of some regulation. "There ought to be responsible regulation. In some states, all you have to be is breathing" to get a payday loan, Geller said. "In my mind that's not responsible."

Geller said he's thought about lobbying for changes in the law. "But the perception of the industry is so volatile, you could get hurt as much as helped" once proposed legislation opened up for debate at a state legislature.

The industry has also been working with different states to create "reasonable regulation that will allow [payday vendors] to stay in business," said Shyne of FSCA. "They feel it's better [to do so] rather than have something that's being pushed by consumer groups."

Consumer advocates have been pushing APR caps of 36 percent. Wisconsin saw just such a proposal last spring for title and payday lenders. At these rates, the interest on a typical two-week loan would be about 1.5 percent. Given a client's high-risk credit history, "how do you stay in business doing that?" Shyne asked.

Caskey believed that the profitable middle ground for payday lenders was "roughly in the range" of 10 percent monthly (120 percent APR, or roughly 5 percent of face value for a two-week loan). "If you don't [charge this much], you can't really do payday lending."

The industry has also tried to improve its image. The Community Financial Services Association, representing about half of the payday industry, requires members to adhere to a "best practices" guideline. This includes compliance with all applicable disclosure laws, truthful advertising, the right to rescind a loan within 24 hours, and allowing no more than four rollovers even where there are no rollover prohibitions.

Tarpey of Indiana called the best practices strategy "a good PR document." But Caskey said it was a step in the right direction because "it's in their best interest to get rid of the poster child [of abusive vendors] for journalists," he said. "I think there's some good in that."

Several sources in the industry said too many consumer advocacy groups suffer from a superiority complex. "I know they mean well," Don Tucker, a lobbyist with the title loan industry, said of consumer groups. "They seem to think they know better. ... 'I know better for you than you know for yourself,'" Tucker said.

A common belief among industry critics is that "if you don't do what your neighbor does, you're wrong," Geller said. "They [consumer advocates] simply don't have their finger on the pulse of the people using our services. They think they do, but they don't."

"The real issue here isn't high interest, it's whether or not certain segments of society have access to credit," Reich said. He pointed out that various caps have made providers pull out of some markets. While that might make advocates happy, it might not serve the consumer in question very well. "Credit at a higher rate is better than no credit at all."

The dilemma facing the fringe banking industry "is like cigarette companies," Caskey said. A person knows that having a cigarette can be bad for your health, he said. But if that person nonetheless wants to start or continue that habit, "is it bad for you to sell a cigarette to that person?"

Chapter 29

What Is Predatory Lending?

Most lenders are reputable and community-minded and charge a fair price for the use of borrowed money. Unfortunately, there are also a rather small group of lenders, called predatory lenders, who take advantage of others.

- Predatory lenders market to vulnerable populations, such as the elderly, minorities, and people with poor credit histories, and they charge extremely high interest rates and fees.

- Predatory lending has recently become an increasing problem nationwide. Predatory lenders include both mortgage lenders that prey on homeowners and non-mortgage lenders that offer both secured and unsecured loans.

- Predatory lenders make money, regardless of whether loans are repaid. Either they receive loan payments from borrowers, charging high interest rates and up-front fees, or collect high fees from the borrowers and sell the loan, often collecting another fee from the loan purchaser; or foreclose on a borrower's home or seize any other property pledged as security (for example, repossessing a car with a car title loan).

- Foreclosure is a legal process by which a home is taken by a lender for non-payment of a mortgage.

About This Chapter: "Reality Check: Lending Rip-Offs," excerpted from Money...What Young Adults Need to Know, a publication of the New Jersey Coalition for Financial Education, © 2007. Reprinted with permission.

How To Identify Predatory Lenders

Predatory lenders can take advantage of you, which can often result in the loss of your home and life savings.

- You are often lent more than you can afford to pay back.

- Interest rates and fees are well above what is needed to pay the lender for the risk and earn a good profit.

- Six characteristics of predatory loans, applicable to mortgage loans, include:

    - High interest rates (for example, 20% + interest plus the financing of loan insurance)

    - Outrageous fees (one lender charged 25 points; that is, 25% of loan amount)

    - High pressure salespeople (for example, claims that a loan rate won't last long)

    - Unaffordable repayment terms (lenders know that borrowers can't repay)

    - Harassing collection tactics (for example, punitive late fees, abusive callers, etc.).

    - Deceptive advertisements and practices (for example, intentionally overstating a borrower's income)

High-Cost Borrowing Practices

Here are some of the most expensive ways to borrow money.

Payday Loans

- Small, short-term, high-rate loans (usually made for a 14-day loan period).

- Fees can be very expensive. Fees are usually calculated by charging a certain amount per face value of the loan, such as $20 on a $100 check, which means you pay $120 to get $100.

- If you don't have enough money in your checking account at the end of the loan period, the lender will charge another fee.

- Payday lenders try to avoid state usury laws that limit the amount of interest a lender can charge for a loan. They do this by calling their charges "fees" instead of "interest." They avoid these limits by starting their company in a state without usury laws.

Table 29.1. High-Cost Borrowing Practices.

Payday loans (also called paycheck loans, cash-advance loans, fast check loans, or deferred deposit loans)	You write a postdated check (a check with a future date on it) and pay a high fee to a lender to get cash immediately. The check is held by the lender until the future date and then it is cashed or deposited.
Pawnshop loans	You get immediate cash by giving items (such as jewelry and watches) to pawnbrokers to hold as security for a loan. Pawnbrokers keep the item 30 to 45 days. If you do not pay back the loan plus interest, they can sell your items.
Car title loans	High-interest loans in exchange for possession of your car title. If you don't repay the loan, the car can be repossessed (taken).
Check-cashing store	You pay a fee to cash a check. Sometimes these fees can be high.
Advanced fee loan scams	A person or company "guarantees" you'll qualify for a loan if you pay an up-front fee (e.g., $100 or more). Instead, they take your money and you don't get the loan. This is fraud.
Rent-to-own plans	You rent new or used items (for example, furniture, appliances) by the week or month. After the item has been rented for a specified period, you own the item.

Check-Cashing Stores

Check-cashing stores are similar to payday lenders. They charge fees to cash checks. This can be an expensive alternative for getting cash, especially if you must cash checks on a regular basis, such as payroll checks. Try not to use check cashers, but if you have to, shop around for the lowest fees.

Alternatives To Check-Cashing Stores: There are reasonable alternatives to check-cashing stores:

- Banks: In New Jersey, Consumer Checking accounts allow low balances with low fees.

- Credit Unions: Credit unions are non-profit financial institutions that serve a group of people with something in common, such as the same employer or church affiliation.

- Electronic Transfer Accounts (ETAs): This is an account that allows you to receive federal government payments electronically through direct deposit for a cost of $3 per month or less.

- Supermarkets: Some supermarkets will cash your check for free with a check-cashing card, if you buy a certain amount of groceries.

Rent-To-Own Agreements

Before you can take a rent-to-own item out of the store, the store will require you to sign a rent-to-own agreement. This is a contract where you need to read the terms (or guidelines). Consider the following items before signing a rent-to-own agreement:

- This method of ownership is expensive.

- Agreements usually consist of a rental contract that is renewed on a weekly or monthly basis.

- Usually, the terms are for 78 weeks or 18 months.

- At the end of the agreement, the customer may own the item or need to return it to the store.

Alternatives To Rent-to-Own: There are less expensive options than rent-to-own. When looking at different purchase options, you can:

- Save up and then buy with cash.

- Buy with a credit card (if available). If you pay less than the full amount due when the bill comes, you will also pay interest. The total amount you pay will depend on the annual percentage rate (APR) of the credit card and how many billing periods it takes to pay off the purchase.

- Buy through a store layaway plan. Many retail stores will allow you to make regular payments on an item. The store keeps the item in storage while you make these payments. Usually, you pay a certain up-front fee (depending on the store's policy) and make regular payments for a limited amount of time. At the end of the payment period, you can pick up the item at the store. The store may charge an additional handling fee, but this is still less expensive than rent-to-own.

- Save money for a month to put down on an item, and then put it on layaway or buy on credit.

- Consider buying a used item from a second-hand store or yard sale.

- Before you buy anything, ask yourself "Do I really need this item now?" Unfortunately in our culture today, many wants are being marketed as if they are needs and we are encouraged to have now and pay later. You might not need it or you might be able to wait until you save the money to purchase it with cash.

Compare The Costs Of Buying Options

There are many ways to buy large items, such as electronics, appliances, or furniture. Use the following list and chart to help you decide which purchase option is best for you before you buy:

- Make sure you are comparing the same item, make, and model in advertisements and local retail stores. For example, in the case of an HD-TV (high definition television), there are many different makes and models to choose from, and these will have a wide range of prices, depending on the features available.

- Using the chart in Table 29.2, look at the second row, "Time to pay off." This is how to work out what goes in each column:

  - Rent-to-Own: The number of rental payments until the item is owned.

  - Credit: The number of payments until the credit is paid off.

  - Layaway: The number of payments until the item is paid off. Some stores add a service fee and some do not.

  - Cash: Zero, since there are no payments.

- In the third row, look for the "Initial payment required" by the "Rent-to-own contract" or the "Layaway" plan. Some stores add service fees to the initial payment.

- For the "Total paid," multiply the "payment" by the "Time to pay off" and then add the "Initial payment required."

Table 29.2. Compare The Costs Of Buying Options

Item: Tower of Power Mini Stereo System with CD Player

	Rent-to-Own	Credit	Layaway	Cash (Local Retail Store)
Cash price	$521.56	$330.00	$330.00	$330.00
Time to pay off	22 months	20 months	3 months	0 months
Initial payment required	$11.99	$20.00	$35.00 (a $5.00 service fee is required)	$330.00
Weekly/monthly payment	$47.96/month	$20.00/month	$100.00/month	$0
Total to be paid	$1,039.00	$381.99	$335.00	$330.00
Amount above original cash price	$517.44	$51.99	$5.00	$0

(Rent-to-Own APR=100%; Credit APR=18%)

- For "Cash (Local Retail Store)," use the cash price.

- For "Amount above cash price," subtract the "Cash price" from "Total paid" for each option. This will tell you how much more you are paying above the original cash price of the item.

✔ **Quick Tip**
How To Avoid Rip-Offs

- Find out how much a loan will cost you over time. Compare at least three lenders before making a decision.

- Always check out a lender before signing loan documents, especially if he/she contacted you first and they are not located in the city or county where you live.

- Check out lenders by asking friends, relatives, and co-workers. They may have had experience with a particular lender or know someone else who has.

- Call the Better Business Bureau (BBB). To get the name of the Better Business Bureau closest to you, visit www.bbb.org.

- Local or state consumer protection agencies can provide information about any complaints about a particular lender.

- Ask lots of questions and be suspicious of anyone who threatens to withdraw the loan if you don't keep quiet.

- Remember, if a loan sounds too good to be true, it probably is. Trustworthy lenders do not go door-to-door or lend more than borrowers can afford to repay.

Chapter 30

Payday And Title Loans

Payday Loans

Deferred deposit loans, commonly known as "payday loans" (also called cash advance loans, check advance loans, and post-dated check loans), have become an increasingly popular method for consumers to access fast cash.

How It Works

Bad credit? No credit? Not a problem. All a consumer needs to obtain a payday loan is a job, a phone, a utility bill, a checking account, and a driver's license. The borrower writes a personal check payable to the lender for the amount he wishes to borrow, plus a fee—typically 10% to 25% of the check. The check is held for one to four weeks, usually until the customer's next payday, at which time he either redeems the check by paying the face amount, or allows the check to be cashed. If the borrower can't afford to cover the check, he may roll it over for another term by writing another check, which will result in another set of fees being added to the balance.

About This Chapter: This chapter begins with "Payday Loans," © 2005 Balance. Reprinted with permission. For additional information, visit the Balance website at www.balancepro.net or call 888-456-2227. It continues with "Banking on the Fringe" by Joe Mahon, *fedgazette*, July 2004. Reprinted with permission from the Federal Reserve Bank of Minneapolis, www.minneapolisfed.org.

Consumers may be mislead into thinking that payday loans are a cheap and convenient way of borrowing money for the short term. However, with average annual interest rates ranging from 390% to 871%, payday loans are no bargain. Consider this example:

- Face value of a check: $200

- 15% fee: $30

- Amount paid to the customer: $170

- Lender receives $30, which translates to an annual percentage rate (APR) of 458% if the loan is repaid in two weeks

- If it is rolled into a new payday loan, an additional fee of $30 is charged, the loan is raised to $230, and the APR jumps to 917%

- In other words, it cost $60 to borrow $170 for one month. Table 30.1. compares the costs to other types of credit.

Consumers often have difficulty repaying the entire loan when their payday arrives because it will leave them with little or no money for their living expenses. Result: The consumer pays another round of charges and fees and obtains no additional cash in return.

Table 30.1. To Borrow $200 and Repay in One Month

Type of Credit	Terms	Finance Charge	Total Payment
Credit Card,	19.9% APR, no grace period, 2.5% fee	$8	$208
Cash Advance Personal Loan	36% APR Cap	$6	$206
Payday Loan	$17.50 per $100, 15-day term with 1 rollover	$70	$270

Source: © 2005 Balance

Collection tactics for payday loans can be very aggressive. A default on a payday loan involves a worthless check, and some state credit laws allow for triple damages when a bad check is used in a retail transaction. Lenders may also require customers to sign an "Assignment of Salary and Wages" authorizing them to go directly to the borrower's employer to ask for the amount owed to be deducted from the borrower's paycheck and paid to the lender.

Breaking The Payday Loan Cycle

The average payday loan customer makes eleven transactions a year—and maintains an endless sequence of debt. If you find yourself caught in the payday loan cycle, follow the steps below for relief:

- Analyze your financial situation in its entirety:

    - Set reasonable and achievable financial goals.

    - Understand your earning potential: Can you work overtime, obtain a second job, or turn a hobby into income?

    - Review your expenses: Can you reduce or eliminate anything in the short or long term?

    - Review your debt: List everything, then set priorities. Because the interest rates on payday loans are well above other types of debt, treat it as a financial priority.

    - Track your spending and regularly review your budget.

- Commit yourself to not using payday loans in the future.

- If you are using payday loans because you inadvertently overdraw on your account, consider overdraft protection.

- Develop a savings plan. Three to six months' worth of expenses in an accessible savings account is recommended, but anything is better than nothing. A hundred dollars set aside for emergencies can save you a trip to the payday loan company—and a tremendous amount in fees.

- Understand the root of the problem. Are you spending beyond your means because you're income is insufficient to live on or because you're spending more than you need to on non-necessities?

Other Ways To Generate Money

Difficult financial situations do happen. It is recommended that consumers consider all available options before choosing to use a payday loan:

- Ask your bank or credit union for a loan. The interest rate cap for unsecured loans is currently 36%—significantly lower than a payday loan.

- Request an extension on what you owe. If you have had a good payment history, this may be the best option. Ask about finance and late charges for delinquent payments and payment plans.

- In an emergency, consider using a credit card to pay your bill.

- A cash advance on your credit card is often more expensive than a credit card purchase, but still an option. Check with your credit card company to compare rates.

- Borrow from a friend or family member.

- Take inventory of your belongings. You may be able to sell an asset.

- Some employers will give an advance on a paycheck. Check with your human resources department for specific regulations.

Laws That Protect Consumers

Under the Truth in Lending Act, the cost of payday loans—like other types of credit—must be disclosed. Among other information, you must receive, in writing, the finance charge (a dollar amount) and the annual percentage rate or APR (the cost of credit on a yearly basis). Collectors for payday loans must comply with the Fair Debt Collection Practices Act. Any complaint against a lender may be filed with the Federal Trade Commission: 877-FTC-HELP, or http://www.ftc.gov.

Banking On The Fringe

Payday and title loans continue to be popular, and states continue to seek tougher regulation for an industry adept at finding ways to grow.

It seems state regulators can't do enough to stem the tremendous growth in the usage of short-term credit.

Over the first few months of this year [2004] two Ninth District states, Michigan and Wisconsin, have seen their governors veto bills that would regulate the practice of payday advance lending. In each case those governors, prodded by consumer advocacy groups, claimed their particular bill did not go far enough to protect the public from unfair lending practices.

Consumer advocates point to interest rates for these short-term loans (typically one to four weeks) that average 391 percent when annualized, and

♣ It's A Fact!!

In the late 1990s, observers began to note the swift rise of an industry that marketed loans to working families at annual percentage rates (APRs) of interest that were previously unheard of in the conventional market. Payday lenders were offering what they described as short-term cash advances on their customer's next paycheck for fees starting around $15 per $100 borrowed. This product was revealed to be a loan carrying APRs that generally ranged from 391 percent to 443 percent.

Researchers soon found additional cause for concern: the loans are structured so that borrowers routinely have difficulty paying them off when they are due. By requiring full repayment within a short period of time (generally two weeks), with no option to make payments in installments, lenders compel payday borrowers to return again and again, renewing a loan for another large fee without being able to pay down the principal. This loan flipping is the foundation of the payday lending business model.

Even as the abusive nature of the payday loan product has become clear, the industry continues to grow at a significant pace. From our analysis based on state regulator data, we conclude that payday loan volume is at least $28 billion a year, growing by well over 100 percent over the past 5 years. The payday lending industry's growth is based on their success in getting the practice of loan flipping legalized in one state after another.

Source: Excerpted from "Financial Quicksand," a publication from the Center for Responsible Lending, www.responsiblelending.org, © 2006. Reprinted with permission.

many borrowers renew their loans again and again, sinking deeper into debt. Many have called for increasingly stringent regulation on the industry.

Lenders, for their part, argue that the cost of borrowing reflects the higher credit risks involved, and growing demand shows that a real need is being served. Payday and auto title loan businesses have continued growing extraordinarily fast, particularly in some states, since the *fedgazette* last reported on the subject in October 2000. For example, in August 2000 there were 195 licensed payday lenders in Wisconsin, and as of April 2003 there were 351, according to the Wisconsin Department of Financial Institutions. In 1995 there were only 17.

But the number of locations is only part of the picture. Loan volumes speak, well, volumes about the industry's growth. In 1996, when the state began keeping track, Wisconsin's 64 payday lending stores made 80,000 loans worth around $11 million. In 2000, the number of loans was 955,666 for roughly $242 million. And for 2003 a total of 1,324,405 loans were made, amounting to a value of nearly $430 million.

Nationally, the trend is similar. Stephens Inc., an investment bank that tracks payday and title lending, also called "fringe" banking, estimates there are 22,000 payday lenders nationwide doing $40 billion in loan volume and collecting $6 billion in fees. Not bad for a business that didn't exist before the 1990s.

States have been trying to catch up as a regulator ever since. As a new industry, payday lending sprang up in some states without regulation. This led to a call for consumer protection laws, which many states passed, including some in the Ninth District. Such laws have limited the size of the business in those states. But as the numbers reflect, the industry has managed to grow in the face of increased regulation, for a number of reasons.

In fact, many payday lenders have welcomed legislative efforts. Regulations have helped change the industry "in a constructive way," said Robert Reich, president of Community Loans of America, a multistate payday and auto title lender that operates locations in Montana, South Dakota, and Wisconsin. "I think any good operator should prefer to work in a better-regulated environment."

Credit Report On The Industry

The reason payday and title lenders need special regulations, it's argued, is the unique characteristics of such loans that separate them from other bank loans.

Payday loans are intended to be repaid within a week to a month. They are backed by a check, written by the borrower for the loan amount plus a fee, and postdated for their payday. When the loan is due, the lender cashes the check or, if the borrower cannot repay it, may renew the loan. The typical loan is for around $200 to $300 and usually costs $15 to $20 per $100 borrowed, although the fees can be much greater.

Auto title loans are also small, short-term arrangements, but they are secured by the borrower's car. The lender places a lien on the car, and if the loan is not paid back the lender may take possession of it. The car must be wholly owned by the borrower and may not have any other liens on it.

According to most observers, the auto title lending business has also grown rapidly, but it is not as easy to track as payday lending because it is not explicitly defined and regulated in most Ninth District states. In several states, pawnshops can get into the business with no special license. Montana, for example, has formal licensing procedures, and the number of licensed title lenders has gone from 21 in 2000 to 45 in April 2004, not counting pawnshops offering the service. In 2002, these licensed lenders granted almost 16,000 loans.

The perception given by consumer groups and some lawmakers is that these businesses prey on the poor because they generally have few other credit alternatives and encourage them to get further into debt. In the last few years, studies looking into the demographics of payday borrowers suggest the stereotype might not fit all that well.

A 2001 survey of payday customers by Georgetown University's Credit Research Center found that borrowers are typically moderate-income younger families—35 percent are married with children and nearly a quarter are single parents. Fully half of all borrowers have household incomes between $25,000 and $49,999. Over half have some education beyond high school. As might be expected, payday customers tend to have credit problems. By and large, however, borrowers are informed about their alternatives and are aware of the high costs of payday loans, although not in terms of annual percentage rates, the study concluded.

However, it did show that payday borrowers tend to be repeat customers, with 48 percent taking out seven or more total advances in a year, and 22 percent taking 14 or more. Borrowers also tend to roll over or renew the same loan, postponing final payment and accruing significant interest charges; about 40 percent had renewed loans five times or more. These numbers jibe with a study by Michael Stegman of the University of North Carolina at Chapel Hill, which found that the practice of payday lending encourages repeat usage and debt rollovers.

Even so, the Georgetown study revealed that three of four borrowers are satisfied or very satisfied with their most recent new advance.

Nanny States

Strong growth in the industry has been met with equally strong calls for regulation. In many cases, the payday lenders have encouraged legislation, in hopes it will improve their legitimacy and allow them to expand. The Community Financial Services Association, the industry's self-regulation and lobbying group, has spearheaded initiatives in several states, including Wisconsin.

Nationwide, 35 states now regulate payday lenders explicitly. Some states, like Georgia, have set rate caps so low that the business is effectively outlawed. In other states that do not have clear laws or strict lending rules, payday lenders have found ways to get around restrictions. In the Ninth District, several states have added new regulations since 2000.

South Dakota has limited loan amounts to $500 and will not allow borrowers to hold more than one loan at a time. The state also requires borrowers to pay loan fees before renewing a loan, to prevent them from piling up, and forbids borrowers from rolling over a loan more than four times. When one out-of-state lender tried to claim the regulations didn't apply to its business, the Legislature promptly redefined the industry in a bill that will take effect in July [2004].

"I don't think that anything that has dealt with consumer education or disclosure has affected the industry all that much, and they've welcomed it," said Rex Hagg, a former South Dakota state legislator who now works as a lobbyist with the Short-Term Lending Association, an industry trade group. "What they don't welcome is attempts to regulate the business to make it significantly more awkward for these people to obtain loans," Hagg said. "That is a big distinction for them."

♣ It's A Fact!!

The data show that payday loans are, in fact, designed to be renewed. Contrary to prudent lending practices, payday lenders do not make loans based on the borrower's ability to repay. Borrowers need only a checking account and a pay stub verifying employment to qualify for a payday loan, which averages about $300. The loans are secured by the borrower's signed personal check, which is dated on the borrower's next payday. The lender may submit this "live" check to the bank for payment should the borrower default. But most borrowers are unable to pay the loan back in full when it is due and still have enough cash to make it to their next payday.

The prospect of bouncing the check left in the hands of the lender, often accompanied by fear of criminal prosecution for writing a "bad check," puts tremendous pressure on the borrower to avoid default. So the borrower generally pays another fee, typically $50 on a $300 loan, to renew or float the loan for another pay period. This transaction is called a rollover.

Or the lender may close out the loan and reopen it in short order to the same effect, called a back-to-back transaction. Back-to-back transactions and rollovers cost the borrower exactly the same amount, typically $50 every payday until they can pay off the loan in full and walk away. However, back-to-back transactions can be particularly confusing for the borrower. Though they have to repay the first loan before taking out the second loan, the second loan can seem like "new money" since they walk out with cash in their pocket like the first time. In reality, they are borrowing back their own money minus the fee, still paying $50 every payday to keep from defaulting on their $300 loan.

Source: Excerpted from "Financial Quicksand," a publication from the Center for Responsible Lending, www.responsiblelending.org, © 2006. Reprinted with permission.

South Dakota, like several other states, doesn't have such strict rules for auto title lenders. "They're not even regulated," said Hagg. "So they're out there making $2,000 loans and there's no requirement that they pay down the interest each time they roll it over, so you tack on that interest all the time and all the sudden it is out of hand and people's cars are at risk." An attempt to tighten regulations for title lenders fizzled in this year's legislative session, but Hagg said there may be another initiative next year.

North Dakota has adopted a licensing system for payday lenders, limiting rollovers to one, restricting fees to 20 percent of the loan and protecting borrowers who default from prosecution. Montana has set up regulations for title loans and extended its payday laws to include electronic debits, because its original law covered only paper checks. Wisconsin continues to have no specific payday laws, which is one reason why business has flourished there.

Minnesota hasn't changed its laws for payday loans since 1995, but the rules are relatively strict. The industry doubled there from 34 licensed locations in 2000 to 68 by early May and lent out almost $54 million in 2002—significant growth until you look at neighboring Wisconsin, which has five times the number of payday outlets.

For Rent: Bank Charters?

Whether or not a state wants to allow payday lending, however, may be of little consequence, thanks to national banking laws. The same laws that allow credit card issuers to evade state interest rate caps can work for payday lenders if they partner with a bank that issues the loans. That is, one state cannot prevent a national bank from conducting business in accordance with the laws of another state in which the bank is chartered.

So in some states, payday chains have partnered with banks to market payday loans technically issued by a bank. In the industry, this is referred to as "the bank model." The lender and the bank share the loan fees. The practice is, therefore, almost exclusive to states that have tough restrictions, since where payday lending is allowed, lenders would prefer to issue the loans themselves and keep all the fees.

♣ It's A Fact!!

What is an auto title loan?

An auto title loan is a short-term loan, usually no longer than 30 days. Your car title is used to secure the loan. This means if the loan is not repaid, the lender may take the car and sell it to get the loan money back. Most title lenders will only make the loan if you do not owe anything else on the car.

Who are auto title lenders?

Auto title lenders often target people with bad credit, low-income individuals, military members, and elderly people. The lenders make money from high interest rates and the repossession of cars when consumers cannot pay off the loans.

Why should I be careful with an auto title loan?

When a person is facing financial problems, a short-term auto title loan seems like a good option, especially to someone with credit problems. However, the solution is short term and the effects can be devastating. You can end up paying very high interest rates and lots of money or lose your car.

How high are the interest rates?

The loan is written with an interest rate for a short time period. For example, the loan will show a 25% interest rate for one month. But this rate over a year is actually 300%. Auto title lenders will usually write a loan for 30 days or less. At the end of the month, the lender will accept the interest payment and allow the debt to be "rolled over" for another month. On a $600 loan, the interest would be approximately $150. This means you owe $750. If you only pay $150 for the month, you will owe $750 the next month.

What if I can't pay the loan off within the proper time?

If you can't pay off the loan it will be rolled over. In many cases the borrower will not be able to pay the loan off in full, and the interest will begin to build up all over again at the high rate. This is called "rolling over" or 'flipping" the loan.

Source: From "Auto Title Loans and the Law," © 2004 South Carolina Appleseed Legal Justice Center (www.scjustice.org). Reprinted with permission.

"It's not the norm; almost the only [payday lenders] who are doing it are the big ones that operate in multiple states," said John Caskey, an economics professor at Swarthmore College and an expert on fringe banking. "So most of the small independents, if they're located in a state where the state laws are favorable, they don't bother partnering, because it's kind of a hassle to set it up and so on. It was the bigger ones, that operate across multiple states where they wanted a common way of doing things, that tended to do it."

Since South Dakota has no usury laws, a number of small banks there have been courted by payday chains. There are now seven South Dakota banks partnering with lenders in states like Pennsylvania, Georgia, Michigan, and Texas. For small banks in South Dakota, often sensitive to the volatility of agriculture, the opportunity to partner with a payday lender is tempting.

One of those banks is First Fidelity in Burke, which partnered with Advance America in October 2001 to lend in Michigan. President and CEO George Kenzie is pleased with the results. "We were just looking for a line of business that we could minimize risk and increase some profits. We didn't have to put a lot of our loan portfolio into this business, and it has some definite profits to it. And it diversifies some of our portfolio and some of our income, so we're not reliant strictly on agriculture."

The practice has steamed consumer groups, who call the practice "charter renting," and it has attracted the attention of some regulators. The attorney general's office in Georgia, for example, is pursuing legal action against Advance America and Bank West in South Dakota, which could determine if and how states can stop payday lenders from using banks to get around usury laws.

"If consumers in South Dakota don't want to be protected from usury that's one thing," said Jean Ann Fox, director of consumer protection for the Consumer Federation of America, "but the folks in North Carolina would like to have the benefit of their 36 percent annual rate cap for small loans, and payday lenders are ignoring that by partnering with these banks. Georgia is a state that has made it a crime to do this kind of lending, where the criminal usury cap is 60 percent. But you have South Dakota banks helping storefronts evade that."

Starting in 2000, the Office of the Comptroller of the Currency (OCC) and the Office of Thrift Supervision (OTS)—two federal agencies that regulate the lending industry—decided the risks involved in bank partnerships were dangerous, and eventually the OCC ordered all nationally chartered banks to end the practice. In January 2003, as part of the crackdown, the OCC ordered First National Bank in Brookings, South Dakota, to end its association with payday lender Cash America International, threatening to charge the bank with violating the Federal Trade Commission Act.

But payday lenders were already one step ahead, having begun to move toward partnerships with state-chartered banks, whose right to export rates to other states has been consistently upheld by federal courts. In the case of First National, its holding company, Fishback Financial, continued its partnership with Cash America through a different state-chartered bank.

Last July, the Federal Deposit Insurance Corporation (FDIC) issued guidelines on the practice (which are available on its website). The FDIC has declared that it will conduct on-site reviews at third-party lending locations partnered with banks to make sure they are in compliance with the guidelines and, if they are not, take appropriate action. The FDIC says that this kind of lending is one of the riskiest activities a bank can get involved in and requires banks partnering with payday lenders to hold more capital, while limiting the amount of a bank's total capital that can be extended in payday loans.

For its part, the Federal Reserve declared in 2000 that payday lenders, even though many are not considered banks under state laws, are nevertheless subject to the Truth in Lending Act, enforced under Regulation Z. Lenders are therefore required to fully disclose all costs and details of loans to customers, including what fees amount to as annual percentage rates. Many in the industry believe treating the fees as APRs is irrelevant, though. Hagg, from South Dakota, said that fees on other financial transactions like ATM withdrawals are comparable when annualized. "I think the best analogy that I have heard in a long time is that it's like taking a taxi somewhere. You would never buy a car at the rate that you pay for a taxi," Hagg said, "but what it is for is to fill short-term need."

"You did have the setback from the OCC forcing the national banks out of it," said Dennis Telzrow, an analyst at Stephens Inc. "I think there were a lot of different issues, some of which may or may not have been economically driven, shall we say."

Caskey agrees with Telzrow. "In some states, the state regulators have not minded state banks partnering with payday lenders, and even though they're members of the FDIC, the FDIC did not take the same hard-line view as the OCC and the OTS. So the payday lenders who are still partnering with banks now partner with state-chartered banks to get around state usury laws. A lot of them had to find new banks because originally most of them were partnered with national banks. After the OCC crackdown on that, then they started looking for new banks and so on. So there was a lot of juggling and fear as this went on."

Because of the bank model, consumer groups have focused more recently on national regulations. If the FDIC doesn't take steps similar to those of the other regulatory agencies, Fox said, "then the only other avenues for solving this problem are Congress clarifying that they had no intention for state banks to be able to rent their charters to third parties to evade state law, or the courts."

Fox hinted that other state-level actions, like prohibitions on partnering with third parties, might be forthcoming. Such actions may make it harder for payday lenders to do business and may limit their number. But if the past is any indication, they will not stop the demand for these services.

"There is such an unmet demand in the marketplace for this kind of lending, that we have people lining up at the stores as they're nearing completion," said Reich of Community Loans of America. "It's kind of, 'build it and they will come.'"

Chapter 31

Refund Anticipation Loans

The Risks And Costs Of Tax Refund Anticipation Loans

The "Tax Refund" That Really Isn't One: It's A Refund Anticipation Loan

How would you like to pay a super-high price to borrow money that already belongs to you? Sounds ridiculous, right? But that's pretty much what happens to many folks at tax time in the crazy world of RALs, or refund anticipation loans.

You may be tempted by tax-time advertisements for "Fast Cash Refunds," "Express Money," or "Instant Refunds." These ads will offer to get you your refund in just a day or two, or even on the spot. Beware! Many of these "fast refunds" are really loans, refund anticipation loans (RALs).

When you get a RAL, you're borrowing against your own tax refund money. And RALs are often marketed to people who need money the most—low- and moderate-income workers who receive the Earned Income Tax Credit.

Don't Pay Triple-Digit Interest Rates To Borrow Your Own Refund

RALs are extremely expensive. Loan fees typically range from $30 to $90, which translates into Annual Percentage Rates (APRs) of about 60% to over 700%. If you paid those rates on all your borrowing you'd probably go broke. And all to get your tax refund just a few days earlier than you can for free from the IRS. You're lining someone else's pockets with your hard-earned money.

RAL fees, combined with tax preparation, electronic filing, and other fees, can end up eating away a big chunk of your refund.

Table 31.1. RAL Example

For a tax refund of $2000, you might pay to get a RAL:

RAL loan fee:	$75
Electronic filing fee:	$40

Combine that with the fee you will need to pay

to the tax preparer:	$100
Total:	$215

This is over 10% of your refund!

This RAL has an APR (Annual Percentage Rate) of 142% if it beats the IRS by 10 days.

Source: Copyright © National Consumer Law Center.

RALs Can Be Hazardous To Your Financial Health

In addition to their high costs, RALs can be risky. Since a RAL is a loan from a bank in partnership with a tax preparer, it must be repaid even if the IRS denies or delays your refund, or your refund is smaller than expected. If you don't pay back the RAL, the lender will take actions to hurt your credit rating and may send your account to a debt collector. In addition, when you apply for a RAL, you are giving the lender the right to grab your tax refund to pay for old tax loan debts that the lender claims you owe.

Ways To Save At Tax Time

Here are ways to take a pass on that RAL—most folks don't need one—and save money at tax time:

E-File With Direct Deposit: File your tax return electronically (E-file) to speed up your refund. Tell the IRS to deposit the refund directly into your bank account—you provide your account number right on your tax return. You can get a refund in about 10 days this way—without paying one cent extra for a loan. Some of the free tax preparation programs (called "VITA" sites) can file taxes electronically. If you have internet access, you may be able to get free tax preparation and electronic filing at http://www.icanefile.org.

Get A Bank Account: If you don't have a bank account, open one up to take advantage of direct deposit. You can use a savings account to receive your tax refund, and maybe save some of it for a down payment on a house or a car, or to build a nest egg.

Wait Just A Bit Longer: Do you really have to get cash from your tax refund today? Can you wait a few weeks to save almost $100? If you have an urgent bill to pay, ask for more time until the tax refund check comes from the IRS. Don't take on a new expensive debt to pay an old bill.

✔ Quick Tip
Have your tax refund deposited electronically into your bank account: Direct deposit is the fastest way to get your tax refund, especially if you file your return electronically. Direct deposit also is the safest way to obtain a refund because paper checks can be lost, misplaced, or stolen.

Source: Excerpted from "Expecting a Tax Refund? Beware of Costly Loans and Other Pitfalls," *FDIC Consumer News*, Federal Deposit Insurance Corporation (FDIC), Winter 2004/2005.

Avoid Check Cashers: Check cashers charge an extra fee to cash RAL and tax refund checks. Some check cashers charge up to 7% to cash a RAL check—the average is about 3%. So if you receive a $2,000 refund, it would cost you an average of $60 to cash the RAL check—on top of the RAL and tax preparation fees. A smarter move is to use a bank account.

Use A VITA Site: A great way to save money at tax time is to go to a volunteer income tax assistance (VITA) site. VITA sites provide free tax preparation to low- and moderate-income taxpayers. VITA sites are sponsored by the IRS and can be found in libraries, community centers, and other locations during tax time. For the nearest VITA site, call the IRS general help line at 800-TAX-1040 or go to www.tax-coalition.org.

✔ Quick Tip

- **Make the best use of your refund:** Sure, you can treat yourself to something special, but consider some "sensible" alternatives: Pay down or pay off your debts, starting with the ones that charge the highest interest rates on unpaid balances. Start or add to an existing savings account. Or, fund a college savings plan.

- **Consider ways to reduce or eliminate a tax refund in the future:** You wouldn't intentionally overpay your electric bill each month just because you knew you'd eventually get the extra payments back at the end of the year. So why pay your taxes that way? A tax refund of $2,000 breaks down to about $167 per month that you lent the U.S. government interest-free each month. Review your current year's tax situation to be fairly sure you won't have a significantly higher tax bill than in the past. If a change is appropriate, fill out a new W-4 form from your employer increasing the number of your "personal allowances." This adjustment will reduce the tax money withheld each pay period and increase your take-home pay. On the other hand, if you owed a lot of money on last year's taxes, consider decreasing your take-home pay.

Source: Excerpted from "Expecting a Tax Refund? Beware of Costly Loans and Other Pitfalls," *FDIC Consumer News*, Federal Deposit Insurance Corporation (FDIC), Winter 2004/2005.

Chapter 32

Overdraft Loans: Courtesy Or Debt Trap?

Big Banks Bury High "Courtesy Overdraft" Loan Charges In Fine Print

Over eighty percent of the nation's largest banks charge consumers high overdraft fees without their permission, according to a study released by the Consumer Federation of America. Consumers are only informed of these charges in the fine print of their account agreements, which can cause them to inadvertently overdraw their accounts when making an ATM (automated teller machine) or debit card transaction.

"Large banks are increasingly allowing consumers to unwittingly overdraw their accounts and then hit them with hidden fees," said Jean Ann Fox, director of consumer protection for Consumer Federation of America (CFA). "A loophole in Federal rules actually permits this deceptive and abusive practice."

While recent regulatory action by the Federal Reserve singles out smaller depository institutions that promote "courtesy" overdraft loans, the nation's largest banks have also included identical provisions in their checking accounts but do not advertise them.

"The Federal Reserve missed an opportunity to require banks to give customers information about the true cost of overdraft loans. As a result, banks can continue to hide the cost of these products," said Eric Halperin, policy counsel at the Center for Responsible Lending, "Federal regulators must do more to protect consumers from these abusive loans."

CFA's study, "Overdrawn: Consumers Face Hidden Overdraft Charges From Nation's Largest Banks," documents that the nation's biggest banks charge fees for discretionary overdrafts without consumer consent and that the overdraft fees charged by these banks exceed industry averages. CFA surveyed large banks controlling over half of all assets held in consumer deposit accounts. The fees at the banks CFA surveyed average $28.57, five percent higher than average overdraft fees at two hundred bank accounts surveyed by *BankRate.com* in May 2005. Banks that offer this discretionary "courtesy" overdraft coverage in their account agreement disclosures also state they are not bound to pay transactions that overdraw depositors' accounts. If consumers who receive "courtesy" overdraft loans do not repay the overdraft quickly enough, many banks tack on an additional sustained overdraft surcharge.

Penalty fees for insufficient funds checks and overdrafts are a huge and growing burden for account holders. Consumers pay at least $10 billion per year and as much as $22.7 billion just for overdraft loans, according to estimates by the Center for Responsible Lending. These estimates are based on reports by industry analysts and publicly disclosed checking account service fee revenue.

"These days, consumers are having a much harder time managing their bank accounts to avoid unwanted overdraft fees," said Ms. Fox.

Increasing overdraft fees are the result of changes in the marketplace and in federal law and the broader use of overdraft fees for transactions other than those involving paper checks, including ATM withdrawals and debt card purchases. Money moves out of consumers' bank accounts faster than ever due to electronic processing allowed under the Federal "Check 21" act, while deposits can be held up for days before consumers are allowed access to their funds. Big banks permit consumers to overdraw their accounts without warning them on more types of transactions. Many larger banks are also increasing the chances that consumers will overdraw their accounts by processing the largest checks ahead of smaller checks, whether or not the bank received the larger checks first. This can cause a larger number of smaller transactions to bounce for consumers with low account balances and increase fee revenue for banks.

♣ It's A Fact!!

Traditionally, depository institutions have selectively covered checks that exceed account balances as an occasional courtesy to depositors. A customer who wanted and qualified for a formal program to protect against overdrafts was offered transfers from a line-of-credit (LOC), a credit card, or linked savings account.

Customers who did not qualify for such contractual programs and who demonstrated a pattern of overdrawing a checking account were typically counseled that future overdrafts would not be honored. Financial institutions returned the check to the presenter, charged a Not Sufficient Funds (NSF) fee, and/or closed the customer's account.

Today's customers are placed in overdraft loan programs, the most expensive credit program that the institution offers, often without their consent. The overdraft loan programs extend credit by paying customer's checks, debit card transactions, and ATM withdrawals when customers have insufficient funds in their accounts to cover the withdrawal(s). The institution pays the transaction and charges the customer a fee for lending the money necessary to cover the transaction.

These fee-based overdraft loan programs have proliferated in the past few years. From 2003 to 2005, the number of financial institutions using a vendor-based overdraft loan program increased almost 80 percent to 3,500 institutions. The amount of overdraft fee income has increased as dramatically as the number of programs. Although automating the programs has lowered the costs of making these loans, the average fee charged for overdrafts increased 24 percent from 1998 to 2006, to $26.90. From 2001 to 2004, total service charges on deposit accounts increased 27 percent from $29.7 billion to $37.8 billion. In comparison, the Consumer Price Index (CPI) grew only 6.7 percent from 2001 to 2004.9

Source: Excerpted from "Overdraft Loans: Survey Finds Growing Problem for Consumers," an Issue Paper from the Center for Responsible Lending, www.responsiblelending.org, © 2006. Reprinted with permission.

The new generation of overdraft loans are more expensive than traditional overdraft protection, which requires that consumers agree ahead of time to pay for an overdraft from a linked savings accounts, credit card, or revolving line of credit. CFA's study found that most of the largest banks offered these contractual overdraft protection policies and these options would be cheaper for consumers than "courtesy" overdraft.

"Big banks should encourage consumers to use lower cost services that are already available. Responsible overdraft protection involves a guarantee that overdrafts will be paid, reasonable fees that are clearly disclosed, and affordable repayment terms," Ms. Fox stated.

Key Findings Of The Report

- The vast majority of large banks' checking account agreements contain discretionary overdraft provisions for paper checks, ATM, and point of service transactions. At least 27 of the 33 institutions surveyed (81.8 percent) have courtesy overdraft provisions written into the fine print of their account agreements that say that the bank may or may not, at its discretion, cover debits to checking accounts that would overdraw the account. All of these

♣ It's A Fact!! Vulnerable Consumers Caught In Overdraft Cycle

The Center for Responsible Lending (CRL) has conducted a survey of overdraft loan customers. Our findings suggest that:

- Sixteen percent of overdraft loan users account for 71 percent of fee-based overdraft loan fees.

- Repeat users are more often low-income, single, non-white renters.

- Repeat users are in effect using the overdraft loans as an expensive substitute for a line-of-credit, and are paying fees that can be as costly as payday loans.

Source: Excerpted from "Overdraft Loans: Survey Finds Growing Problem for Consumers," an Issue Paper from the Center for Responsible Lending, www.responsiblelending.org, © 2006. Reprinted with permission.

banks allowed depositors to overdraw their accounts at the ATM, 26 (78.8 percent) allow overdrafts at point-of-sale debit transactions at merchants, and 17 (51.5 percent) allow overdrafts from automated or scheduled electronic payments.

- Fees for overdrafts are rising. Current fees for overdrafts and bounced checks at the surveyed banks are higher than the fees charged for these services at larger banks in 2002. Current average overdraft fees of $28.57 are $1.73 (6.4 percent) higher than the $26.84 the Federal Reserve reported larger banks were charging in 2002.

- Overdraft fees at big banks are higher than average bank fees. Overdraft fees at the largest banks are 5.3 percent higher than they are at average banks. The average overdraft fee at the banks CFA surveyed was $28.57, compared to the $27.13 that *bankrate.com* found in a May 2005 study of more than 200 checking accounts.

- Nearly half of banks charge sustained overdraft fees. Twelve of the banks (36.4 percent) charge additional fees for not repaying the overdraft within a certain period. These sustained overdraft charges begin on average after the fifth day the account is deficient. Seven banks charge an average $5.57 per-day sustained overdraft fee and five banks charge an average $27.50 single sustained overdraft fee.

- Contractual overdraft protection is cheaper that discretionary "courtesy" overdraft protection. Fees for overdraft transfers from savings accounts averaged $7.38 per transfer, about one-fourth the average overdraft loan fee of $28.57, although four of the banks with this service (14.1 percent) have an average annual fee for this service of $23.75. The average credit card overdraft transfer fee of $10.00 is less than half (35.0 percent) the average "courtesy" overdraft fee. (Interest charges in this case would be extra if the consumer did not pay the card's full balance.) Fees for transfers from lines of credit were also cheaper—an average of $5.20 per transfer, although some banks also charged an annual fee.

- Many banks do not adequately disclose a key factor: check processing order. Others inform consumers that they process checks in a manner that will maximize fee income. As cited above, the order in which checks are processed has a major impact on how many checks a consumer might bounce or overdraw and what they might be charged. Depository institutions do not generally disclose the order they process debits (paper checks, ATM withdrawals, POS purchases, or electronic transfers) and many state they could change their processing order without notice to depositors. CFA found that nearly one fourth of banks (24.2 percent) refuse to disclose any debit processing order beyond "any order"; one seventh (15.2%) of banks reserve the right to process debits in any order

---

♣ It's A Fact!!
Consumer Service Or Debt Trap?

Vendors and bankers say their overdraft loan programs appeal to a broad range of bank customers who occasionally use the service to cover a missed deposit or math error. One vendor says, "The primary users of overdraft services are middle-income, employed consumers with $50,000 or more in annual household income who have lived at their current address 4 ½ years. They have an average of four years in their present job and 32% own their homes and our studies show that they not only welcome but are demanding such discreet, value-added programs."

However, consumer advocates have raised concerns that the vast majority of fee income is collected from a small number of vulnerable customers who struggle to make ends meet on a recurring basis. The repeat usage by these families suggests that they have become trapped in a payday loan-like cycle of debt.

This cycle begins when an overdraft is paid and the corresponding fee is deducted from an account balance, which then causes additional items to overdraft and additional fees deducted from the account. Only when a deposit is made to the account does the account become positive again. However, the continual deduction of overdraft fees leaves the consumer without enough money in the account to cover monthly expenses, so the pattern repeats itself.

Source: Excerpted from "Overdraft Loans: Survey Finds Growing Problem for Consumers," an Issue Paper from the Center for Responsible Lending, www.responsiblelending.org, © 2006. Reprinted with permission.

but disclose they generally process debits from largest to smallest; and one third (33.3%) disclose they process debits largest to smallest.

About The Study: CFA surveyed 33 of the nation's largest financial institutions with checking accounts. These institutions have 35,151 branches and $2.8 trillion in deposits (or 51.7 percent of all U.S. deposits). These institutions are listed as among the 50 largest depository institutions by the Federal Deposit Insurance Corporation in its *Summary of Deposits* database. The list of 50 depository institutions was reduced to 33 by consolidating affiliates, taking mergers and acquisitions into account, eliminating three institutions that did not offer checking accounts, and not surveying an institution in the midst of a merger for which CFA could obtain no fee information.

Chapter 33

Rent-To-Own Stores And No-Interest Financing

Rent-To-Own: Worth The Convenience?

A Maryland woman signed a rent-to-own agreement for a computer. The weekly payments were $28 for a period of 52 weeks. If she made all the payments, she would pay a total of $1,364 to own the computer—which was used and had a cash price of only $649.

If you need a television, major appliance, or furniture but you don't have the cash or credit to buy it outright, you might be tempted to go to a rent-to-own store. These stores advertise that you can take home the item immediately, simply by agreeing to make a weekly or monthly payment. You're obligated only to pay each rental payment as it comes due, and you are free to end the arrangement by returning the merchandise to the store.

This arrangement may sound convenient, but it comes at a very high price. Buying on a rent-to-own plan will often cost you double what you would pay for the item with cash, on layaway, or on an installment plan.

About This Chapter: This chapter includes "Rent-to-Own: Worth the Convenience?" © 2003 Maryland Office of the Attorney General, Consumer Protection Division. Reprinted with permission. And, "No-Interest Financing Can Cost You Plenty," © 1996 Maryland Office of the Attorney General, Consumer Protection Division. Reprinted with permission.

For example, a new $400 washing machine purchased on an 18-month installment plan at the maximum allowable interest[1] (24%) would cost $480 total. Under an 18-month rent-to-own plan, you'd typically pay $1,000 or more for the same washing machine. Plus, the rent-to-own washing machine might be a couple of years old and previously rented to many other people.

Maryland law[2] does not place any limits on the finance charges or interest rent-to-own dealers can charge. The dealers are also not required to disclose as an annual percentage rate (APR) the finance charge or interest consumers end up paying to own the product. Therefore, you cannot easily compare the cost of buying under a rent-to-own plan with buying on, for example, an installment plan. If rent-to-own dealers did have to disclose an APR, consumers would see that their rates are often as high as 120% to 150%.

Consider All Your Options

Rent-to-own stores market to people who may think they have no other options, because of low income or bad credit. But there may be less-expensive alternatives:

- Can you do without the item until you have saved enough money in the bank to pay cash? If the woman who wanted a computer could wait a few months, perhaps by using a friend's computer or one at the public library, she could save $28 a week instead of paying a rent-to-own dealer. In six months she would have enough to buy a new computer priced at $650. She would own the computer in half the time and save more than $700.

- Can you buy the item on a layaway plan? You may only need a small down payment.

- Can you buy the item on an installment plan at a retail store? With an installment plan you can take the item home immediately, as with rent-to-own. The law limits the amount of interest that can be charged on installment plans (maximum 24%[1]), so these plans are less costly than rent-to-own agreements.

- Can you get a short-term loan from a lending institution such as a bank or credit union to purchase the item?

- Can you find a used item through the classified ads, a yard sale, or second-hand store? You may be able to find what you need for the cost of only a few rent-to-own payments.

Your Rights Under The Law

If you do decide to enter a rent-to-own agreement, be aware that Maryland law[2] provides some protections for rent-to-own consumers. Rent-to-own contracts must disclose the following important information:

Whether The Item Is New Or Used: This information may be especially important to know when considering purchasing an appliance, a TV or a computer.

What It Will Cost You: The contract must state how much the item would cost if you paid cash, how many rental payments you must make to own the item, how much each payment will be, and how much you'll have to pay in total to own the item. With this information, you can look at the total amount you will pay to own the item and consider if it is worth it.

Your Early Purchase Option: The contract must give you the option to purchase the item earlier than originally planned by paying a certain amount. The method for determining that amount must be described.

Your Right To "Reinstate" After Late Payments Or Repossession: The law allows consumers who are late in making payments to retain their rights to the item, even after it has been repossessed, if they make all outstanding payments. These provisions protect consumers who have made a substantial investment toward owning the property.

If the dealer repossesses an item you were renting because you failed to make a payment, the dealer must give you a written notice that states your right to reinstate the rent-to-own agreement, the last date by which you can reinstate the agreement, and the amount you will have to pay to reinstate. You may reinstate the rent-to-own agreement within 15 days of the repossession by paying all past due charges, the reasonable costs of pickup and redelivery, and a reinstatement fee of $5.

Maintenance And Damage: The dealer is responsible for keeping your rented items in good working order without extra charge to you, as long as you have not damaged it. You are responsible for loss, damage, theft, or destruction of the property while it is in your possession. If the item is lost, damaged, or stolen while in your possession, you must pay the dealer the early purchase option price of the item.

Warranties: If any part of a manufacturer's warranty covers the rental item at the time you acquire ownership, the warranty will be transferred to you if allowed by the warranty.

Notes

1. Based on Maryland law; rates in other states vary.
2. Regulations in other states vary.

No-Interest Financing Can Cost You Plenty

- "0% Interest for 6 months"
- "No Interest for 12 months"
- "No Interest, No Payments until ..."

"Free Financing" offers seem to be everywhere these days. If you are a careful consumer and read all of the fine print, you might be able to save some money with a "no-interest" buying plan. But beware—many no-interest offers carry hidden charges that can more than make up for the interest charges, or are not really offering what they say.

> **♣ It's A Fact!!**
> **"No Payments on Merchandise Until Next Year."**
> Even though you won't make payments for several months, if interest is being charged from the date of purchase, as is often the case, you can end up paying much more for an item than you expected. Also, if you don't pay for the merchandise in full by the end of the specified period, you may be charged interest from the date of purchase.
>
> Source: Excerpted from "There's No Such Thing as a Free-Lunch Loan," *FDIC Consumer News*, Spring 2002, Federal Deposit Insurance Corporation (www.fdic.gov).

Here are some questions to ask before you sign up for a "no-interest" financing plan:

- Will you have to pay interest and then get it refunded back to you at a later date?

- What happens if you cannot pay off the full purchase price by the designated date?

- If you end up having to pay interest because you cannot pay off the full purchase price, what is the interest rate you will be charged and when will it begin accruing? Would you be better off using your lower-interest bank card?

- Is the price of the item inflated to make up for the lack of interest?

Hidden Costs

"No interest" financing plans can carry some hidden costs. Here are some you might encounter:

- **0 Interest Only If Full Payment Is On Time:** In many "zero-interest" programs, you do not have to pay interest for the first six months, or whatever period of time is advertised. However, if you do not pay off the full price of the purchase within that time period, you will then be charged interest on the entire purchase amount dating back to the purchase date, even if you have paid off most of the balance. Often, the interest rate charged by the store is 20 percent or more—higher than most bank credit cards. More than half of the consumers who signed up for "no interest" financing plans with one company did not pay off the balance in the time required and ended up paying interest.

- **Interest Paid But Rebated:** In some no interest programs, your payment each month does include an interest charge. If you make all of your payments on time and pay off the entire purchase price by the agreed-upon date, the interest you have paid is credited back to you. If you miss a payment, pay late one month, or do not pay off the whole balance by the end of the agreed upon period, you don't get your rebate.

- **Inflated Prices:** Some stores offer "no-interest" financing but inflate the selling price to make up the difference. A recent advertisement from a large appliance chain offered a choice: no interest for six months or $150 off the purchase price. Another chain offered comparable 35-inch televisions: $1,499 with no interest for 15 months, or a similar TV for $999 without the no-interest offer.

- **Minimum Purchase Requirements:** "No-interest" financing offers can include minimum-purchase requirements or may apply only to specific brands.

- **Store Credit Card Catches:** If you make your purchase on a store credit card on which you carry a balance or make other purchases that are not "no-interest" financing, you might have to make two payments each month: a minimum monthly payment and the payment due under the zero-interest program. Read your billing statement carefully to understand what payments you have to make and when they are due.

If you are interested in a "zero interest" offer, read the fine print in the advertisement and the financing agreement. Make certain you understand exactly how the store's "zero interest" program works. There are many different types of programs. Also, if you are not familiar with the product's price, do comparison shopping to make certain the product is not available elsewhere at a substantially lower price. A "zero interest" purchase will save you money only if you

♣ It's A Fact!!
"Zero Percent Interest" on a credit card: These offers usually are for limited purposes and time periods, such as no interest charges for three months on new purchases on any balance you transfer from another credit card. "This may be a good option, but you've got to read all the documentation and do the math," says Janet Kincaid, a senior consumer affairs officer with the Federal Deposit Insurance Corporation. For example, if you don't pay the balance by the due date, you will incur interest. Also find out if there's a balance transfer fee or an annual fee. These charges could be sizable—so high, in fact, that the zero-percent offer may cost more than a card with a higher interest rate but not the other fees.

Source: Excerpted from "There's No Such Thing as a Free-Lunch Loan," *FDIC Consumer News*, Spring 2002, Federal Deposit Insurance Corporation (www.fdic.gov).

are able to comply with the terms of the program and the purchase price is a reasonable one.

Can You Compare The Costs Of Paying For Things Over Time?

Unfortunately the answer is not always. In 1968, Congress passed the Truth in Lending Act requiring merchants to disclose to consumers borrowing money or purchasing goods over time the Annual Percentage Rate ("APR") of interest. For transactions regulated by that law, all merchants must compute the APR the same way and consumers can easily compare the cost of credit.

In recent years, however, alternative forms of consumer credit transactions, such as rent-to-own and auto leases, have emerged in the marketplace. For the time being, merchants using these forms of credit transactions are not required to disclose the APR. It is therefore extremely difficult for consumers to compare the cost of credit when entering into such transactions. Although it is not as accurate or easy as comparing APRs, consumers entering into these transactions need to find out the total amount of money they will end up spending under the contract. They can then compare that total cost with the total cost they will pay under other forms of credit. The bottom line is that consumers must always learn the cost of the credit before signing on the dotted line in any contract.

♣ It's A Fact!!

"Zero Percent Financing" on auto loans: Often these loans are for 12, 24, or 36 months, not the 48 or 60 months many people choose to keep monthly payments down. If you opt for a shorter loan term, be sure you can make the monthly payments. Also look for any hidden fees.

Source: Excerpted from "There's No Such Thing as a Free-Lunch Loan," *FDIC Consumer News*, Spring 2002, Federal Deposit Insurance Corporation (www.fdic.gov).

Chapter 34

The Truth About Advance-Fee Loan Scams

Advance-fee loan sharks are preying on unwary consumers, taking their money for the promise of a loan or credit, and leaving them in hot water. The scam artists often impersonate legitimate lenders to entice consumers into falling for their bogus offer.

Many advance-fee loans are promoted in the classified sections of daily and weekly newspapers and magazines. Often, the ads feature toll-free 800, 866, or 877 numbers, or area codes from Canada, such as 416, 647, 905, or 705. The loans also are promoted through direct mail, radio, and cable TV spots. The fact that an ad is in a legitimate media outlet—like the local newspaper or radio station—doesn't guarantee that the company placing it is trustworthy.

Legitimate offers of credit do not require an up-front payment. Although legitimate lenders may charge application, appraisal, or credit report fees, the fees generally are taken from the amount borrowed. And the fees usually are paid to the lender or broker after the loan is approved. Legitimate lenders may guarantee firm offers of credit to "credit-worthy" consumers, but first, they evaluate the consumer's creditworthiness and confirm the information in the application. Canadian law enforcers caution that it is highly

About This Chapter: "The Truth About Advance-Fee Loan Scams," Federal Trade Commission (http://www.ftc.gov), May 2005.

unlikely that legitimate Canadian lenders would take a risk on U.S. citizens whose credit problems preclude them from getting a loan in the U.S.

Often, advance-fee loan sharks claim that their fees will go to a third party for credit insurance or a related service. Sometimes, they even fax materials using stolen or forged logos and letterheads from legitimate companies. The materials are fakes, according to enforcement officials, and the contracts the scam artists ask consumers to sign are worthless. Adding insult to injury, some scammers have used the information they collect from consumers to commit identity theft.

☞ **Remember!!**

- Don't pay for the promise of a loan. It's illegal for companies doing business by phone in the U.S. to promise you a loan and ask you to pay for it before they deliver. Requiring advance fees for loans also is illegal in Canada.

- Check out questionable ads by calling Project Phonebusters in Canada toll-free at 888-495-8501. If you live in the U.S. and think you've been a victim of an advance-fee loan scam, report it to the Federal Trade Commission (FTC) online at http://www.ftc.gov or by phone, toll-free, at 877-FTC-HELP (877-382-4357).

Often, advance-fee loan scammers direct applicants to send the fees via Western Union money transfers payable to an individual, rather than a business. They ask applicants to use a "password code" with their Western Union payment, which allows the scammers to hide their identity.

Chapter 35

Be Wary Of "Gold" And "Platinum" Cards Offering "Easy Credit"

If you're looking for credit, be wary of some 'gold' or 'platinum' card offers promising to get you credit cards or improve your credit rating.

While sounding like general-purpose credit cards, some 'gold' or 'platinum' cards permit you to buy merchandise only from specialized catalogues. Marketers of these credit cards often promise that by participating in their credit programs, you will be able to get major credit cards (such as an unsecured Visa or MasterCard), lines of credit from national specialty and department stores, better credit reports, and other financial benefits.

Rarely, however, can you improve your credit rating or get major credit cards by buying 'gold' or 'platinum' credit cards. Often the only major credit card you might get is a secured credit card that requires a substantial security deposit with a bank. In addition, many of these credit-card offerors do not report to credit bureaus as they promise, and their cards seldom help secure lines of credit with other creditors.

Watch Out

Be wary of 'gold' and 'platinum' card promotions that:

About This Chapter: "Gold and Platinum Cards," Federal Trade Commission (http://www.ftc.gov), October 1996.

- Charge upfront fees, without saying there may be additional costs.

- Use '900' or '976' telephone exchanges.

- Misrepresent prices and payments for merchandise.

- Promise to easily get you "better credit."

How To Protect Yourself

Follow these precautions to avoid becoming a victim of 'gold' and 'platinum' card scams:

♣ **It's A Fact!!**

'Gold' and 'platinum' credit-card offers usually are promoted through television or newspaper advertisements, direct mail, or telephone solicitations using automatic dialing machines and recorded messages. People who live in lower-income areas often are the target of these sales pitches.

Think twice about any offer to get "easy credit." Be skeptical of promises to erase bad credit or to secure major credit cards regardless of your past credit problems.

Investigate an offer before enrolling. Contact your local Better Business Bureau, consumer protection agency, or state Attorney General's office to see if any complaints have been filed against a particular promoter of 'gold' or 'platinum' cards. If a marketer promises that a card is accepted at certain retail chains, verify it with the stores. If a marketer assures you that reliable information about you will be reported to credit bureaus, call the bureaus to confirm that the merchant is a member. Unless 'gold' or 'platinum' card merchants are subscribers to credit bureaus, they won't be able to report information about your credit experience.

Be cautious about calling '900' or '976' telephone numbers. Calls to numbers with '900' or '976' prefixes cost money. Don't confuse these exchanges with toll-free '800' numbers. If you dial a pay-per-call number mistakenly, contact your local phone company immediately. They may be able to remove the charge from your bill.

Part Five

Preventing And Resolving
Debt-Related Problems

Chapter 36

How To Avoid Common Debt Mistakes

Everybody makes mistakes with their money. The important thing is to keep them to a minimum. And one of the best ways to accomplish that is to learn from the mistakes of others. Here is the Federal Deposit Insurance Corporation's list of the top mistakes young people (and even many not-so-young people) make with their money, and what you can do to avoid these mistakes in the first place.

Buying Items You Don't Need (and paying extra for them in interest): Every time you have an urge to do a little "impulse buying" and you use your credit card but you don't pay in full by the due date, you could be paying interest on that purchase for months or years to come. Spending money for something you really don't need can be a big waste of your money. But you can make the matter worse, a lot worse, by putting the purchase on a credit card and paying monthly interest charges.

Research major purchases and comparison shop before you buy. Ask yourself if you really need the item. Even better, wait a day or two, or just a few hours, to think things over rather than making a quick and costly decision you may come to regret.

About This Chapter: "If at First You Don't Succeed," *FDIC Consumer News*, Federal Deposit Insurance Corporation (FDIC), 2005.

There are good reasons to pay for major purchases with a credit card, such as extra protections if you have problems with the items. But if you charge a purchase with a credit card instead of paying by cash, check, or debit card (which automatically deducts the money from your bank account), be smart about how you repay. For example, take advantage of offers of "zero-percent interest" on credit card purchases for a certain number of months (but understand when and how interest charges could begin).

♣ It's A Fact!!

If you pay only the minimum payment due on a $1,000 computer, let's say it's about $20 a month, your total cost at an annual percentage rate (APR) of more than 18 percent can be close to $3,000, and it will take you nearly 19 years to pay it off.

And, pay the entire balance on your credit card or as much as you can to avoid or minimize interest charges, which can add up significantly.

"If you pay only the minimum amount due on your credit card, you may end up paying more in interest charges than what the item cost you to begin with," said Janet Kincaid, FDIC (Federal Deposit Insurance Corporation) Senior Consumer Affairs Officer.

Getting Too Deeply In Debt: Being able to borrow allows us to buy clothes or computers, take a vacation, or purchase a home or a car. But taking on too much debt can be a problem, and each year millions of adults of all ages find themselves struggling to pay their loans, credit cards, and other bills.

Learn to be a good money manager by following the basic strategies outlined in this chapter. Also recognize the warning signs of a serious debt problem. These may include borrowing money to make payments on loans you already have, deliberately paying bills late, and putting off doctor visits or other important activities because you think you don't have enough money.

If you believe you're experiencing debt overload, take corrective measures. For example, try to pay off your highest interest-rate loans (usually your credit cards) as soon as possible, even if you have higher balances on other loans. For new purchases, instead of using your credit card, try paying with cash, a check, or a debit card.

"There are also reliable credit counselors you can turn to for help at little or no cost," added Rita Wiles Ross, an FDIC attorney. "Unfortunately, you also need to be aware that there are scams masquerading as 'credit repair clinics' and other companies, such as 'debt consolidators,' that may charge big fees for unfulfilled promises or services you can perform on your own."

Paying Bills Late Or Otherwise Tarnishing Your Reputation: Companies called credit bureaus prepare credit reports for use by lenders, employers, insurance companies, landlords, and others who need to know someone's financial reliability, based largely on each person's track record paying bills and debts. Credit bureaus, lenders, and other companies also produce "credit scores" that attempt to summarize and evaluate a person's credit record using a point system.

While one or two late payments on your loans or other regular commitments (such as rent or phone bills) over a long period may not seriously damage your credit record, making a habit of it will count against you. Over time you could be charged a higher interest rate on your credit card or a loan that you really want and need. You could be turned down for a job or an apartment. It could cost you extra when you apply for auto insurance. Your credit record will also be damaged by a bankruptcy filing or a court order to pay money as a result of a lawsuit.

✔ **Quick Tip**

For more guidance on how to get out of debt safely or find a reputable credit counselor, start at the Federal Trade Commission (FTC) website at www.ftc.gov/bcp/conline/edcams/credit/coninfo _debt.

So, pay your monthly bills on time. Also, periodically review your credit reports from the nation's three major credit bureaus—Equifax, Experian and TransUnion— to make sure their information accurately reflects the accounts you have and your payment history, especially if you intend to apply for credit for something important in the near future.

Having Too Many Credit Cards: Two to four cards (including any from department stores, oil companies, and other retailers) is the right number for most adults. Why not more cards?

The more credit cards you carry, the more inclined you may be to use them for costly impulse buying. In addition, each card you own—even the ones you don't use—represents money that you could borrow up to the card's spending limit. If you apply for new credit you will be seen as someone who, in theory, could get much deeper in debt and you may only qualify for a smaller or costlier loan.

Also be aware that card companies aggressively market their products on college campuses, at concerts, ball games, or other events often attended by young adults. Their offers may seem tempting and even harmless—perhaps a free T-shirt or Frisbee, or 10 percent off your first purchase if you just fill out an application for a new card—but you've got to consider the possible consequences we've just described. "Don't sign up for a credit card just to get a great-looking T-shirt," Kincaid added. "You may be better off buying that shirt at the store for $14.95 and saving yourself the potential costs and troubles from that extra card."

Not Watching Your Expenses: It's very easy to overspend in some areas and take away from other priorities, including your long-term savings. Our suggestion is to try any system—ranging from a computer-based budget program to hand-written notes—that will help you keep track of your spending each month and enable you to set and stick to limits you consider appropriate. "A budget doesn't have to be complicated, intimidating, or painful—just something that works for you in getting a handle on your spending," said Kincaid.

Not Saving For Your Future: We know it can be tough to scrape together enough money to pay for a place to live, a car, and other expenses each month. But experts say it's also important for young people to save money for their long-term goals, too, including perhaps buying a home, owning a business, or saving for your retirement (even though it may be 40 or 50 years away).

Start by "paying yourself first." That means even before you pay your bills each month you should put money into savings for your future. Often the simplest way is to arrange with your bank or employer to automatically transfer a certain amount each month to a savings account or to purchase a U.S. Savings Bond or an investment, such as a mutual fund that buys stocks and bonds.

Even if you start with just $25 or $50 a month you'll be significantly closer to your goal. "The important thing is to start saving as early as you can—even saving for your retirement when that seems light-years away—so you can benefit from the effect of compound interest," said Donna Gambrell, a Deputy Director of the FDIC's Division of Supervision and Consumer Protection. Compound interest refers to when an investment earns interest, and later that combined amount earns more interest, and on and on until a much larger sum of money is the result after many years.

Banking institutions pay interest on savings accounts that they offer. However, bank deposits aren't the only way to make your money grow. "Investments, which include stocks, bonds, and mutual funds, can be attractive alternatives to bank deposits because they often provide a higher rate of return over long periods, but remember that there is the potential for a temporary or permanent loss in value," said James Williams, an FDIC Consumer Affairs Specialist. "Young people especially should do their research and consider getting professional advice before putting money into investments."

Paying Too Much In Fees: Whenever possible, use your own financial institution's automated teller machines or the ATMs owned by financial institutions that don't charge fees to non-customers. You can pay $1 to $4 in fees if you get cash from an ATM that isn't owned by your financial institution or isn't part of an ATM "network" that your bank belongs to.

Try not to "bounce" checks—that is, writing checks for more money than you have in your account, which can trigger fees from your financial institution (about $15 to $30 for each check) and from merchants. The best precaution is to keep your checkbook up to date and closely monitor your balance, which is easier to do with online and telephone banking.

☞ Remember!!
Remember to record your debit card transactions from ATMs and merchants so that you will be sure to have enough money in your account when those withdrawals are processed by you bank.

Financial institutions also offer "overdraft protection" services that can help you avoid the embarrassment and inconvenience of having a check returned to a merchant. But be careful before signing up because these programs come with their own costs.

Pay off your credit card balance each month, if possible, so you can avoid or minimize interest charges. Also send in your payment on time to avoid additional fees. If you don't expect to pay your credit card bill in full most months, consider using a card with a low interest rate and a generous "grace period" (the number of days before the card company starts charging you interest on new purchases).

Not Taking Responsibility For Your Finances: Do a little comparison shopping to find accounts that match your needs at the right cost. Be sure to review your bills and bank statements as soon as possible after they arrive or monitor your accounts periodically online or by telephone. You want to make sure there are no errors, unauthorized charges, or indications that a thief is using your identity to commit fraud.

"Many young people don't take the time to check their receipts or make the necessary phone calls or write letters to correct a problem," one banker told FDIC Consumer News. "Resolving these issues can be time consuming and exhausting but doing so can add up to hundreds of dollars."

☞ **Remember!!**
Remember that being financially independent doesn't mean you're entirely on your own. There are always government agencies, including the FDIC and the other organizations that can help with your questions or problems. A great resource provided by the FDIC that contains more information on organizations that can help you can be found at http://www.fdic.gov/consumers/consumer/news/cnspr05/info.html.

Even if you are fortunate enough to have parents or other loved ones you can turn to for help or advice as you start handling money on your own, it's really up to you to take charge of your finances. Doing so can be intimidating for anyone. It's easy to become overwhelmed or frustrated. And everyone makes mistakes. The important thing is to take action.

Start small if you need to. Stretch to pay an extra $50 a month on your credit card bill or other debts. Find two or three ways to cut your spending. Put an extra $50 a month into a savings account. Even little changes can add up to big savings over time.

Chapter 37

Avoiding Costly Banking Mistakes

Avoiding Costly Banking Mistakes: No Trivial Pursuit

To err is human...and sometimes it can be expensive. That's the case for many consumers who have to pay fees and penalties because of mistakes they've made when using banking services. The Federal Deposit Insurance Corporation (FDIC) wants you to know about some of the more common and costly slip-ups.

Not Checking Up On Your Checking Account

Many people write checks and use their debit card without paying attention to their account balance. The results can be costly and may include fees from $20 to $35 for each "bounced" check you write when you don't have enough money in your account. Similar fees can be imposed if you overdraw your account using your debit card at the ATM. There may also be fees if your checking account goes below a required minimum balance. And, if you fail to spot fraudulent transactions, fixing those can be costly and time consuming.

About This Chapter: This chapter includes information from articles the originally appeared in *FDIC Consumer*, Federal Deposit Insurance Corporation (FDIC): "Avoiding Costly Banking Mistakes: No Trivial Pursuit," Fall 2006; "High-Tech Banking, 24/7," Spring 2005; "Shopping for a Bank Account That Fits Your Style," Summer 2006; "The Right Way to Right a Wrong: How to Fix a Problem with a Financial Institution," Spring 2005; and "Five Things You Should Know About Checks and Checking Accounts," Spring 2005.

Your lack of attention could make a bad situation worse if fees are assessed for several days or even months. "Account holders can get very frustrated when they suddenly find out that multiple checks and payments have been returned, and a fee has been assessed for each one," said Eloy Villafranca, a Community Affairs Officer with the FDIC.

Villafranca recalled a situation involving a consumer who "was confident that her bank statements were correct so she didn't open them for six months." Unfortunately for her, a recurring, electronic payment she thought had been stopped continued to be charged against her account, and her account balance was lower than she thought. "As she wrote checks month after month," Villafranca explained, "she was being hit with charges for insufficient funds."

✔ Quick Tip
How can you avoid unnecessary costs?

- Keep your check register up to date. Deduct for all withdrawals—not only for checks but also for ATM transactions, bank fees, and debit card purchases. Do not rely on your ATM receipt for balance information because it may not reflect outstanding checks or debit card transactions.

- Promptly compare your check register with your bank statement to look for errors or unauthorized transactions. Open and review your monthly statement as soon as it arrives in the mail or check your account information more frequently online or by telephone.

- Take additional precautions to avoid fees for insufficient funds. For instance, make sure you have enough money in your account before you write a big check, use your debit card, or arrange for an automatic payment. Also remember that, under federal rules that allow banking institutions to put a temporary "hold" on certain deposits, you may have to wait from one to five business days (in most situations) before you can withdraw funds deposited into your account, and longer in other circumstances (such as deposits over $5,000 or if your account has been repeatedly overdrawn).

Source: Federal Deposit Insurance Corporation, 2006.

Remember!!

Remember that just because an account is advertised as "free" or "no cost" doesn't mean you'll pay nothing. Under Federal Reserve Board rules, an account may be described as free even if certain fees are charged, such as for ATM withdrawals or overdrafts.

Source: Federal Deposit Insurance Corporation, 2006.

Be aware that if bounced checks are not repaid in a timely fashion they may become part of your record. That could make it difficult to get a merchant to accept your checks. And if your account is closed by the bank because of repeated problems with insufficient funds that you do not repay, you may have difficulty opening a new account elsewhere.

Not Considering Fees When Opening A Bank Account

A high interest rate or annual percentage yield (APY) on a checking account is definitely an attention grabber. But that great rate shouldn't divert your attention from fees that can significantly reduce, if not wipe out, your earnings. Examples include monthly fees for going below a minimum balance, monthly or quarterly "inactivity" fees if you've had no deposits or withdrawals for a certain time period, and annual service charges on individual retirement accounts (IRAs).

To get the best deal possible, first think about how you plan to use the account and how much you expect to keep on deposit, then compare different accounts at a few different institutions. Do the math as best you can, figuring your interest earnings after a year and then subtract the estimated fees for services or a low balance based on your expected use of the account. Sometimes an account that pays no interest can be a better deal than an interest-bearing account that's heavy with fees you are likely to pay.

High-Tech Banking, 24/7

For young adults today, it's hard to imagine life without gadgets and high-tech helpers. There are several attractive electronic banking services beyond ATMs that you should know about.

- **Internet Banking** (online banking): Enables you to transfer money between your accounts at the same bank and view account information, deposits as well as loans, at any time.

- **Internet Bill Paying:** Allows you to pay monthly and one-time bills over the internet. Some banks offer electronic bill payment free of charge, others charge a fee that is usually less than what you would spend on postage.

- **Debit Cards:** Look like credit cards but they automatically withdraw the money you want from your account. You can use a debit card to get cash from an ATM or to pay for purchases.

- **Direct Deposit:** Enables your paycheck and certain other payments to be transmitted automatically to your bank account. "Direct deposit is free and it's fast—there's no waiting for the check to arrive at home and no waiting in the teller lines," said Kathryn Weatherby, an Examination Specialist for the FDIC.

- **Telephone Banking:** Allows you to use your touch-tone phone to confirm that a check or deposit has cleared, get your latest balance, transfer money between separate accounts at the same bank, and obtain details about services.

- **Automatic Withdrawals:** Withdrawals from your bank account can be arranged free of charge to pay recurring bills (such as phone bills or insurance premiums) or to systematically put a certain amount of money into a savings account, a U.S. Savings Bond, or an investment.

♣ It's A Fact!!

One example of a common bank product is a "certificate of deposit," which enables you to earn a higher interest rate the longer you leave the money untouched in the bank, but these accounts usually require a large amount of money (perhaps $1,000 or more) to open. But many banks also offer special savings accounts designed just for young people and can be opened with very little money.

Source: FDIC, Summer 2006.

"Your banking can be so much more convenient and easier to monitor and control when you have access to your accounts 24 hours a day, seven days a week, from your home or practically anywhere else," added Weatherby.

However, she also stressed the need to take security precautions with your electronic transactions and your computer.

Shopping For A Bank Account That Fits Your Style

How To Choose And Use A Checking Or Savings Product

You probably started saving money years ago in a piggy bank and may now have another favorite place at home to stash your cash. That's fine for smaller bills and coins, but what if you've got checks and large sums of money from birthday gifts or your job? Maybe your parents (or other trusted adults) have been keeping your money in their bank accounts. Now may be a good time to talk with them about opening your own bank account which, if you are under 18, you'll probably have to do with their help.

There are lots of good reasons for opening a checking or savings account at a bank, including these:

- **Safety:** Money in the bank is better protected against loss or theft than it is at home. And if the bank has financial troubles and goes out of business, your FDIC-insured money will be fully protected.

- **More Ways To Save:** Banks offer several different ways to save money and earn interest, which is what banks pay customers to keep their money in the bank. "It's also less tempting to spend your money if it's in the bank rather than in your room," said Sachie Tanaka, an FDIC Consumer Affairs Specialist.

- **Easy Access:** Bank customers have different ways to send or receive their money—from going to the bank to writing checks or using the internet from home. Some banks even have "branches" at schools. If your parents approve, you also may want to start using a debit card to make purchases. It looks like a credit card but you won't pay interest or get into debt because the money is automatically deducted from your bank account.

Whether you open a checking or savings account, it pays to be smart in how you choose and use the account. Here are some suggestions:

Shop around for a good deal before you open an account. Banks usually offer several accounts to choose from with different features, fees, interest rates, opening balance requirements, and so on. These accounts also may differ significantly from bank to bank. Some banks have special accounts for teens and even younger kids featuring parental controls on withdrawals.

> **☞ Remember!!**
> Keep your account records up to date. Record all transactions—deposits and withdrawals.
>
> Source: Federal Deposit Insurance Corporation, 2006.

It's usually best to choose an account that takes very little money to start and involves low fees or no fees for having the account. "The fees charged may be more important than any interest you may earn on the account, especially if the account has a small balance," said James Williams, an FDIC Consumer Affairs Specialist.

Pay attention to your bank statements and immediately report any errors. If your account has a minimum balance requirement, avoid going below it. Your bank may charge you a fee, which would mean less money in your account.

Use the account responsibly. Even a "free" checking account can involve some fees, such as when you use another bank's ATM to withdraw money, so do your best to keep costs down. Also, never share your account numbers, bank cards or passwords with friends or strangers—this could give them access to your money.

The Right Way To Right A Wrong: How To Fix A Problem With A Financial Institution

Got a question or a complaint involving a financial institution but you're not sure about the best or quickest ways to resolve the matter? Here's a good game plan.

1. Contact the institution directly. Experience has shown that's the quickest way to resolve most problems. Also keep your cool. Be as professional as possible.

2. Put your complaint in writing, even if you also call the institution. Some consumer protection laws require that written complaints be filed. Be sure to send your letter to the address that the institution recommends for complaints and keep a copy of all correspondence and supporting documents. With phone calls, get the name of the person you spoke to and keep good notes of your conversation, including the date.

3. Act as soon as possible. Some laws require consumers to report a problem within a certain time period to be fully protected.

4. If you can't fix a problem on your own you may contact the institution's government regulator for help or guidance. To find out who regulates a bank or other deposit-taking institution, you can write or call the FDIC (http://www.fdic.gov). Find contact information and tips for solving problems with non-bank financial companies, such as insurance companies or brokerage firms, at http://www.consumeraction.gov.

Five Things You Should Know About Checks And Checking Accounts

1. Shop around for a good deal, preferably an account without a monthly maintenance fee. Banks usually offer several accounts to choose from with different features, fees, interest rates, opening balance requirements, and so on.

☞ Remember!!

Remember that what's good for your
parents or your friends may not be best for you.

Source: Federal Deposit Insurance Corporation, 2005.

2. Keep your checkbook up to date by recording all transactions, including ATM withdrawals, bank fees, purchases you make using a debit card, and any other deductions that do not involve writing a check. Also, promptly compare your checkbook with your monthly statement or review your account information online or by telephone.

3. Avoid "overdrawing your account," which can happen if you write a check or otherwise attempt to withdraw (by mistake) more money than you have in your account. It also is possible to overdraw your account using your debit card at the ATM or when making a purchase. These transactions can be costly.

4. Consider internet (online) banking. This service allows you to make payments or move money from one account to another through your bank's website instead of (or in addition to) writing and mailing paper checks. This saves on the costs of postage and buying paper checks. Online banking also allows you to monitor your account without having to wait for a statement in the mail.

5. Pay attention to your bank statements. Immediately report any errors or unauthorized transactions (to protect yourself from accusations that you were negligent in managing your account). Look at your statement as soon as possible after it arrives in the mail or monitor your account more regularly on the internet or through your bank's telephone banking service.

Chapter 38

How To Budget And Save

As a consumer, you face many choices on how to manage your money.

Knowing how to manage money can help you make smart choices. Your money will work harder for you. You'll be more likely to avoid traps that can undermine your ability to attain your financial goals. You'll be in a better position to pay off debt and build savings.

Being smart about money can help you buy a house, finance higher education, or start a retirement fund. A money management game plan can help you get started and stay with it until you achieve the goals you set for yourself.

A Game Plan For Learning About Money Management

A few simple steps can make a big difference in making your money work harder for you.

Establish goals. Where do you want to be?

Use the work sheets in Figures 38.1, 38.2, and 38.3 to help you identify your goals. Print them and fill them in.

About This Chapter: Reprinted from "How to Budget and Save," an online financial education publication of the Federal Reserve Bank of Chicago, http://www.chicagofed.org, 2006.

Without goals, it's difficult to accomplish anything. When you think about your future and what you want to achieve, it's helpful to establish a timeframe.

- **Short-Term:** Such as paying off credit card debt, saving for a vacation or buying new clothes

- **Intermediate:** Such as saving to buy a car

- **Long-Term:** Such as saving for education or for retirement.

Estimate the cost of each goal and the date you want to achieve it. Then figure out how much you need to save each month. Try to set realistic goals and saving requirements.

Short-term Goals	Cost	Completion Date	Saving Needed per Month
Example: Vacation*	$1,200	12 months	$100
*For example, if your goal is to save for a vacation that will cost $1,200, you need to save $100 for 12 months. (Please note that these examples do not include the interest that would accrue over time.			

Figure 38.1. Short-Term Goals.

Intermediate-term Goals	Cost	Completion Date	Saving Needed per Month
Example: Car*	$18,000	36 months	$500
*For example, if your goal is to buy a car that costs $18,000 in three years, you need to save $500 for 36 months.			

Figure 38.2. Intermediate-Term Goals.

Long-term Goals	Cost	Completion Date	Saving Needed per Month
Example: Educational Fund*	$36,000	60 months	$600
*For example, if your goal is to save for an education costing $36,000 you need to save $600 a month for 60 months.			

Figure 38.3. Long-Term Goals.

Create a budget. Determine your current situation. Where are you today?

Now that you've figured out your financial goals, you are ready to create a budget that will help you attain them. Print the budget work sheets shown in Figure 38.4 and write in your budget figures. Start by writing down your expenses (under Current Monthly Expenses).

Current Monthly Expenses

Fixed	
Savings	$
Rent/Mortgage	$
Gas (Cooking/Heating)	$
Electric	$
Water/Sewer/Trash	$
Home Upkeep/Repairs	$
Home Insurance	$
Life Insurance	$
Disability Insurance	$
Auto Insurance	$
Telephone	$
Groceries	$
Car Loans	$
Car Stickers/License	$
Bus, Train, Cabs	$
Laundry/Dry Cleaning	$
Haircuts/Hair Care Cosmetics	$
Newspapers/Publications	$
Other	$
Other	$
Other	$
Other	$
Total Fixed Expenses:	$

Variable	
Credit Card Bills	$
Other Loans	$
Clothing/Shoes	$
Gasoline	$
Parking/Tolls	$
Car Maintenance	$
Postage	$
Restaurants	$
Entertainment	$
Charity	$
Gifts	$
Vacation	$
Tobacco/Beverages	$
Medical/Dental/Prescriptions	$
Eye Glasses/Contacts	$
Home Cleaning Supplies	$
Personal	$
Other	$
Other	$
Other	$
Total Variable Expenses:	$
	$
Total Expenses:	$

Monthly Income

Wages/Salary	$
(after taxes & deductions)	$
Part-time Work	$
Child Support/Alimony	$
Other	$
Other	$
Other	$
Other	$
Total Net Income:	$

Financial Summary

Total Net Income	$
Minus Total Expenses	$
Surplus or Deficit:*	$

*If you are spending less than you are bringing home, you have a surplus; otherwise, you have a deficit.

Your monthly surplus or deficit:	$

Figure 38.4. Create A Budget

Monthly Fixed Expenses: Start with monthly fixed expenses such as regular savings, housing, groceries, utilities, and car payments. Put these continuing obligations under the heading: Fixed.

Use checking account statements, credit card statements, receipts, and other records to help you complete this estimate. Be realistic—it's better to estimate high than low.

Remember that savings is considered an expense even though you keep the money. You work hard. You deserve to keep some of what you earn every month. Savings is the key to meeting your financial goals.

Make estimates for all money spent—regardless of how you pay: cash, check, credit card, debit card, automatic checking account withdrawals, or savings through work plans such as 401K or 403B plans.

Monthly Variable Expenses: Once you have noted all your fixed expenses, write down your expenses that vary each month such as clothing, vacations, gifts, and personal spending money. Put these expenses under the heading: Variable. You might have these expenses every month, but the amount you spend could change.

Get a handle on variable expenses by writing down every expense for a month—even small purchases. Use a small note book or other informal method to track your spending. This is very important because it's the best way to understand your current spending behavior. Get receipts for all purchases—especially those you make with cash. Record and categorize each transaction. You may be surprised at how much you spend in certain categories.

Use a notebook to write down every purchase you make for one month. This is the best way to understand your current spending behavior.

List Your Monthly Income: Now that you have figured out your expenses, write down your monthly income after all taxes and deductions. Write this under the heading: Monthly Income. Make sure this figure reflects the total take-home pay for your household after all taxes and deductions.

Now Compare Expenses To Income: One of the advantages of doing a comparison of expenses to income is that it provides a quick reality check. If you are spending more than you're bringing home every month in income, you have a deficit. If you're spending less than you're bringing home, you have a surplus. In either case, it's time to step back and consider some options.

If you have a deficit—spending more than you're bringing home—ask yourself:

• Can I spend less in some of my variable expenses?

• How much interest am I paying with credit card and other loans?

- Where did my money go? (Consider writing down everything you spend for a month.

If you have a surplus—spending less than you're bringing home—ask yourself:

- Am I saving enough to meet my goals?
- Are my spending estimates accurate?
- Have I included all my fixed and variable expenses?

♣ **It's A Fact!!**

Why Build An Emergency Fund

Having an emergency savings fund may be the most important difference between those who manage to stay afloat and those who are sinking financially. That's because maintaining emergency savings of $500 to $1,000 allows you to easily meet unexpected financial challenges.

The emergency fund not only allows you to cover these expenses, it also gives you the "peace of mind" that you can afford these types of financial emergencies. Not having an emergency savings fund is an important reason that many individuals borrow too much money at high interest rates. For example, with emergency savings, Americans probably would not have to take out $2 billion a year in payday loans at interest rates that average 300 to 500 percent.

Where To Keep Emergency Savings

It's usually best to keep emergency savings in a bank or credit union savings account. These types of accounts offer easier access to your money than certificates of deposit, U.S. Savings Bonds, or mutual funds.

But not too easy. Keeping your money in a savings account makes it much less likely that you will use these savings to pay for everyday, non-emergency expenses. That's why it is usually a mistake to keep your emergency fund in a checking account.

Source: From "The Importance of Emergency Savings", © 2007 America Saves. All rights reserved. For additional information, visit www.americasaves.org.

Ages And Stages Of Money Management: A To-Do List

✔ **Quick Tip**

To successfully reach your financial goals, a lot depends on what you do and when. Here are just a few ideas young adults can consider at key stages of their life.

You're In High School

- Consider earning money outside of your home, whether it's baby-sitting, lawn mowing, or working in a movie theater or another "real" business. A job can provide a sense of accomplishment and responsibility. It also can be a good opportunity to learn about careers and to "network" with professionals.

- Learn the concept of "paying yourself first"—that is, automatically putting some money into savings or investments before you're tempted to spend it. Start small if you have to and gradually build up.

- Consider opening a bank account, either on your own or with a parent or other adult. It's a good way to learn about managing money. You also may want to start using a debit card—you can use it to make purchases but you won't pay interest or get into debt because the money is automatically deducted from your bank account.

- Take a personal finance class or join an investment club at school.

- If you're planning to go to college, learn about your options for saving or borrowing money for what will be a major expense.

- If you (and your parents) are comfortable with getting a credit card, you should know that there are cards designed just for teens. One is a credit card with a low credit limit that can keep you from getting deeply in debt. Another is a pre-paid card that comes with parental controls, including spending limits.

Save Your Way To A More Secure Future

An estimated seventy-five percent of families will experience a major financial setback in any given ten-year period. The economy and the job market are good now, but that could change. It's smart to be prepared for financial thunderstorms.

You're In College

- Realize that as you pay bills and debts on your own you are building a "credit record" that could be important when you apply for a loan or a job in the future. Pay your bills on time...and borrow only what you can repay.

- If you decide to get your own credit card, choose carefully. Take your time, understand the risks as well as the rewards, and do some comparison shopping. Don't apply for a credit card just because you received an invitation in the mail or a sales person was offering a free gift on campus.

- Protect your Social Security number (SSN), credit card numbers, and other personal information from thieves who use someone else's identity to commit fraud. Examples: Use your SSN as identification only if absolutely necessary and never provide it to a stranger. Safeguard your personal information when using the internet or borrowing a computer provided by your school.

- Consider a paying job or even an unpaid internship at a workplace related to a career you're considering.

- If possible, set aside money into savings and investments.

- Try to take a class in personal finance. Read money-related magazine and newspaper articles.

Source: Excerpted from "Ages and Stages of Money Management: A To-Do List," *FDIC Consumer News*, Federal Deposit Insurance Corporation (FDIC), Spring 2005.

Save Early, Save Often: A consistent, long-term saving program can help you achieve your goals. It also can help you build a financial safety net. Experts recommend that you save from three to six months worth of living expenses for emergencies.

Savings grow beyond what you contribute because of compound interest. Over time, the value of compound interest works to every saver's advantage. For example, if you save $75 a month for five years and earn five-percent interest, the $4,500 you contributed would grow to $5,122 because of the compounding interest.

It's easy to figure out how long it will take you to double the money you save. It's called the Rule of 72. You take the interest you're earning on your money and divide that number into 72. The result is roughly the number of years it will take your principal to double. For example, if you're earning 5 percent on your money, you divide 72 by 5 and you get 14.4. Your principal will double in 14.4 years without further contributions.

Keep in mind, however, that inflation reduces the return on your money. For example, five percent-interest, adjusted for three-percent inflation, only nets a two-percent real return.

What You Don't See, You Don't Spend: Saving means giving up something now, so you will have more in the future. It's not easy deferring or eliminating purchasing things you want today.

It helps to pay yourself first. Take a portion of savings from every paycheck before you pay any bills. Use your company's payroll deduction plan if available. Arrange for a fixed amount to be taken out so that you never see it. What you don't see, you don't spend. You also can direct automatic checking account withdrawals into a savings account or money market.

Join the company's retirement-savings plan (such as a 401K or 403B). Your contribution avoids current taxes and accumulates tax deferred. Also, companies sometimes match some of your contributions. For example, for every dollar you contribute, the company could contribute 25 cents. That would be a 25-percent return on your money.

Here are some other saving tips:

• When you get a raise, save all or most of it.

• Pay off your credit card balances and save the money you're no longer spending on interest.

✔ Quick Tip
Simple, Everyday Things You Can Do To Save Money

Everyone can use a little guidance on how to save more money. Here are some suggestions for simple things you can do.

Set Goals: "Saving money now for use in the future gets easier if you know what you want and how much you'll need," said Janet Kincaid, Senior Consumer Affairs Officer with the Federal Deposit Insurance Corporation (FDIC). It helps to set savings goals you can easily achieve. If you want to buy a $500 item within the next year, plan to save $50 a month for 10 months, which is just $12.50 a week. (We're not including any "interest" you could earn on your savings.)

Have A Strategy: Every time you receive money—from your allowance, a gift, a summer job or some other source—try to automatically put some of it into savings instead of spending it. That approach to saving money is known as "paying yourself first."

Here's One Suggestion: Consider putting about 25 percent ($1 out of every $4) or more into savings that you intend to let build for a few years, perhaps for a down payment on your first car. Separately you can save a similar amount of money for clothes, video games, electronics or other items you might want to buy within the next few months. With what's left, keep some handy for spending money (maybe for snacks or a movie) and also consider donating some of your money to charity.

Cut Back, Not Out: Are you spending $5 a week on snacks? If you save $2 by cutting back, after a year you'll have $104 to put in a savings or investment account that earns interest.

Source: From "Simple, Everyday Things You Can Do to Save Money," *FDIC Consumer News*, Federal Deposit Insurance Corporation (FDIC), Summer 2006.

- Shift credit card balances to a card with a lower interest rate and use the savings to pay off the balance.

- Keep your car a year or two longer. Do routine maintenance and make regular repairs. Save the money you would have spent on a new car.

- Stop smoking.

- Take $5 from your wallet everyday and put it in a safe place. That will add up to $1,825 in a year.

- Shop with a list and stick to it.

- Don't buy any new clothes until you've paid off your current wardrobe.

- Eat more meals at home.

- Look for inexpensive entertainment: zoos, museums, parks, walks, biking, library books, concerts, movies, and picnics.

- Shop for less expensive insurance.

- Save any tax refund.

- Drop subscriptions to publications you don't read.

- Postpone purchases or consider fewer features on the items you plan to purchase.

The less you spend, the more you can save. And the longer you can consistently save, the faster your savings will grow.

Conserve—Spend Sensibly; Pay Wisely

Experts recommend paying with cash whenever possible. This helps you spend less than you otherwise would have spent if you had charged the purchase. You'll also avoid credit card interest charges and check-cashing fees.

Applying For A Credit Card: When you choose to apply for a credit card, shop carefully. There is a wide range of annual fees, interest rates, grace periods for which you do not pay interest, late fee charges, cash advance charges and other fees. Watch out for "teaser" rates that offer low rates initially but increase dramatically soon after.

To get a card with a low interest rate, you'll first need to pay down your current debt. Second, let a year go by without applying for any new cards or loans, or accepting a higher credit limit on your current cards. Third, cancel cards you're not currently using. As a rule, limit yourself to two credit cards. Fourth, get a copy of your credit report and check it for accuracy.

Credit Cards: Visa, MasterCard, and Discover are revolving-credit cards. You can charge up to a certain limit and carry most of the balance forward from month to month. Be careful about only paying the minimum amount due. This is a very expensive form of credit because of interest charges. The best rule is to charge only what you can afford to pay off in full every month. Then actually pay the entire balance when you get the bill.

When you are paying down credit card debt, start with the card with the highest interest rate. Pay your bills as quickly as possible.

Charge Cards: Some cards require that you pay the balance every month. They provide the convenience of not using cash and the discipline of requiring that you pay what you owe every thirty days.

Charge cards also provide the additional benefit of not charging interest, although you may pay an annual fee and other transaction fees.

♣ It's A Fact!!
How A Small Savings Account Can Get Big Over Time

People who put even a small amount of money into a savings account as often as they can and leave it untouched for years may be amazed at how big the account grows. The reason? A combination of saving as much as possible on a regular basis and the impact of interest payments (what the financial world calls "the miracle of compounding").

Here's how you can slowly build a large savings account and experience the miracle of compounding. Let's say you put money into a savings account that pays you interest every month. After the first month, the interest payment will be calculated based on the money you put in. But the next time the bank pays you interest, it will calculate the amount based on your original deposit plus the interest you received the previous month. Later, that larger, combined amount will earn more interest, and after many years it becomes a much larger sum of money. The earnings are called compound interest. You can earn even more in compound interest if you make deposits regularly and stretch to put in as much as you can and leave it untouched. For example, assume you start with a savings account with $50 earning interest at a rate of 3.5 percent each month. If you add just $10 each month, the account can grow nicely to $714 after five years. If you instead put in a slightly higher amount—$15 each month—you'd have a balance of $1,042 after five years. But if you had increased your deposits to $50 a month, those extra dollars plus the compounding of interest would give you a balance of $3,333 after five years.

Source: From *FDIC Consumer News*, Federal Deposit Insurance Corporation (FDIC), Summer 2006.

Debit Cards: A debit card looks like a credit card, but it works like the electronic equivalent of a check. You use it when you want to pay cash instead of using credit. When you pay with a debit card, your checking account will be debited for the amount of the purchase.

ATM cards (automated teller machine) are debit cards. They automatically withdraw money from your account.

Some consumers prefer to use debit cards rather than credit cards because debit cards don't incur interest charges.

✔ Quick Tip
Five Ways To Cut Spending...
And Still Get To Do And Buy Cool Things

Do you want to find ways to stretch your money, so it goes farther and is there when you really need it? Here are some suggestions for knowing how much money you have, how much you need for expenditures, and how to reach your goals by cutting back on what you spend.

Practice Self-Control: To avoid making a quick decision to buy something just because you saw it featured on display or on sale:

• Make a shopping list before you leave home and stick to it.

• Before you go shopping, set a spending limit (say, $5 or $10) for "impulse buys"—items you didn't plan to buy but that got your attention anyway. If you are tempted to spend more than your limit, wait a few hours or a few days and think it over.

• Limit the amount of cash you take with you. The less cash you carry, the less you can spend and the less you lose if you misplace your wallet.

Research Before You Buy: To be sure you are getting a good value, especially with a big purchase, look into the quality and the reputation of the product or service you're considering. Read "reviews" in magazines or respected websites. Talk to knowledgeable people you trust. Check other stores or go online and compare prices. Look at similar items. This is known as "comparison shopping," and it can lead to tremendous savings and better quality purchases.

Paying Off Debt Versus Saving

If you have credit card or other debt, it usually makes sense to pay off this debt first before contributing to savings. The interest rate you'll get on savings is likely to be far less than the amount of credit interest you're paying.

Act—Implement Your Plan/Assess/Adjust

Once you have set goals, estimated your fixed and variable expenses, and identified monthly savings targets, it's time to put your plan to work.

And if you're sure you know what you want, take advantage of store coupons and mail-in "rebates."

Keep Track Of Your Spending: This helps you set and stick to limits, what many people refer to as budgeting. "Maintaining a budget may sound scary or complicated, but it can be as simple as having a notebook and writing down what you buy each month," said Janet Kincaid, FDIC Senior Consumer Affairs Officer. "Any system that helps you know how much you are spending each month is a good thing."

Also pay attention to small amounts of money you spend. "A snack here and a magazine there can quickly add up," said Paul Horwitz, an FDIC Community Affairs Specialist. He suggested that, for a few weeks, you write down every purchase in a small notebook. "You'll probably be amazed at how much you spend without even thinking."

Think "Used" Instead Of "New": Borrow things (from the library or friends) that you don't have to own. Pick up used games, DVDs and music at "secondhand" stores around town.

Take Good Care Of What You Buy: It's expensive to replace things. Think about it: Do you really want to buy the same thing twice?

Source: From *FDIC Consumer News*, Federal Deposit Insurance Corporation (FDIC), Summer 2006.

Give it some time. Then see how you're doing. Were you able to meet your savings goals? If so, stick with it. If not, look at your variable expenses for opportunity areas to cut back spending and increase savings.

Evaluate your plan every three months and make adjustments as needed. If you're not saving enough to meet your monthly goals, you may need to spend less.

Saving is the key to successful financial plans. Use payroll deductions or automatic transfers to checking, savings or money market accounts. It's easier to save if you never see the money.

Use budget plans for paying utilities if they're available. Use cash for purchases rather than charging if you can.

Enter each check you write in a check register. Balance the account every month. If you use a debit card, enter those amounts in your check register.

Select A Financial Institution

Creating a safety net is easier if you work with a good financial institution such as a credit union, a bank or a thrift.

Interview employees at several locations. Look for people who are willing and able to answer your questions. Be ready to talk about the services and the advice you need.

For example, if it's important to you to conduct transactions face-to-face rather than by automatic teller machines (ATM), ask if the financial institution charges for the services of a person at the counter. If you prefer to use ATMs, make sure they're readily accessible and don't charge transaction fees.

Once you select a financial institution, consider opening a checking account if you don't have one. A checking account can save you fees you may now be paying for cashing your paycheck and paying your bills.

Start now and stick with it. You'll find that being smart about money is well worth it.

Chapter 39

Smart Shopping

Smart Shoppers Save While They Spend

6 Ways To Save

There are ways of getting what you want without paying top dollar. Here are some of them:

1. **Don't shop as entertainment.** When you hang out at the mall on a Saturday afternoon, you see things you don't need. But because you see them, you want them.

2. **Shop the sales.** If you shop the big sales to buy needed items, your shopping stays focused, and you get more for your money.

3. **Wait for the sale.** When you see something you like, you should approach a salesperson to ask if the item will go on sale anytime soon.

4. **Shop places other than the mall.** There are plenty of them.

    • Outlet stores offer good deals on popular designer names. The clothing may be leftovers or very slightly flawed (like crooked

About This Chapter: This chapter includes "Smart Shoppers," "What's It Worth," "Buy It Or Not?" "Try A Real Life Decision," and "I Paid How Much?" This information is from www.mint.org, which was conceived, written, and sponsored by the Northwestern Mutual Foundation, the charitable arm of Northwestern Mutual, to help families educate young people about personal money management. © 2007 The Northwestern Mutual Life Insurance Company, Milwaukee WI. Reprinted by permission. All rights reserved.

stitching in a seam). But you can get logo wear that's still in style at much lower prices.

- Discount stores. Not every-thing you own has to have a logo on it. Use discount stores to cut corners on less important wardrobe items, like underwear, belts, socks, etc. If the current look is to layer shirts, buy the "under" shirts at the discount store. If oversized shirts are in style and they hang over your jeans, who will know if there's a logo on your back pocket? Buy your jeans at the discount store and spend your money on the shirt.

♣ It's
A Fact!!
How Small
Savings Add Up

Don't underestimate saving a little here and a little there. Let's take a really common way of saving that everyone is familiar with: grocery shopping. If you buy sale items, clip coupons, and save $12 a week—which doesn't sound like so much—at year's end, you will have saved $624. That's a bundle of cash you could probably find a use for.

Source: © 2007 North-western Mutual.

- Consignment or second-hand stores. These stores are usually choosy about accepting only clothes in good condition. You can get some real buys.

5. **Go to matinees and discount theaters.** You know that movie you've been dying to see? You can go to a full-price theater and pay big bucks or...

    - look in the newspaper for a discount theater and get a couple bucks off the ticket price.

    - get a group of friends together on a weekend or a day off and go to a matinee (tickets are cheaper).

    - another trick: don't spend all that money on drinks and popcorn. Without too much trouble, you can spend more on snacks than on the price of admission. Eat before you go to the movie, buy a beverage during the movie, and then catch a pizza or a burger afterwards. You'll at least be getting more food for your money.

6. Check out purchases that perform tasks. Be a smart consumer. Believe it or not, advertisers sometimes exaggerate what their products will do! Buying speakers, sports gear, a computer? Go to a consumer magazine or a specialty magazine that tests products for you. Get smart. You and your family work too hard for your money to believe what ads tell you.

♣ It's A Fact!!
Small Savings Add Up To Big Money

How much does a cup of coffee cost you? Would you believe $465.84? Or more?

If you buy a cup of coffee every day for $1.00 (an awfully good price for a decent cup of coffee, nowadays), that adds up to $365.00 a year. If you saved that $365.00 for just one year, and put it into a savings account or investment that earns 5% a year, it would grow to $465.84 by the end of 5 years, and by the end of 30 years, to $1,577.50.

That's the power of "compounding." With compound interest, you earn interest on the money you save and on the interest that money earns. Over time, even a small amount saved can add up to big money.

If you are willing to watch what you spend and look for little ways to save on a regular schedule, you can make money grow. You just did it with one cup of coffee.

If a small cup of coffee can make such a huge difference, start looking at how you could make your money grow if you decided to spend less on other things and save those extra dollars.

If you buy on impulse, make a rule that you'll always wait 24 hours to buy anything. You may lose your desire to buy it after a day. And try emptying your pockets and wallet of spare change at the end of each day. You'll be surprised how quickly those nickels and dimes add up!

Source: Excerpted from "Make A Financial Plan," U.S. Securities and Exchange Commission (www.sec.gov), October 2004.

Judging An Item's Worth

It's Only $79.99

Only $79.99. How many times have you heard those words? Did you ever notice that almost every price tag has an ONLY on it? Even big screen TVs—they're only $1,799.

So let's take a better look at this only business. How long does it take you to earn $79.99? What do you have to do to get that money? Let's say you stock shelves at a discount store, and you're making $7.00 an hour. The little item that's only $79.99 is worth almost 12 hours of your work.

✔ Quick Tip
Do You Really Need
Those $125 Designer Sneakers?

A "need" is something you cannot live without. A "want" is something that would be nice to have but isn't necessary.

"A need may be a pair of sneakers, but a want is the $125 pair advertised by your favorite athlete," explained Paul Horwitz of the Federal Deposit Insurance Corporation (FDIC).

When you can control your spending on life's wants, you'll have more money available to save for what you need in the future.

Janet Kincaid of the FDIC offered this tip: "Take a day or two to think about any purchase that will cost a significant portion of your savings," she said. "If you really need to buy the item, it will probably still be there for you. If you don't need it but you still want it, perhaps you can buy something similar that's a lot less expensive and save the remaining money for other things."

Source: From "Start Smart: Money Management for Teens," *FDIC Consumer News*, Federal Deposit Insurance Corporation (FDIC), Summer 2006.

And if your job is easier, let's say, working at the counter of a fast-food place, your salary is probably lower, maybe around minimum wage. Now how long does it take you to earn $79.99 at a little more than $5 an hour? About 15 hours.

What's It Worth?

So as you stand in a store, getting excited about a purchase, think of how long it takes you to earn the money to pay for it. Is that $65 plain white cotton shirt with the logo on the pocket really worth the time and effort it takes you to earn $65? It's something to think about. You could probably find a $27 shirt of equal quality without the logo. And you could do something else with the $38 you saved.

P.S. Even if your parents are still buying your clothes, they work hard for their money too. Even with parents, there's only so much money to go around. If you spend it on one item, you don't have it to spend on others.

Buy It Or Not?

Here's the trick. You don't want to run out of your spending money before you get paid again. Many adults moan about having more month than they have money—they're out of cash by the 21st and they don't get paid again until the 1st of the next month.

Resist Impulse Buying

So learn to stretch those dollars! One way is to get into the habit of asking yourself questions before you buy. Advertisers would shudder at this idea. Their job is to make their products so tempting you will buy impulsively. Advertisers don't want you to think about what you're doing. They want you to buy right now—if you stop to think, you might not buy.

Advertisers study buyers and buying habits all the time, so these people have got some pretty clever ways to convince you that you must have this item. How do you hang on to your cash so you don't just buy impulsively? Ask yourself these questions:

- Do I really need this item?
- If I don't need it, do I at least really want it?

- Am I sure that I'll use it? Wear it?

- If I buy it now, will I have enough money for other things I might need later on—this week, this month, next month?

- Will this purchase take money away from paying off any debts I might owe?

- Is there any risk in delaying this purchase in order to think about it longer?

- What are the chances this item might go on sale soon?

- Could I find this item somewhere else cheaper?

- Could I find an item like this, but without a brand name? It will probably cost less.

Answer honestly: If you answer HONESTLY, (very important) chances are you'll still have spending money when you need it. Think about this: If you're out of money, and then you find something you really, really want to buy—you're stuck.

Don't Ever Touch Savings

Well, why can't you just dip into your savings—just this once—to make the purchase? Don't even think about it. That's the path to instant destruction. Once you start spending your savings, it'll be gone before you know it.

Try A Real-Life Decision

Buy it? Pass it up? Charge it? These are the questions that should occur to you each time you are thinking of buying something. How do you decide? You should ask yourself a series of questions—to test if and how to make the purchase.

What Would You Do?

Kirsten is a high school junior. Her parents gave her a credit card, but she is supposed to use it only for emergencies. She is in the mall one day and sees the perfect dress for prom in a store window. The price tag reads $125, but the store is running a One-Day-Only Sale, all items are 25% off the ticketed price.

Kirsten's grandmother, a dressmaker, has offered to make Kirsten's prom dress, and Kirsten has only $50 in her savings account. What should she do?

- What is the need?
    - A prom dress
- What are all the alternatives?
    - Buy the dress
    - Don't buy dress—wear the dress that Grandma sews.
    - Call home and talk about it.
    - Look for another dress.
- What's the money situation?
    - Doesn't have the money in her wallet to buy the dress; she'll have to use the credit card.
- What are the benefits of charging the purchase?
    - The dress is on sale.
- What are the disadvantages of charging the purchase?
    - The "sale" dress costs more than twice what Kirsten's has now in her spending money budget.
    - Even though the dress is on sale, Kirsten will have to pay finance charges on the dress until she pays it off.
    - Her grandmother can make a dress for the cost of the fabric. Under $35.
    - Grandma's feelings may be hurt.
    - Kirsten will be using the credit card for other than an emergency—her parents may be upset.

Weigh the advantages against the disadvantages. What would you do?

It may be easy for you to see what Kirsten should do. There are lots of disadvantages. In fact, there's no real advantage for Kirsten except that she loves the dress. You see that clearly because you're on the outside looking in—you're not emotionally involved in the purchase. Kirsten may want to deny the answers that stare her in the face because she WANTS the dress. Remember that when you find yourself in a similar situation.

Anytime you are thinking of making a purchase, run through these questions. If you answer them honestly, they will help you combat your impulses and make a good decision.

☞ **Remember!!**

Credit card debt can be an expensive mistake.

Source: © 2007 Northwestern Mutual.

I Paid How Much?

Let's look at finance charges in action.

You charge a bunch of items during the month. Some are on sale, and some you just can't live without. Then at the end of the month, you find this terrific audio system on clearance. It's a once-in-a-lifetime deal. You cave-in and charge the system. It's going to make your life so great.

The bill arrives. You can't believe it. How did you charge $2,000? None of these items were that expensive. You check over the bill, and they do add up to $2,000. You cut up your card—with a little pressure from your parents—and you begin the slow process of paying off what you owe.

You are paying 18.9% interest on the $2,000, and you can manage to pay $100 a month. If you continue to pay only $100 a month, how long will it take to pay off your debt? You may be surprised at the answer. It will take 25 months (more than two years), and it will cost you $2,421.00. (It may cost even more if you incur any late charges or other penalties).

Chapter 40

Signs of Compulsive Debting

1. Being unclear about your financial situation. Not knowing account balances, monthly expenses, loan interest rates, fees, fines, or contractual obligations.

2. Frequently "borrowing" items such as books, pens, or small amounts of money from friends and others, and failing to return them.

3. Poor saving habits. Not planning for taxes, retirement, or other not-recurring but predictable items, and then feeling surprised when they come due; a "live for today, don't worry about tomorrow" attitude."

4. Compulsive shopping: Being unable to pass up a "good deal"; making impulsive purchases; leaving price tags on clothes so they can be returned; not using items you've purchased.

5. Difficulty in meeting basic financial or personal obligations, and/or an inordinate sense of accomplishment when such obligations are met.

6. A different feeling when buying things on credit than when paying cash, a feeling of being in the club, of being accepted, of being grown up.

7. Living in chaos and drama around money: Using one credit card to pay another; bouncing checks; always having a financial crisis to contend with.

8. A tendency to live on the edge: Living paycheck to paycheck; taking risks with health and car insurance coverage; writing checks hoping money will appear to cover them.

9. Unwarranted inhibition and embarrassment in what should be a normal discussion of money.

10. Overworking or underearning: Working extra hours to earn money to pay creditors; using time inefficiently; taking jobs below your skill and education level.

11. An unwillingness to care for and value yourself: Living in self-imposed deprivation; denying your basic needs in order to pay your creditors.

12. A feeling or hope that someone will take care of you if necessary, so that you won't really get into serious financial trouble, that there will always be someone you can turn to.

15 Questions

Most compulsive debtors will answer "yes" to at least eight of the following 15 questions.

1. Are your debts making your home life unhappy?

2. Does the pressure of your debts distract you from your daily work?

3. Are your debts affecting your reputation?

4. Do your debts cause you to think less of yourself?

5. Have you ever given false information in order to obtain credit?

6. Have you ever made unrealistic promises to your creditors?

7. Does the pressure of your debts make you careless of the welfare of your family?

8. Do you ever fear that your employer, family or friends will learn the extent of your total indebtedness?

9. When faced with a difficult financial situation, does the prospect of borrowing give you an inordinate feeling of relief?

10. Does the pressure of your debts cause you to have difficulty sleeping?

11. Has the pressure of your debts ever caused you to consider getting drunk?

12. Have you ever borrowed money without giving adequate consideration to the rate of interest you are required to pay?

13. Do you usually expect a negative response when you are subject to a credit investigation?

14. Have you ever developed a strict regimen for paying off your debts, only to break it under pressure?

15. Do you justify your debts by telling yourself that you are superior to the "other" people, and when you get your "break" you'll be out of debt overnight?

How did you score? If you answered yes to eight or more of these questions, the chances are that you have a problem with compulsive debt, or are well on your way to having one. If this is the case, today can be a turning point in your life.

We have all arrived at this crossroad. One road, a soft road, lures you on to further despair, illness, ruin, and in some cases, mental institutions, prison, or suicide. The other road, a more challenging road, leads to self-respect, solvency, healing, and personal fulfillment. Debtors Anonymous (www.debtorsanonymous.org) urges you to take the first difficult step onto the more solid road now.

Chapter 41

Take Control Of Debt

Remember the definition of net worth (wealth):

$$\text{Assets} - \text{Liabilities} = \text{Net Worth}$$

Liabilities are your debts. Debt reduces net worth. Plus, the interest you pay on debt, including credit card debt, is money that cannot be saved or invested—it's just gone. Debt is a tool to be used wisely for such things as buying a house. If not used wisely, debt can easily get out of hand. For example, putting day-to-day expenses—like groceries or utility bills—on a credit card and not paying off the balance monthly can lead to debt overload.

Why People Get Into Trouble With Debt

Lots of people are mired in debt. In some cases, they could not control the causes of their debt. However, in some instances they could have. Many people get into serious debt because they:

- Experienced financial stresses caused by unemployment, medical bills, or divorce.

About This Chapter: This chapter begins with text reprinted with permission from "Building Wealth: A Beginner's Guide to Securing Your Financial Future, revised edition 2006," Federal Reserve Bank of Dallas (www.dallasfed.org). Text under the heading "Managing Debt" is © 2007 America Saves. All rights reserved. For additional information, visit www.americasaves.org.

Tips For Controlling Debt   ✔ **Quick Tip**

- Develop a budget and stick to it.

- Save money so you're prepared for unforeseen circumstances. You should have at least three to six months of living expenses stashed in your rainy day savings account, because as the poet Longfellow put it, "Into each life some rain must fall."

- When faced with a choice of financing a purchase, it may be a better financial decision to choose a less expensive model of the same product and save or invest the difference.

- Pay off credit card balances monthly.

- If you must borrow, learn everything about the loan, including interest rate, fees, and penalties for late payments or early repayment.

Source: Federal Reserve Bank of Dallas, 2006.

- Could not control spending, did not plan for the future, and did not save money.

- Lacked knowledge of financial and credit matters.

Speaking Of Interest

When you take out a loan, you repay the principal, which is the amount borrowed, plus interest, the amount charged for lending you the money. The interest on your monthly balance is a good example of compound interest that you pay. The interest is added to your bill, and the next month interest is charged on that amount and on the outstanding balance. The bottom line on interest is that those who know about interest earn it; those who don't, pay it.

Avoid Credit Card Debt

Planners rarely use credit cards. When they do, they pay off their balances every month. When a credit card balance is not paid off monthly, it means paying interest—often 20 percent or more a year—on everything purchased. So think of credit card debt as a high-interest loan. Do you need to reduce your credit card debt? Here are some suggestions.

- Pay cash.

- Set a monthly limit on charging, and keep a written record so you don't exceed that amount.

- Limit the number of credit cards you have. Cut up all but one of your cards. Stash that one out of sight, and use it only in emergencies.

- Choose the card with the lowest interest rate and no (or very low) annual fee. But beware of low introductory interest rates offered by mail. These rates often skyrocket after the first few months.

- Don't apply for credit cards to get a free gift or a discount on a purchase.

- Steer clear of blank checks that financial services companies send you. These checks are cash advances that may carry a higher interest rate than typical charges.

- Pay bills on time to avoid late charges or increased interest rates.

♣ It's A Fact!!
The Tale Of Two Spenders And The Big-Screen TV

Betty is a planner. She saved up for "extras." When she had enough money in her savings account, she bought a big-screen TV for $1,500. She paid cash.

Her friend Tim is an impulsive spender. He seeks immediate gratification using his credit cards, not realizing how much extra it costs. Tim bought the same TV for $1,500 but financed it on a store credit card with an annual interest rate of 22 percent. At $50 a month, it took him almost four years to pay off the balance.

While Betty paid only $1,500 for her big-screen TV, Tim paid $2,200— the cost of the TV plus interest. Tim not only paid an extra $700, he lost the opportunity to invest the $700 in building his wealth.

Source: Federal Reserve Bank of Dallas, 2006.

Beware The Perils Of Payday Loans And Predatory Lenders

People can get deep in debt when they take out a loan against their paycheck. They write a postdated check in exchange for money. When they get paid again, they repay the loan, thus the name payday loan. These loans generally come with very high, double-digit interest rates. Borrowers who can't repay the money are charged additional fees for an extension, which puts them even deeper in debt. Borrowers can continue to pay fees to extend the loan's due date indefinitely, only to find they are getting deeper in debt because of the steep interest payments and fees.

Predatory lenders often target seniors and low-income people they contact by phone, mail or in person. After her husband died, 73-year-old Pauline got plenty of solicitations from finance companies. She was struggling to make ends meet on her fixed income. To pay off her bills, she took out a $5,000 home equity loan that carried a high interest rate and excessive fees. Soon she found she was even deeper in debt, so she refinanced the loan once, then again, and again, paying fees each time.

Pauline's children discovered her situation and paid off the loan. The lessons here are:

- Don't borrow from Peter to pay Paul.
- Never respond to a solicitation that makes borrowing sound easy and cheap.
- Always read the fine print on any loan application.

Seek assistance from family members, local credit counseling services, or others to make sure a loan is right for you.

Know What Creditors Say About You

Those who have used credit will have a credit report that shows everything about their payment history, including late payments. The information in your credit report is used to create your credit score. A credit score is a number generated by a statistical model that objectively predicts the likelihood that you will repay on time. Banks, insurance companies, potential landlords and other lenders use credit scores.

Credit scores range from under 500 to 800 and above and are determined by payment history, the amount of outstanding debt, length of your credit history, recent inquiries on your credit report, and the types of credit in use. Factors not considered in a credit score include age, race or ethnicity, income, job, marital status, education, length of time at your current address, and whether you own or rent your home.

A credit report that includes late payments, delinquencies, or defaults will result in a low credit score and could mean not getting a loan or having to pay a much higher interest rate. The higher your score, the less risk you represent to the lender.

Review your credit report at least once a year to make sure all information is accurate. If you find an error, the Fair Credit Reporting Act requires credit reporting companies and those reporting information to them to correct the mistake. To start the process of fixing an error:

- Contact the credit reporting company online, by fax or certified letter, identifying the creditor you have a dispute with and the nature of the error.

- Send the credit reporting company verifiable information, such as canceled checks or receipts, supporting your complaint.

- The credit reporting company must investigate your complaint within 30 days and get back to you with its results.

- Contact the creditor if the credit reporting company investigation does not result in correction of the error. When you resolve the dispute, ask the creditor to send the credit reporting company a correction.

If the issue remains unresolved, you have the right to explain in a statement that will go on your credit report. For example, if you did not pay a car repair bill because the mechanic didn't fix the problem, the unpaid bill may show up on your credit report, but so will your explanation.

Keep Your Good Name

Every month, go back to your budget and plan carefully to ensure your bills are paid before their due dates. Betty is a planner. She makes sure she pays her bills on time. Betty gets paid twice a month. She has her paycheck set up for direct deposit so she doesn't have to scramble to get to the bank on payday. With her first paycheck each month, she pays her mortgage (which she has set up on auto debit), cable TV, and utility bills. Out of the second check, Betty makes her car payment (also on auto debit) and has a monthly deposit automatically made to her savings account. Betty has found that "autopilot" really simplifies budgeting and saving.

If you believe you are too deep in debt:

- Discuss your options with your creditors before you miss a payment.

- Seek expert help, such as Consumer Credit Counseling Services, listed in your local telephone directory.

- Avoid "credit repair" companies that charge a fee. Many of these are scams.

Save Money By Choosing The Right Loan

If you have good credit, you may want to take out a loan to purchase a house or to cover educational expenses—both are investments in the future. But regardless of how the money is spent, a loan is a liability, or debt, and decreases your wealth. So choose loans carefully.

Shop and negotiate for the lowest interest rate. The interest you save can be invested to build wealth. Take a look at the chart in Table 41.1. In this example, it is obvious that Pixley Bank and Trust would charge the lowest

Table 41.1. Choose The Right Loan

$15,000 Car Loan for 5 Years

Lender	Interest Rate	Total Interest
Pixley Bank and Trust	6.5%	$2,609.53
XYZ Savings and Loan	7.5%	$3,034.15
Joe's Auto Sales	15.0%	$6,410.94

$15,000 Car Loan at 8 Percent Interest

	3-year	4-year	5-year
Number of payments	36	48	60
Payment	$470	$366	$304
Total paid	$16,922	$ 17,577	$ 18,249

interest over the term of the loan. What's not obvious is that your credit score may determine which interest rate you are offered. Use an online auto loan calculator to compare rates.

Save Money By Paying Loans Off Early

You can save interest expense by increasing your monthly payments or choosing a shorter payment term on your loan. Betty, the planner, knew her new car would cost more than the sticker price because she would have to pay interest on the loan from the bank. After checking her options, she chose a shorter payment term with higher payments. Betty budgeted enough money each month to make the higher payments. By doing this, she will reduce the amount of interest she ultimately pays. Table 41.1 shows how shorter terms with higher payments would affect the total amount and interest on Betty's $15,000 car loan.

Avoid the trap of getting "upside down"—owing more on the car than it is worth when you sell or trade it in. Betty's car will be paid for in three years, and she plans on driving it for at least eight years. Once her car is paid for, she will continue to budget for the car payment but will invest the money to further build her wealth.

Take Steps To Control Your Debt

As you can see, a big part of building wealth is making wise choices about debt. You need to maximize assets and minimize liabilities to maximize net worth. To manage debt, you need to know how much you have and develop strategies to control it.

When Bob decided to reduce his $3,000 credit card debt, he analyzed his debt and developed a strategy. He listed the balance, interest rate, and monthly interest on each credit card. He checked his credit score and shopped for the best rate on a new credit card. Then he transferred all his balances to that card. He cut up the old credit cards and used the interest he saved to pay toward the principal balance. He used the new card only for emergencies.

What is your credit card debt situation? See Table 41.2 for an example and to do an analysis of your own.

Table 41.2. Evaluate Your Credit Card Debt Situation

Example

Credit Card	Debt	Interest Rate	Monthly Interest*
Department Store A	$500	19.5%	$8.13
XYZ Bank	$1,250	17%	$ 17.71
BHA Finance Co.	$1,000	22%	$18.33
Store B	$250	15%	$3.13
Total	$3,000		$ 47.30

Analyze Your Situation

Credit Card	Debt	Interest Rate	Monthly Interest*
_____	_____	_____	_____
_____	_____	_____	_____
_____	_____	_____	_____
_____	_____	_____	_____
Total	_____		_____

*Interest rate divided by 12 months multiplied by the amount of debt.

✔ **Quick Tip**
Some Tips To Protect Your Identity

Shred or destroy your bank and credit card statements and all other private records before tossing them in the trash.

Give out your Social Security number only when absolutely necessary, and never carry both your Social Security card and driver's license in your wallet.

Pick up mail promptly from your mailbox, and never leave outgoing mail with paid bills in an unsecured mailbox.

Don't give out personal information on the phone, through the mail or on the internet unless you're sure you know whom you're dealing with.

Source: Federal Reserve Bank of Dallas, 2006.

Guard Your Identity

Just as you protect the security of your home with locks for your windows and doors, you should take steps to protect your identity. Secure your financial records, Social Security number and card, account numbers, and all passwords and PINs (personal identification numbers). A periodic check of your credit report can alert you if someone is illegally using credit products in your name. If you suspect unauthorized access, contact the three major credit reporting companies and place a fraud alert on your name and Social Security number.

Managing Debt

Large consumer debts are the most important financial reason that people have trouble saving and building wealth. The good news is that there is hope. With planning, discipline, patience, and maybe some outside help, almost anyone can reduce their debts and start to accumulate wealth.

Are You In Trouble?

If you answer "yes" to any of the following questions, then you probably need to get your debts under better control:

- Can you only afford to make minimum payments on your credit cards?

- Do you worry about finding the money to make monthly car payments?

- Do you borrow money to pay off old debts?

- Have you used a home equity loan to refinance credit card debts, then run up new revolving balances on your cards?

How To Reduce Your Debts

The first step in getting out of debt is to stop borrowing. To do that, you have to stop spending more than you earn. So, make a budget and cut out any expenses you can. It may help to cut up your credit cards or lock them away in a safe place.

While you are making a budget, figure out the most you can afford to pay each month to reduce your debts, then make those payments without fail. If you have debts on more than one credit card, either pay off the card with the highest interest rate first and work your way down to the card with the lowest rate, or pay off the smallest loan first and work your way up to the largest. Once you've paid off your debts, don't give in to the temptation to start overspending again. Instead, take the money you were paying each month on your debts and begin to save it. That will give you a financial cushion the next time an emergency strikes.

Where To Get Help

In most communities, there are agencies that can help you manage your debts.

The most helpful and most widely available are non-profit Consumer Credit Counseling Services (CCCS). CCCS counselors can work with you privately to help you develop a budget, figure out your options, and negotiate with creditors to repay your debts. Call 800-388-2227 to locate the office nearest you.

Some national credit counseling non-profits, who provide advice online or over the phone, can also be helpful. However, others charge high fees for little service, so be sure to shop carefully. In many communities, Cooperative Extension offices offer workshops, home-study courses, and other services to help people manage their money, including their debts. Cooperative Extension offices are listed in the blue pages of the phone book under county government.

If your debts are too large, you may want to consider bankruptcy. Bankruptcy can give you a fresh start, but it is a serious step that can make it harder to get credit for years after you declare bankruptcy. Call your local Legal Aid or Legal Services office for advice. If you don't qualify for their services, ask them for a referral to a bankruptcy attorney.

♣ It's A Fact!!
Why Too Much Debt Is Costly

Borrowing more money than you can afford is costly in many ways. Americans spend well over $75 billion a year just on credit card interest and fees. That means that families who revolve credit card balances pay an average of $1,500 a year in interest and fees. If they saved that $1,500 in an account with a five percent yield, in 40 years they would have nearly $200,000! Taking on too much debt also lowers your credit score. That means you will end up paying higher interest rates on all your consumer and mortgage loans. A low credit score can also make it harder to rent an apartment, get utility services, and even get a job.

Too much debt isn't just expensive. People with lots of debt often say they lack peace of mind. They worry constantly about paying off debts and making ends meet. The stress of these worries affects their family life, work performance, and other areas of their lives.

Source: Excerpted "Managing Debt" © 2007 America Saves. All rights reserved. For additional information, visit www.americasaves.org.

Chapter 42

If You Are Contacted By A Debt Collector

Fair Debt Collection

If you use credit cards, owe money on a personal loan, or are paying on a home mortgage, you are a "debtor." If you fall behind in repaying your creditors, or an error is made on your accounts, you may be contacted by a "debt collector."

You should know that in either situation, the Fair Debt Collection Practices Act requires that debt collectors treat you fairly and prohibits certain methods of debt collection. Of course, the law does not erase any legitimate debt you owe.

How may a debt collector contact you?

Collector may contact you in person, by mail, telephone, telegram, or fax. However, a debt collector may not contact you at inconvenient times or places, such as before 8 A.M. or after 9 P.M., unless you agree. A debt collector also may not contact you at work if the collector knows that your employer disapproves of such contacts.

You can stop a debt collector from contacting you by writing a letter to the collector telling them to stop. Once the collector receives your letter, they may

About This Chapter: "Fair Debt Collection," March 1999, and "Time-Barred Debts," October 2004, Federal Trade Commission (http://www.ftc.gov).

not contact you again except to say there will be no further contact or to notify you that the debt collector or the creditor intends to take some specific action.

May a debt collector contact anyone else about your debt?

If you have an attorney, the debt collector must contact the attorney, rather than you. If you do not have an attorney, a collector may contact other people, but only to find out where you live, what your phone number is, and where you work. Collectors usually are prohibited from contacting such third parties more than once. In most cases, the collector may not tell anyone other than you and your attorney that you owe money.

What must the debt collector tell you about the debt?

Within five days after you are first contacted, the collector must send you a written notice telling you the amount of money you owe, the name of the creditor to whom you owe the money, and what action to take if you believe you do not owe the money.

May a debt collector continue to contact you if you believe you do not owe money?

A collector may not contact you if, within 30 days after you receive the written notice, you send the collection agency a letter stating you do not owe money. However, a collector can renew collection activities if you are sent proof of the debt, such as a copy of a bill for the amount owed.

What types of debt collection practices are prohibited?

Harassment: Debt collectors may not harass, oppress, or abuse you or any third parties they contact. For example, debt collectors may not take these actions:

- Use threats of violence or harm
- Publish a list of consumers who refuse to pay their debts (except to a credit bureau)
- Use obscene or profane language
- Repeatedly use the telephone to annoy someone

False Statements: Debt collectors may not use any false or misleading statements when collecting a debt. For example, debt collectors may not take these actions:

- Falsely imply that they are attorneys or government representatives
- Falsely imply that you have committed a crime
- Falsely represent that they operate or work for a credit bureau
- Misrepresent the amount of your debt
- Indicate that papers being sent to you are legal forms when they are not
- Indicate that papers being sent to you are not legal forms when they are

Debt collectors also may not make these statements or claims:

- You will be arrested if you do not pay your debt.
- They will seize, garnish, attach, or sell your property or wages (unless the collection agency or creditor intends to do so, and it is legal to do so).
- Actions, such as a lawsuit, will be taken against you, when such action legally may not be taken, or when they do not intend to take such action.

In addition, debt collectors may not give false credit information about you to anyone, including a credit bureau, send you anything that looks like an official document from a court or government agency when it is not, or use a false name.

Unfair Practices: Debt collectors may not engage in unfair practices when they try to collect a debt. For example, collectors may not take these actions:

- Collect any amount greater than your debt, unless your state law permits such a charge
- Deposit a post-dated check prematurely
- Use deception to make you accept collect calls or pay for telegrams
- Take or threaten to take your property unless this can be done legally
- Contact you by postcard

Time-Barred Debts

Federal law imposes limitations on how debt collectors can collect debts, including time-barred debts. The Fair Debt Collection Practices Act (FDCPA) prohibits debt collectors from engaging in any unfair, deceptive, or abusive practices while collecting debts. It does not erase any legitimate debt that you owe.

Most courts that have addressed the issue have ruled that the FDCPA does not prohibit debt collectors from trying to collect time-barred debts, as long as they do not sue or threaten to sue you for the debt. If a debt collector sues you to collect a time-barred debt, you can have the suit dismissed by letting the court or judge know the debt is, indeed, time-barred.

✎ What's It Mean?

Time-Barred Debts: Debts that are so old they are beyond the point at which a creditor or debt collector may sue you to collect. State law varies as to when a creditor or debt collector may no longer sue to collect: in most states, the statute of limitations period on debts is between 3 and 10 years; in some states, the period is longer. Check with your State Attorney General's Office to determine when a debt is considered time-barred in your state. You can get contact information for your state's Attorney General online at http://www.naag.org.

Source: Federal Trade Commission, 2004.

Chapter 43

Credit Counseling

Living paycheck to paycheck? Worried about debt collectors? Can't seem to develop a workable budget, let alone save money for emergencies or retirement? If this sounds familiar, you may want to consider the services of a credit counselor. Many credit counseling organizations are nonprofit and work with you to solve your financial problems. But beware—just because an organization says it is "nonprofit" doesn't guarantee that its services are free or affordable, or that its services are legitimate. In fact, some credit counseling organizations charge high fees, some of which may be hidden, or urge consumers to make "voluntary" contributions that cause them to fall deeper into debt.

Most credit counselors offer services through local offices, the internet, or on the telephone. If possible, find an organization that offers in-person counseling. Many universities, military bases, credit unions, housing authorities, and branches of the U.S. Cooperative Extension Service operate nonprofit credit counseling programs. Your financial institution, local consumer protection agency, and friends and family also may be good sources of information and referrals.

About This Chapter: Excerpted from "Fiscal Fitness: Choosing a Credit Counselor," Federal Trade Commission (http://www.fdc.gov), December 2005.

Choosing A Credit Counseling Organization

Reputable credit counseling organizations advise you on managing your money and debts, help you develop a budget, and usually offer free educational materials and workshops. Their counselors are certified and trained in the areas of consumer credit, money and debt management, and budgeting. Counselors discuss your entire financial situation with you, and help you develop a personalized plan to solve your money problems. An initial counseling session typically lasts an hour, with an offer of follow-up sessions.

Once you've developed a list of potential counseling agencies, check them out with your state Attorney General, local consumer protection agency, and Better Business Bureau. They can tell you if consumers have filed complaints about them. (But even if there are no complaints about them, it's not a guarantee that they're legitimate.) The United States Trustee Program (http://www.usdoj.gov/ust) also keeps a list of credit counseling agencies that have been approved to provide pre-bankruptcy counseling. After you've done your background investigation, it's time for the most important research— you should interview the final "candidates."

Questions To Ask

Here are some questions to ask to help you find the best counselor for you.

> **☞ Remember!!**
> A reputable credit counseling agency should send you free information about itself and the services it provides without requiring you to provide any details about your situation. If a firm doesn't do that, consider it a red flag and go elsewhere for help.

- **What services do you offer?**
  Look for an organization that offers a range of services, including budget counseling, and savings and debt management classes. Avoid organizations that push a debt management plan (DMP) as your only option before they spend a significant amount of time analyzing your financial situation.

- **Do you offer information? Are educational materials available for free?**
  Avoid organizations that charge for information.

- In addition to helping me solve my immediate problem, will you help me develop a plan for avoiding problems in the future?

- What are your fees? Are there set-up or monthly fees? Get a specific price quote in writing.

- What if I can't afford to pay your fees or make contributions? If an organization won't help you because you can't afford to pay, look elsewhere for help.

- Will I have a formal written agreement or contract with you? Don't sign anything without reading it first. Make sure all verbal promises are in writing.

- Are you licensed to offer your services in my state?

- What are the qualifications of your counselors? Are they accredited or certified by an outside organization? If so, by whom? If not, how are they trained? Try to use an organization whose counselors are trained by a non-affiliated party.

- What assurance do I have that information about me (including my address, phone number, and financial information) will be kept confidential and secure?

- How are your employees compensated? Are they paid more if I sign up for certain services, if I pay a fee, or if I make a contribution to your organization? If the answer is yes, consider it a red flag and go elsewhere for help.

Debt Management Plans

If your financial problems stem from too much debt or your inability to repay your debts, a credit counseling agency may recommend that you enroll in a debt management plan. A DMP alone is not credit counseling, and DMPs are not for everyone. Consider signing on for one of these plans only after a certified credit counselor has spent time thoroughly reviewing your financial situation, and has offered you customized advice on managing your money. Even if a DMP is appropriate for you, a reputable credit counseling organization still will help you create a budget and teach you money management skills.

✔ Quick Tip
Debt Negotiation Programs

Debt negotiation is **not** the same thing as credit counseling or a DMP. It can be very risky and have a long-term negative impact on your credit report and, in turn, your ability to get credit. That's why many states have laws regulating debt negotiation companies and the services they offer.

Steer clear of debt negotiation companies that make the following claims:

- guarantee they can remove your unsecured debt

- promise that unsecured debts can be paid off with pennies on the dollar

- require substantial monthly service fees

- demand payment of a percentage of savings

- tell you to stop making payments to or communicating with your creditors

- require you to make monthly payments to them, rather than with your creditor

- claim that creditors never sue consumers for non-payment of unsecured debt

- promise that using their system will have no negative impact on your credit report

- claim that they can remove accurate negative information from your credit report

If you decide to work with a debt negotiation company, be sure to check it out with your state Attorney General, local consumer protection agency, and the Better Business Bureau. They can tell you if any consumer complaints are on file about the firm you're considering doing business with. Also, ask your state Attorney General if the company is required to be licensed to work in your state and, if so, whether it is.

How A DMP Works

You deposit money each month with the credit counseling organization. The organization uses your deposits to pay your unsecured debts, like credit card bills, student loans, and medical bills, according to a payment schedule the counselor develops with you and your creditors. Your creditors may agree to lower your interest rates and waive certain fees, but check with all your creditors to be sure that they offer the concessions that a credit counseling organization describes to you. A successful DMP requires you to make regular, timely payments, and could take 48 months or longer to complete. Ask the credit counselor to estimate how long it will take for you to complete the plan. You also may have to agree not to apply for—or use—any additional credit while you're participating in the plan.

How To Make A DMP Work For You

The following steps will help you benefit from a DMP, and avoid falling further into debt.

- Continue to pay your bills until the plan has been approved by your creditors. If you stop making payments before your creditors have accepted you into a plan, you'll face late fees, penalties, and negative entries on your credit report.

- Contact your creditors and confirm that they have accepted the proposed plan before you send any payments to the credit counseling organization for your DMP.

- Make sure the organization's payment schedule allows your debts to be paid before they are due each month. Paying on time will help you avoid late fees and penalties. Call each of your creditors on the first of every month to make sure the agency has paid them on time.

- Review monthly statements from your creditors to make sure they have received your payments.

- If your debt management plan depends on your creditors agreeing to lower or eliminate interest and finance charges, or waive late fees, make sure these concessions are reflected on your statements.

Chapter 44

Credit Repair

You see the advertisements in newspapers, on TV, and on the internet. You hear them on the radio. You get fliers in the mail. You may even get calls from telemarketers offering credit repair services. They all make the same claims:

- "Credit problems? No problem!"

- "We can erase your bad credit—100% guaranteed."

- "Create a new credit identity—legally."

- "We can remove bankruptcies, judgments, liens, and bad loans from your credit file forever!"

Do yourself a favor and save some money, too. Don't believe these statements. Only time, a conscious effort, and a personal debt repayment plan will improve your credit report.

This chapter explains how you can improve your creditworthiness and gives legitimate resources for low or no-cost help.

The Scam

Everyday, companies nationwide appeal to consumers with poor credit histories. They promise, for a fee, to clean up your credit report so you can

About This Chapter: Excerpted "Credit Repair: Self Help May Be Best," Federal Trade Commission (http://www.ftc.gov), December 2005.

get a car loan, a home mortgage, insurance, or even a job. The truth is, they can't deliver. After you pay them hundreds or thousands of dollars in fees, these companies do nothing to improve your credit report; most simply vanish with your money.

The Warning Signs

If you decide to respond to a credit repair offer, look for these tell-tale signs of a scam:

> ♣ **It's A Fact!!**
> Under the Credit Repair Organizations Act, credit repair companies cannot require you to pay until they have completed the services they have promised.

- companies that want you to pay for credit repair services before they provide any services

- companies that do not tell you your legal rights and what you can do for yourself for free

- companies that recommend that you not contact a credit reporting company directly

- companies that suggest that you try to invent a "new" credit identity—and then, a new credit report—by applying for an Employer Identification Number to use instead of your Social Security number

- companies that advise you to dispute all information in your credit report or take any action that seems illegal, like creating a new credit identity (If you follow illegal advice and commit fraud, you may be subject to prosecution.)

You could be charged and prosecuted for mail or wire fraud if you use the mail or telephone to apply for credit and provide false information. It's a federal crime to lie on a loan or credit application, to misrepresent your Social Security number, and to obtain an Employer Identification Number from the Internal Revenue Service under false pretenses.

The Truth

No one can legally remove accurate and timely negative information from a credit report. The law allows you to ask for an investigation of information in your file that you dispute as inaccurate or incomplete. There is no charge for this. Everything a credit repair clinic can do for you legally, you can do for yourself at little or no cost.

You can dispute mistakes or outdated items for free. Under the Fair Credit Reporting Act (FCRA), both the consumer reporting company and the information provider (that is, the person, company, or organization that provides information about you to a consumer reporting company) are responsible for correcting inaccurate or incomplete information in your report. To take advantage of all your rights under this law, contact the consumer reporting company and the information provider.

Step One

Tell the consumer reporting company, in writing, what information you think is inaccurate. Include copies (not originals) of documents that support your position. In addition to providing your complete name and address, your letter should clearly identify each item in your report you dispute, state the facts and explain why you dispute the information, and request that it be removed or corrected. You may want to enclose a copy of your report with the items in question circled. Send your letter by certified mail, "return receipt requested," so you can document what the consumer reporting company received. Keep copies of your dispute letter and enclosures.

Consumer reporting companies must investigate the items in question—usually within 30 days—unless they consider your dispute frivolous. They also must forward all the relevant data you provide about the inaccuracy to the organization that provided the information. After the information provider receives notice of a dispute from the consumer reporting company, it must investigate, review the relevant information, and report the results back to the consumer reporting company. If the information provider finds the disputed information is inaccurate, it must notify all three nationwide consumer reporting companies so they can correct the information in your file.

When the investigation is complete, the consumer reporting company must give you the results in writing and a free copy of your report if the dispute results in a change. If an item is changed or deleted, the consumer reporting company cannot put the disputed information back in your file

✔ **Quick Tip**

If you need to dispute an item in your credit report, use this sample to help you write a dispute letter.

Sample Dispute Letter

Date
Your Name
Your Address
Your City, State, Zip Code

Complaint Department
Name of Company
Address
City, State, Zip Code

Dear Sir or Madam:

I am writing to dispute the following information in my file. The items I dispute also are encircled on the attached copy of the report I received.

This item (identify item(s) disputed by name of source, such as creditors or tax court, and identify type of item, such as credit account, judgment, etc.) is (inaccurate or incomplete) because (describe what is inaccurate or incomplete and why). I am requesting that the item be deleted (or request another specific change) to correct the information.

Enclosed are copies of (use this sentence if applicable and describe any enclosed documentation, such as payment records, court documents) supporting my position. Please investigate this (these) matter(s) and (delete or correct) the disputed item(s) as soon as possible.

Sincerely,

Your name

Enclosures: (List what you are enclosing)

unless the information provider verifies that it is accurate and complete. The consumer reporting company also must send you written notice that includes the name, address, and phone number of the information provider.

If you request, the consumer reporting company must send notices of any correction to anyone who received your report in the past six months. You can have a corrected copy of your report sent to anyone who received a copy during the past two years for employment purposes.

Step Two

Tell the creditor or other information provider, in writing, that you dispute an item. Be sure to include copies (NOT originals) of documents that support your position. Many providers specify an address for disputes. If the provider reports the item to a consumer reporting company, it must include a notice of your dispute. And if you are correct—that is, if the information is found to be inaccurate—the information provider may not report it again.

Reporting Accurate Negative Information

When negative information in your report is accurate, only the passage of time can assure its removal. A consumer reporting company can report most accurate negative information for seven years and bankruptcy information for 10 years. Information about an unpaid judgment against you can be reported for seven years or until the statute of limitations runs out, whichever is longer. There is no time limit on reporting: information about criminal convictions; information reported in response to your application for a job that pays more than $75,000 a year; and information reported because you've applied for more than $150,000 worth of credit or life insurance. There is a standard method for calculating the

✔ Quick Tip

If an investigation doesn't resolve your dispute with the consumer reporting company, you can ask that a statement of the dispute be included in your file and in future reports. You also can ask the consumer reporting company to provide your statement to anyone who received a copy of your report in the recent past. You can expect to pay a fee for this service.

seven-year reporting period. Generally, the period runs from the date that the event took place.

The Credit Repair Organizations Act

By law, credit repair organizations must give you a copy of the "Consumer Credit File Rights Under State and Federal Law" before you sign a contract. They also must give you a written contract that spells out your rights and obligations. Read these documents before you sign anything. The law contains specific protections for you. For example, a credit repair company cannot:

- make false claims about their services;

> ## ♣ It's A Fact!!
> ## Have You Been Victimized?
>
> Many states have laws regulating credit repair companies. State law enforcement officials may be helpful if you've lost money to credit repair scams.
>
> If you've had a problem with a credit repair company, don't be embarrassed to report it. While you may fear that contacting the government will only make your problems worse, remember that laws are in place to protect you. Contact your local consumer affairs office or your state Attorney General (AGs). Many AGs have toll-free consumer hotlines. Check the Blue Pages of your telephone directory for the phone number or check http://www.naag.org for a list of state Attorneys General.

- charge you until they have completed the promised services;

- perform any services until they have your signature on a written contract and have completed a three-day waiting period. During this time, you can cancel the contract without paying any fees.

Your contract must specify:

- the payment terms for services, including their total cost;

- a detailed description of the services to be performed;

- how long it will take to achieve the results;

- any guarantees they offer;

- the company's name and business address.

Chapter 45

Bankruptcy: A Brief Overview

General Concepts

What are the main purposes of bankruptcy?

Bankruptcy laws serve two main purposes. First, bankruptcy law gives creditors some payment on their debts if a debtor (the one who owes the debt) can afford to pay them. Second, bankruptcy law gives debtors a fresh start, by canceling many of their debts, through an order of the court called a discharge.

What are the different kinds of bankruptcy?

There are four types of bankruptcy available to individuals:

- Chapter 7 (a liquidation-style case for individuals or businesses)

- Chapter 13 (a payment plan or rehabilitation-style case for individuals with a regular source of income)

- Chapter 12 (a payment plan or rehabilitation-style case for family farmers and fishermen)

About This Chapter: "General Concepts," reprinted with permission from the American Bankruptcy Institute (http://www.abiworld.org). All rights reserved. © 2006. Additional text under the heading "Before You File for Personal Bankruptcy: Information About Credit Counseling and Debtor Education" is from the Federal Trade Commission (www.ftc.gov), produced in cooperation with the Department of Justice's U.S. Trustee Program, November 2006.

- Chapter 11 (a more complex rehabilitation-style case used primarily by business debtors, but sometimes by individuals with substantial debts and asset)

The two most important types of cases for consumers are chapter 7 and chapter 13. Both provide for some possible payments to creditors, a discharge for debtors, and supervision by a trustee. Chapter 7 involves surrendering some of your property (at least in theory) in return for a discharge of many of your debts. The trustee sells any non-exempt property and pays your creditors. In chapter 13, you keep your property but must commit to a three- to five-year repayment plan. You then obtain a discharge of most of the debts not paid in the plan.

In both types of bankruptcy, most creditors must stop efforts to collect debts after your case is filed. This protection is called the "automatic stay." In a chapter 7, this relief is often temporary.

What is the difference between chapter 7 and chapter 13?

Chapter 7—A Brief Overview: Chapter 7 is designed as a liquidation or sell-out type of bankruptcy. Under this model, debtors give up certain property that they own at the time they file the bankruptcy case, which is sold by a trustee. The trustee uses the proceeds of the sale to pay creditors. This is the way many cases proceed. In other cases, probably most cases, the debtor does not have any assets over and above what the law allows the debtor to keep. Thus, in most chapter 7 cases, the debtor does not give up any property. Still, we call chapter 7 cases liquidation cases.

About 90 days after a chapter 7 case is filed, most debtors get most of their debts discharged. This means the debts have gone away. Some debts do not go away, and must be paid after the case. Examples include past-due child support payments, some taxes, and student loans. Debts for which the debtor has pledged collateral for the loan (such as cars, homes, and household goods) also do not go away in a bankruptcy.

The bankruptcy case addresses only the debts the debtor has at the time of the bankruptcy case. Future debts must always be paid as usual. Debtors are allowed to keep the money that they earn after filing the bankruptcy case, as well as most other property that they obtain after the filing.

Chapter 13—A Brief Overview: Chapter 13 is very different. The model is one of pay out rather than sell out. Debtors pay some of their debts over time.

Debtors in chapter 13 usually keep all of their property, whether or not it is exempt, but they make regular payments on their debts out of the money that they earn after filing the bankruptcy case. The plan payments must total at least as much as creditors would have received if the debtor had just liquidated under chapter 7. The payments are made to a trustee, who distributes the payments to the creditors.

The payments are made in regular installments, according to a payment plan (called a chapter 13 plan) that the debtor proposes, usually with the help of an attorney. The plan lasts either until the debts are paid in full or until the end of a three- to five-year period. The debtor receives a discharge at the completion of the plan.

This was just an overview. More detail is provided throughout this chapter.

Does a debtor have to "qualify" for bankruptcy? How will I know if I am eligible?

Chapter 7 Eligibility: Today's law allows debtors, for the most part, to choose the type of bankruptcy they want to file, though there are reasons a debtor might choose one chapter over another.

For example, a chapter 13 case allows a debtor to catch up on missed payments owed to creditors holding a security interest in collateral, such as a mortgage or auto lender, and therefore might be a better choice for some debtors. As long as the debtor's plan has been approved by the court and the debtor is maintaining payments to the trustee, the collateral will be protected from repossession.

For cases filed on or after October 17, 2005, access to chapter 7 will be more limited. Individual debtors with primarily consumer debts who want to file a case under chapter 7 will have their finances examined to determine if they can afford to pay creditors. If they can, based on a set formula know as the "means test," they will not be eligible to file a chapter 7.

If they want to file a bankruptcy, they will need to file a chapter 13. The "means test" is designed to force people who can afford to pay some of their creditors to do so rather than discharging all their debts in a chapter 7.

The means test compares the debtor's excess monthly income to the amount of unsecured debt to determine how much a debtor could repay to

✎ What's It Mean?

Automatic Stay: An injunction that automatically stops lawsuits, foreclosures, garnishments, and all collection activity against the debtor the moment a bankruptcy petition is filed.

Bankruptcy Code: The informal name for title 11 of the United States Code (11 U.S.C. §§ 101-1330), the federal bankruptcy law.

Consumer Debtor: A debtor whose debts are primarily consumer debts (debts incurred for personal, as opposed to business, needs).

Discharge: A release of a debtor from personal liability for certain dischargeable debts set forth in the Bankruptcy Code. (A discharge releases a debtor from personal liability for certain debts known as dischargeable debts and prevents the creditors owed those debts from taking any action against the debtor to collect the debts. The discharge also prohibits creditors from communicating with the debtor regarding the debt, including telephone calls, letters, and personal contact.)

Exemptions (Exempt Property): Certain property owned by an individual debtor that the Bankruptcy Code or applicable state law permits the debtor to keep from unsecured creditors. For example, in some states the debtor may be able to exempt all or a portion of the equity in the debtor's primary residence (homestead exemption), or some or all "tools of the trade" used by the debtor to make a living (for example, auto tools for an auto mechanic or dental tools for a dentist). The availability and amount of property the debtor may exempt depends on the state the debtor lives in.

Nondischargeable Debt: A debt that cannot be eliminated in bankruptcy. Examples include a home mortgage, debts for alimony or child support, certain taxes, debts for most government funded or guaranteed educational loans or benefit overpayments, debts arising from death or personal injury caused

creditors if he were in a chapter 13. Because this calculation is hypothetical and does not necessarily reflect the debtor's true financial condition, a debtor who appears to be able to repay the minimum portion of his debts but who, in reality, cannot, may be permitted to stay in a chapter 7 case. Unfortunately, the means test is more complicated than we can explain well here.

by driving while intoxicated or under the influence of drugs, and debts for restitution or a criminal fine included in a sentence on the debtor's conviction of a crime. Some debts, such as debts for money or property obtained by false pretenses and debts for fraud or defalcation while acting in a fiduciary capacity may be declared nondischargeable only if a creditor timely files and prevails in a nondischargeability action.

Secured Debt: Debt backed by a mortgage, pledge of collateral, or other lien; debt for which the creditor has the right to pursue specific pledged property upon default. Examples include home mortgages, auto loans, and tax liens.

Trustee: The representative of the bankruptcy estate who exercises statutory powers, principally for the benefit of the unsecured creditors, under the general supervision of the court and the direct supervision of the U.S. trustee or bankruptcy administrator. The trustee is a private individual or corporation appointed in all chapter 7, chapter 12, and chapter 13 cases and some chapter 11 cases. The trustee's responsibilities include reviewing the debtor's petition and schedules and bringing actions against creditors or the debtor to recover property of the bankruptcy estate. In chapter 7, the trustee liquidates property of the estate, and makes distributions to creditors. Trustees in chapter 12 and 13 have similar duties to a chapter 7 trustee and the additional responsibilities of overseeing the debtor's plan, receiving payments from debtors, and disbursing plan payments to creditors.

U.S. Trustee: An officer of the Justice Department responsible for supervising the administration of bankruptcy cases, estates, and trustees; monitoring plans and disclosure statements; monitoring creditors' committees; monitoring fee applications; and performing other statutory duties.

Source: Excerpted from "Bankruptcy Basics, Glossary," Administrative Office of the U.S. Courts (www.uscourts.gov), 2006.

Chapter 13 Eligibility: There are two principal requirements for eligibility in a chapter 13 cases. First, the debtor must have regular income, although this need not be from a job—regular benefit payments or rental income would qualify. Second, the debtor must not have debts over a certain amount. The debt limits are $922,975 in secured debt (like home mortgages and auto loans), and $307,675 in unsecured debt (like most credit card debt). These numbers are good through April 1, 2006, and go up every year.

How does bankruptcy help me in the short run?

By imposing an injunction against all collection efforts by creditors, which means creditors must stop calling, sending letters, or suing you over your debts. This is called the automatic stay.

What is a discharge?

If a debt is discharged, the debtor no longer has an obligation to pay the debt and the creditor may not make any effort to compel the debtor to repay. However, if some other person (such as a relative or friend) also has an obligation to pay, their obligation is not discharged. In addition, if the debtor has property that is collateral for a loan, the creditor may still be able to repossess that collateral.

Do all debts get discharged?

No, not all debts will be discharged through the bankruptcy, even if a debtor has satisfactorily performed all of his duties in a case. First, a bankruptcy case only discharges debts that the debtor owed at the time the case was filed, not those incurred after the case was filed.

Debts that are not discharged include debts for certain taxes, certain unscheduled debts (creditors with debts not listed in your paperwork), alimony, maintenance or support debts, pre-petition fines or restitution, debts for injury or death caused by a debtor's use of drugs or alcohol, some government-backed student loans, and certain condo or co-op fees.

Other debts that may not be discharged include debts incurred through fraud or by willful or malicious actions of the debtor. If the creditor does not ask the court to rule on these debts, they will be discharged.

Also, for cases filed before October 17, 2005, some debts listed above that would not be discharged in a chapter 7 case can be discharged through a chapter 13 case. For example, debts incurred through fraud, through the use of a false financial statement, or for an intentional tort, can be discharged through completion of a chapter 13 case. This is only true if you filed your chapter 13 case before October 17, 2005.

How much does it cost to file bankruptcy?

For cases filed before October 17, 2005, the fee for a chapter 7 was $209 or chapter 13 case was $194. As of October 17, 2005, the fee for a chapter 7 case was $274 and $189 for a chapter 13 case. Some courts also impose an additional administrative fee. Also, as of October 17, 2005, the court may waive the filing fee in a chapter 7 case if the debtor's income is below specified levels and the court finds that the debtor cannot pay the filing fee in installments.

Debtors usually find it necessary to hire attorneys to assist them with filing bankruptcy. Attorneys usually charge a fixed fee for certain services in a bankruptcy case and the fees typically differ depending on the chapter under which a debtor files.

Before You File For Personal Bankruptcy: Information About Credit Counseling And Debtor Education

The Bankruptcy Abuse Prevention and Consumer Protection Act of 2005 launched a new era: With limited exceptions, people who plan to file for bankruptcy protection must get credit counseling from a government-approved organization within 180 days before they file. They also must complete a debtor education course to have their debts discharged.

The Department of Justice's U.S. Trustee Program approves organizations to provide the mandatory credit counseling and debtor education. Only the counselors and educators that appear on the U.S. Trustee Program's lists can advertise that they are, indeed, approved to provide the required counseling and debtor education. By law, the U.S. Trustee Program does not operate in Alabama and North Carolina; in these states, court officials called Bankruptcy Administrators approve pre-bankruptcy credit counseling organizations and pre-discharge debtor education course providers.

✔ Quick Tip
Important Questions To Ask
When Choosing A Credit Counselor

It's wise to do some research when choosing a credit counseling organization. If you are in search of credit counseling to fulfill the bankruptcy law requirements, make sure you receive services only from approved providers for your judicial district. Check the list at www.usdoj.gov/ust/eo/bapcpa/ccde/cc_approved.htm or at the bankruptcy clerk's office for the district where you will file. Once you have the list of approved organizations in your judicial district, call several to gather information before you make your choice. Some key questions to ask are:

- What services do you offer?

- Will you help me develop a plan for avoiding problems in the future?

- What are your fees?

- What if I can't afford to pay your fees?

- What qualifications do your counselors have? Are they accredited or certified by an outside organization? What training do they receive?

- What do you do to keep information about me (including my address, phone number, and financial information) confidential and secure?

- How are your employees paid? Are they paid more if I sign up for certain services, if I pay a fee, or if I make a contribution to your organization?

Source: Federal Trade Commission, 2006.

Counseling And Education Requirements: As a rule, pre-bankruptcy credit counseling and pre-discharge debtor education may not be provided at the same time. Credit counseling must take place before you file for bankruptcy; debtor education must take place after you file.

In general, you must file a certificate of credit counseling completion when you file for bankruptcy, and evidence of completion of debtor education after you file for bankruptcy—but before your debts are discharged. Only credit counseling organizations and debtor education course providers that have been approved by the U.S. Trustee Program may issue these certificates. To protect against fraud, the certificates are produced through a central automated system and are numbered.

Pre-Bankruptcy Counseling: A pre-bankruptcy counseling session with an approved credit counseling organization should include an evaluation of your personal financial situation, a discussion of alternatives to bankruptcy, and a personal budget plan. A typical counseling session should last about 60 to 90 minutes, and can take place in person, on the phone, or online. The counseling organization is required to provide the counseling free of charge for those consumers who cannot afford to pay. If you cannot afford to pay a fee for credit counseling, you should request a fee waiver from the counseling organization before the session begins. Otherwise, you may be charged a fee for the counseling, which will generally be about $50, depending on where you live, the types of services you receive, and other factors. The counseling organization is required to discuss any fees with you before starting the counseling session.

Once you have completed the required counseling, you must get a certificate as proof. Check the U.S. Trustee's website (http://www.usdoj.gov/ust) to be sure that you receive the certificate from a counseling organization that is approved in the judicial district where you are filing bankruptcy. Credit counseling organizations may not charge an extra fee for the certificate.

Post-Filing Debtor Education: A debtor education course by an approved provider should include information on developing a budget, managing money, using credit wisely, and other resources. Like pre-filing counseling, debtor education may be provided in person, on the phone, or online. The debtor education session might last longer than the pre-filing counseling—about two hours—and the typical fee is between $50 and $100. As with pre-filing counseling, if you are unable to pay the session fee, you should seek a fee waiver from the debtor education provider. Check the list of approved debtor education providers at www.usdoj.gov/ust/eo/bapcpa/ccde/de_approved.htm or at the bankruptcy clerk's office in your district.

Once you have completed the required debtor education course, you should receive a certificate as proof. This certificate is separate from the certificate you received after completing your pre-filing credit counseling. Check the U.S. Trustee's website to be sure that you receive the certificate from a debtor education provider that is approved in the judicial district where you filed bankruptcy. Unless they have disclosed a charge to you before the counseling session begins, debtor education providers may not charge an extra fee for the certificate.

♣ It's A Fact!!
For More Information And Assistance

The U.S. Trustee Program promotes integrity and efficiency in the nation's bankruptcy system by enforcing bankruptcy laws, providing oversight of private trustees, and maintaining operational excellence. The Program has 21 regions and 95 field offices, and oversees the administration of bankruptcy in all states except Alabama and North Carolina. For more information, visit www.usdoj.gov/ust.

If you have concerns about approved credit counseling agencies or debtor education course providers, such as the failure to provide adequate service, please contact the U.S. Trustee Program by e-mail at USTCCDE ComplaintHelp@usdoj.gov, or in writing at Executive Office for U.S. Trustees, Credit Counseling and Debtor Education Unit, 20 Massachusetts Avenue, NW, Suite 8000, Washington, DC, 20530. Provide as much detail as you can, including the name of the credit counseling organization or debtor education course provider, the date of contact, and whom you spoke with.

Source: Federal Trade Commission,
2006.

Part Six

If You Need More Information

Chapter 46

Credit And Debt Statistics

This chapter presents data on the nation's finances. The primary sources of these data are publications of several departments of the federal government, especially the Treasury Department, and independent agencies such as the Federal Deposit Insurance Corporation, the Federal Reserve Board, and the Securities and Exchange Commission.

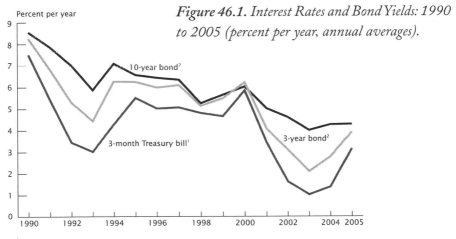

Percent per year

Figure 46.1. Interest Rates and Bond Yields: 1990 to 2005 (percent per year, annual averages).

[1] New issues.
[2] U.S. Treasury, constant maturities.
Source: Chart prepared by U.S. Census Bureau. For data, see Tables 1178 and 1179.

About This Chapter: This chapter includes excerpts from "Section 25: Banking, Finance, and Insurance" of the *Statistical Abstract of the United States, 2007*, U.S. Census Bureau (www.census.gov).

Table 46.1. **Financial Assets Held by Families by Type of Asset: 2001 and 2004**

[Median value in thousands of constant 2004 dollars (29.8 represents $29,800). All dollar figures are adjusted to 2004 dollars using the "current methods" version of the consumer price index for all urban consumers published by U.S. Bureau of Labor Statistics. Families include one-person units.

Age of family head and family income	Any financial asset [1]	Trans- action accounts [2]	Certifi- cates of deposit	Savings bonds	Stocks [3]	Pooled invest- ment funds [4]	Retirement accounts [5]	Life insur- ance [6]	Other man- aged [7]
PERCENT OF FAMILIES OWNING ASSET									
2001, total	93.4	91.4	15.7	16.7	21.3	17.7	52.2	28.0	6.6
2004, total	**93.8**	**91.3**	**12.7**	**17.6**	**20.7**	**15.0**	**49.7**	**24.2**	**7.3**
Under 35 years old.	90.1	86.4	5.6	15.3	13.3	8.3	40.2	11.0	2.9
35 to 44 years old	93.6	90.8	6.7	23.3	18.5	12.3	55.9	20.1	3.7
45 to 54 years old	93.6	91.8	11.9	21.0	23.2	18.2	57.7	26.0	6.2
55 to 64 years old	95.2	93.2	18.1	15.2	29.1	20.6	62.9	32.1	9.4
65 to 74 years old	96.5	93.9	19.9	14.9	25.4	18.6	43.2	34.8	12.8
75 years old and over	97.6	96.4	25.7	11.0	18.4	16.6	29.2	34.0	16.7
Percentiles of income: [8]									
Less than 20	80.1	75.5	5.0	6.2	5.1	3.6	10.1	14.0	3.1
20 to 39.9	91.5	87.3	12.7	8.8	8.2	7.6	30.0	19.2	4.9
40 to 59.9	98.5	95.9	11.8	15.4	16.3	12.7	53.4	24.2	7.9
60 to 79.9	99.1	98.4	14.9	26.6	28.2	18.6	69.7	29.8	7.8
80 to 89.9	99.8	99.1	16.3	32.3	35.8	26.2	81.9	29.5	12.1
90 to 100	100.0	100.0	21.5	29.9	55.0	39.1	88.5	38.1	13.0
MEDIAN VALUE [9]									
2001, total	29.8	4.2	16.0	1.1	21.3	37.3	30.9	10.7	74.6
2004, total	**23.0**	**3.8**	**15.0**	**1.0**	**15.0**	**40.4**	**35.2**	**6.0**	**45.0**
Under 35 years old.	5.2	1.8	4.0	0.5	4.4	8.0	11.0	3.0	5.0
35 to 44 years old	19.0	3.0	10.0	0.5	10.0	15.9	27.9	5.0	18.3
45 to 54 years old	38.6	4.8	11.0	1.0	14.5	50.0	55.5	8.0	43.0
55 to 64 years old	78.0	6.7	29.0	2.5	25.0	75.0	83.0	10.0	65.0
65 to 74 years old	36.1	5.5	20.0	3.0	42.0	60.0	80.0	8.0	60.0
75 years old and over	38.8	6.5	22.0	5.0	50.0	60.0	30.0	5.0	50.0

[1] Includes other types of financial assets, not shown separately.   [2] Checking, savings, and money market deposit accounts, money market mutual funds, and call accounts at brokerages.   [3] Covers only those stocks that are directly held by families outside mutual funds, retirement accounts and other managed assets.   [4] Excludes money market mutual funds and indirectly held mutual funds and includes all other types of directly held pooled investment funds, such as traditional open-ended and closed-end mutual funds, real estate investment trusts, and hedge funds.   [5] The tax-deferred retirement accounts consist of IRAs, Keogh accounts, and certain employer-sponsored accounts. Employer-sponsored accounts include 401(k), 403(b), and thrift saving accounts from current or past jobs; other current job plans from which loans or withdrawals can be made; and accounts from past jobs from which the family expects to receive the account balance in the future.   [6] The value of such policies according to their current cash value, not their death benefit.   [7] Includes personal annuities and trusts with an equity interest and managed investment accounts. [8] Percentiles of income distribution in 2004 dollars: 20th: $18,900; 40th: $33,900; 60th: $53,600; 80th: $89,300; 90th: $129,400. Percentile: A value on a scale of zero to 100 that indicates the percent of a distribution that is equal to or below it. For example, a family with income in the 80th percentile has income equal to or better than 80 percent of all other families.   [9] Median value of financial asset for families holding such assets.

Source: Board of Governors of the Federal Reserve System, "2004 Survey of Consumer Finances"; published 28 February 2006; <http://www.federalreserve.gov/pubs/oss/oss2/2004/scf2004home.html>.

Table 46.2. **Flow of Funds Accounts—Liabilities of Households: 1990 to 2005**

[As of December 31 (3,715 represents $3,715,000,000,000). Includes nonprofit organizations. n.e.c. = Not elsewhere classified]

Type of instrument	Total (bil. dol.)							Percent distribution		
	1990	1995	2000	2002	2003	2004	2005	1990	2000	2005
Total liabilities	3,715	5,055	7,350	8,605	9,605	10,735	11,916	100.0	100.0	100.0
Credit market instruments.	3,593	4,858	6,961	8,297	9,254	10,292	11,497	96.7	94.7	96.5
Home mortgages [1]	2,500	3,326	4,770	5,844	6,680	7,593	8,660	67.3	64.9	72.7
Consumer credit	824	1,168	1,730	1,949	2,038	2,126	2,189	22.2	23.5	18.4
Municipal securities	87	98	143	170	184	194	211	2.3	1.9	1.8
Bank loans, n.e.c.	18	57	77	58	74	79	106	0.5	1.0	0.9
Other loans	82	116	120	121	119	120	119	2.2	1.6	1.0
Commercial mortgages.	83	92	121	156	160	180	212	2.2	1.6	1.8
Security credit	39	79	235	148	183	264	232	1.0	3.2	1.9
Trade payables	67	101	135	140	148	157	164	1.8	1.8	1.4
Unpaid life insurance premiums [2]	16	18	20	20	21	22	23	0.4	0.3	0.2

[1] Includes loans made under home equity lines of credit and home equity loans secured by junior liens.   [2] Includes deferred premiums.

Source: Board of Governors of the Federal Reserve System, "Federal Reserve Statistical Release, Z.1, Flow of Funds Accounts of the United States"; published 9 March 2006; <http://www.federalreserve.gov/releases/z1/20060309/>.

Table 46.3. **Financial Debt Held by Families by Type of Debt: 2001 and 2004**

[Median debt in thousands of constant 2004 dollars (41.3 represents $41,300). See headnote, Table 46.1]

Age of family head and family income	Any debt	Secured by residential property		Lines of credit not secured by residential property	Installment loans	Credit card balances [2]	Other [3]
		Primary residence [1]	Other				
PERCENT OF FAMILIES HOLDING DEBT							
2001, total	75.1	44.6	4.6	1.5	45.2	44.4	7.2
2004, total	76.4	47.9	4.0	1.6	46.0	46.2	7.6
Under 35 years old	79.8	37.7	2.1	2.2	59.4	47.5	6.2
35 to 44 years old	88.6	62.8	4.0	1.5	55.7	58.8	11.3
45 to 54 years old	88.4	64.6	6.3	2.9	50.2	54.0	9.4
55 to 64 years old	76.3	51.0	5.9	0.7	42.8	42.1	8.4
65 to 74 years old	50.0	32.1	3.2	0.4	27.5	31.9	4.0
75 years old and over	40.3	18.7	1.5	(B)	13.9	23.6	2.5
Percentiles of income: [4]							
Less than 20	52.6	15.9	(B)	(B)	26.9	28.8	4.6
20 to 39.9	69.8	29.5	1.5	1.5	39.9	42.9	5.8
40 to 59.9	84.0	51.7	2.6	1.8	52.4	55.1	8.0
60 to 79.9	86.6	65.8	4.1	1.8	57.8	56.0	8.3
80 to 89.9	92.0	76.8	7.5	2.6	60.0	57.6	12.3
90 to 100	86.3	76.2	15.4	2.5	45.7	38.5	10.6
MEDIAN DEBT [5]							
2001, total	41.3	74.6	42.6	4.2	10.3	2.0	3.2
2004, total	55.3	95.0	87.0	3.0	11.5	2.2	4.0
Under 35 years old	33.6	107.0	62.5	1.0	11.9	1.5	3.0
35 to 44 years old	87.2	110.0	75.0	1.9	12.0	2.5	4.0
45 to 54 years old	83.2	97.0	87.0	7.0	12.0	2.9	4.0
55 to 64 years old	48.0	83.0	108.8	14.0	12.9	2.2	5.5
65 to 74 years old	25.0	51.0	100.0	4.0	8.3	2.2	5.0
75 years old and over	15.4	31.0	39.0	(B)	6.7	1.0	2.0

B Base figure too small. [1] First and second mortgages and home equity loans and lines of credit secured by the primary residence. [2] Families that had an outstanding balance on any of their credit cards after paying their most recent bills. [3] Includes loans on insurance policies, loans against pension accounts, borrowing on margin accounts and unclassified loans. [4] See footnote 0, Table 1150. [5] Median amount of financial debt for families holding such debts.

Source: Board of Governors of the Federal Reserve System, "2004 Survey of Consumer Finances"; published 28 February 2006; <http://www.federalreserve.gov/pubs/oss/oss2/2004/scf2004home.html>.

Table 46.4. **Percent Distribution of Amount of Debt Held by Families: 2001 and 2004**

[See headnote, Table 46.1]

Type of debt	2001	2004	Purpose of debt	2001	2004	Type of lending institution	2001	2004
Total	100.0	100.0	**Total**	100.0	100.0	**Total**	100.0	100.0
Secured by residential property:			Primary residence:			Commercial bank	34.1	35.1
Primary residence	75.2	75.2	Purchase	70.9	70.2	Thrift institution	6.1	7.3
Other	6.2	8.5	Improvement	2.0	1.9	Credit union	5.5	3.6
Lines of credit not			Other residential			Finance or loan company.	4.3	4.1
secured by			property	6.5	9.5	Brokerage	3.1	2.5
residential property	0.5	0.7	Investments, excluding			Real estate lender [1] . . .	38.0	39.4
Installment loans	12.3	11.0	real estate	2.8	2.2	Individual lender	2.0	1.7
Credit card balances	3.4	3.0	Vehicles	7.8	6.7	Other nonfinancial	1.4	2.0
Other	2.3	1.6	Goods and services	5.8	6.0	Government	1.1	0.7
			Education	3.1	3.0	Credit card issuer	3.7	3.0
			Other loans	1.1	0.6	Other loans	0.8	0.5

[1] Includes mortgage lender.

Source: Board of Governors of the Federal Reserve System, "2004 Survey of Consumer Finances"; published 28 February 2006; <http://www.federalreserve.gov/pubs/oss/oss2/2004/scf2004home.html>.

Table 46.5. **Household Debt-Service Payments and Financial Obligations as a Percentage of Disposable Personal Income: 1980 to 2005**

[As of end of year, seasonally adjusted. Household debt service ratio is an estimate of the ratio of debt payments to disposable personal income. Debt payments consist of the estimated required payments on outstanding mortgage and consumer debt. The financial obligations ratio adds automobile lease payments, rental payments on tenant-occupied property, homeowners' insurance, and property tax payments to the debt service ratio]

Year	Household debt service ratio	Financial obligations ratio			Year	Household debt service ratio	Financial obligations ratio		
		Total	Home-owner	Renter			Total	Home-owner	Renter
1980 . . .	10.58	15.37	13.31	23.70	2001 . . .	13.20	18.68	16.06	31.73
1990 . . .	11.98	17.37	15.50	24.69	2002 . . .	13.27	18.53	16.10	30.81
1995 . . .	11.84	17.45	15.14	27.00	2003 . . .	13.17	18.18	15.83	30.76
1999 . . .	12.35	17.83	15.41	29.39	2004 . . .	13.17	17.97	15.87	29.22
2000 . . .	12.77	18.14	15.64	30.54	2005 . . .	13.86	18.62	16.77	28.43

Source: Board of Governors of the Federal Reserve System, "Household Debt Service and Financial Obligations Ratios;" <http://www.federalreserve.gov/releases/housedebt/default.htm>.

Table 46.6. **Ratios of Debt Payments to Family Income: 1995 to 2004**

[In percent. All dollar figures are adjusted to 2004 dollars using the "current methods" version of the consumer price index for all urban consumers published by U.S. Bureau of Labor Statistics. Families include one-person units.

Age of family head and family income (constant (**2004**) dollars)	Ratio of debt payments to family income						Percent of debtors with—					
	Aggregate			Median			Ratios above 40 percent			Any payment 60 days or more past due		
	1995	2001	2004	1995	2001	2004	1995	2001	2004	1995	2001	2004
All families	**14.1**	**12.9**	**14.4**	**16.2**	**16.7**	**18.0**	**11.7**	**11.8**	**12.2**	**7.1**	**7.0**	**8.9**
Under 35 years old.	17.8	17.2	17.8	16.8	17.7	18.0	12.1	12.0	12.8	8.7	11.9	13.7
35 to 44 years old	17.2	15.1	18.2	18.3	17.8	20.6	9.9	10.1	12.6	7.7	5.9	11.7
45 to 54 years old	15.1	12.8	15.3	16.6	17.4	18.4	12.3	11.6	13.1	7.4	6.2	7.6
55 to 64 years old	11.8	10.9	11.5	14.2	14.3	15.8	15.1	12.3	10.2	3.2	7.1	4.2
65 to 74 years old	7.2	9.2	8.7	12.3	16.0	15.6	11.3	14.7	11.6	5.3	1.5	3.4
75 years old and over	2.5	3.9	7.1	2.9	8.0	12.8	7.4	14.6	10.7	5.4	0.8	3.9
Percentiles of income: [1]												
Less than 20	19.1	16.1	18.2	13.3	19.2	19.7	27.5	29.3	27.0	10.2	13.4	15.9
20 to 39.9	17.0	15.8	16.7	17.5	16.7	17.4	18.0	16.6	18.6	10.1	11.7	13.8
40 to 59.9	15.6	17.1	19.4	15.7	17.6	19.5	9.9	12.3	13.7	8.7	7.9	10.4
60 to 79.9	17.9	16.8	18.5	18.9	18.1	20.6	7.7	6.5	7.1	6.6	4.0	7.1
80 to 89.9	16.6	17.0	17.3	16.8	17.3	18.1	4.7	3.5	2.4	2.8	2.6	2.3
90 to 100	9.5	8.1	9.3	12.6	11.2	12.7	2.3	2.0	1.8	1.0	1.3	0.3

[1] See footnote 8, Table 46.1.

Source: Board of Governors of the Federal Reserve System, "2004 Survey of Consumer Finances"; published 28 February 2006; <http://www.federalreserve.gov/pubs/oss/oss2/2004/scf2004home.html>.

Table 46.7. **Usage of General Purpose Credit Cards by Families: 1995 to 2004**

[General purpose credit cards include Mastercard, Visa, Optima, and Discover cards. Excludes cards used only for business purposes. All dollar figures are given in constant 2004 dollars based on consumer price index data as published by U.S. Bureau of Labor Statistics. Families include one-person units.

Age of family head and family income	Percent having a general purpose credit card	Median number of cards	Median new charges on last month's bills (dol.)	Percent having a balance after last month's bills	Median balance (dol.) [1]	Percent of cardholding families who—		
						Almost always pay off the balance	Some-times pay off the balance	Hardly ever pay off the balance
1995, total	66.5	2	200	56.0	1,700	52.4	20.1	27.5
1998, total	67.5	2	200	54.7	2,000	53.8	19.3	26.9
2001, total	72.7	2	200	53.7	1,900	55.3	19.1	25.6
2004, total	**71.5**	**2**	**300**	**56.2**	**2,100**	**55.7**	**20.3**	**24.0**
Under 35 years old	60.6	2	200	66.1	1,500	49.0	20.4	30.6
35 to 44 years old.	73.3	2	300	70.8	2,400	41.6	26.2	32.2
45 to 54 years old.	77.5	2	300	61.2	3,000	49.3	23.9	26.8
55 to 64 years old.	78.2	2	400	46.1	2,500	66.8	16.8	16.5
65 to 74 years old.	75.5	2	300	37.7	2,300	70.7	13.4	15.9
75 years old and over	65.4	2	200	32.2	1,100	77.5	12.9	9.7
Less than $10,000	31.5	1	100	59.4	1,200	50.9	17.3	31.9
$10,000 to $24,999	48.6	1	100	59.7	1,200	49.9	17.0	33.1
$25,000 to $49,999	71.2	2	200	64.3	2,000	46.9	20.3	32.8
$50,000 to $99,999	88.2	2	300	56.1	2,800	56.1	22.0	21.8
$100,000 and more.	96.6	2	1,200	42.8	3,400	71.1	20.2	8.7

[1] Among families having a balance.

Source: Board of Governors of the Federal Reserve System, unpublished data.

Chapter 47

A Directory Of Financial Literacy Resources

To Help You Learn About Money And Money Management

American Bankers Association
1120 Connecticut Ave., NW
Washington, DC 20036
Toll-Free: 800-BANKERS
Phone: 202-663-5000
Fax: 202-663-7578
Website: http://www.aba.com

American Bankruptcy Institute
44 Canal Center Plaza, Suite 404
Alexandria, VA 22314
Phone: 703-739-0800
Fax: 703-739-1060
Website: http://www.abiworld.org

American Financial Services Association Education Foundation
919 Eighteenth St., NW, Suite 300
Washington, DC 20006-5517
Phone: 202-466-8611
Fax: 202-223-0321
Website: http://www.afsaef.org

American Institute of Certified Public Accountants
1211 Avenue of the Americas
New York, NY 10036
Phone: 888-777-7077
Website: http://
www.360financialliteracy.org

About This Chapter: The resources listed in this chapter were compiled from many sources deemed accurate. Inclusion does not constitute endorsement, and there is no implication associated with omission. All contact information was verified in June 2007.

American Savings Education Council
2121 K Street, NW, Suite 600
Washington, DC 20037-1896
Phone: 202-659-0670
Fax: 202-775-6312
Website: http://www.asec.org
E-mail: info@choosetosave.org;
info@asec.org

America's Community Bankers (ACB)
900 19th St., NW, Suite 400
Washington, DC 20006
Phone: 202-857-3100
Fax: 202-296-8716
Website: http://www.acbankers.org

Bankrate
11760 U.S. Highway 1, Suite 200
N. Palm Beach, FL 33408
Phone: 561-630-2400
Website: http://www.bankrate.com

Bond Market Foundation
Website: http://
www.tomorrowsmoney.org
E-mail: info@tomorrowsmoney.org

Center for Responsible Lending
301 West Main Street
Durham, NC 27701
Phone: 919-313-8500
Website: http://
www.responsiblelending.org

Certified Financial Planner Board of Standards
Communication and Consumer Services
1670 Broadway, Suite 600
Denver, CO 80202-4809
Toll-Free: 888-237-6275
Phone: 303-830-7500
Fax: 303-860-7388
Website: http://www.CFP-Board.org
E-mail: mail@cfp-board.org

Coalition Against Insurance Fraud
1012 14th St. NW, Suite 200
Washington, DC 20005
Phone: 202-393-7330
Fax: 202-393-7329
Website: http://
www.InsuranceFraud.org
E-mail: info@insurancefraud.org

Consumer Action
P.O. Box 1762
Washington, DC 20013
Complaints: 415-777-9635
Fax: 415-777-5267
TTY: 415-777-9456
Website: http://www
.consumer-action.org
E-mail: info@consumer-action.org

Consumer Credit Counseling Services (CCCS)
Phone: 800-388-2227
Website: http://www.nfcc.org

Consumer Federation of America (CFA)

1620 I Street, NW, Suite 200
Washington, DC 20006
Phone: 202-387-6121
Fax: 202-265-7989
Website: http://
www.consumerfed.org

Cooperative State Research, Education, and Extension Service

U.S. Department of Agriculture
Cooperative State Research,
Education, and Extension Service
1400 Independence Avenue SW,
Stop 2201
Washington, DC 20250-2201
Phone: 202-720-7441
Website: http://www.csrees.usda.gov

Credit Abuse Resistance Education (CARE) Program

Website: http://www.careprogram.us

Credit Union National Association (CUNA)

P.O. Box 431
Madison, WI 53701-0431
Phone: 800-356-9655
Fax: 608-231-4263
Website: http://www.cuna.org

Debtors Anonymous

General Service Board
P.O. Box 920888
Needham, MA 02492-0009
Phone: 781-453-2743
Fax: 781-453-2745
Website: http://
www.debtorsanonymous.org
E-mail:
new@debtorsanonymous.org

Federal Citizen Information Center

Toll-Free: 888-878-3256
Website: http://
www.pueblo.gsa.gov

Federal Deposit Insurance Corporation (FDIC)

Division of Supervision and
Consumer Protection
550 17th St., NW
Washington, DC 20429
Phone: 703-562-2222
Toll-Free: 877-ASK-FDIC
(877-275-3342)
TDD Toll-Free: 800-925-4618
Fax: 202-898-6683
Website: http://www.fdic.gov

Federal Reserve Board

Division of Consumer and
Community Affairs
Board of Governors of the Federal
Reserve System
Constitution Avenue, NW
Washington, DC 20551
Complaints: 202-452-3693
Public Affairs: 202-452-3204
TDD: 202-452-3544
Website: http://
www.federalreserve.gov

Federal Trade Commission (FTC)

Consumer Response Center
600 Pennsylvania Ave., NW
Washington, DC 20580
Toll-Free: 877-FTC-HELP
(877-382-4357)
TDD/TTY: 866-653-4261
Website: http://www.ftc.gov

Financial Literacy 101

Illinois Division of Banks and Real
Estate
Website: http://www.idfpr.com/
finlit101/default.asp

Financial Literacy Two Thousand and Ten

Website: http://www.fl2010.org.

Financial Planning Association (FPA)

4100 E. Mississippi Ave., Suite 400
Denver, CO 80246-3053
Toll-Free: 800-647-6340;
800-322-4237
Fax: 303-759-0749
Website: http://www.fpanet.org
E-mail: fpa@fpanet.org

Government National Mortgage Association

451 7th Street, SW, Room B-133
Washington, DC 20410
Phone: 202-708-1535
Website: http://www.ginniemae.gov

Housing and Urban Development

Website: http://www.hud.gov

InCharge Education Foundation, Inc.

2101 Park Center Dr., Suite 310
Orlando, FL 32835
Website: http://
www.inchargefoundation.org

Institute for Financial Literacy

P.O. Box 1842
Portland, ME 04104
Phone: 207-221-3600
Fax: 207-221-3691
Toll-Free: 866-662-4932
TTY: 866-662-4937
Website: http://www.financiallit.org

Jump$tart Coalition for Personal Financial Literacy

919 18th St., NW, Suite 300
Washington, DC 20006
Phone: 202-466-8610
Toll-Free: 888-45-EDUCATE
Fax: 202-223-0321
Website: http://www.jumpstart.org
E-mail: info@jumpstartcoalition.org

Junior Achievement

One Education Way
Colorado Springs, CO 80906
Phone: 719-540-8000
Fax 719-540-6299
Website: http://www.ja.org
E-mail: newmedia@ja.org

Kansas State University Research and Extension

Website: http://
www.oznet.ksu.edu/
financialmanagement

Mortgage Bankers Association of America

Consumer Affairs
1919 Pennsylvania Ave., N.W.
Washington, DC 20006
Phone: 202-557-2700
Website: http://
www.mortgagebankers.org

National Association of Personal Financial Advisors

3250 North Arlington Heights Rd.
Suite 109
Arlington Heights, IL 60004
Toll-Free: 800-366-2732
Website: http://www.napfa.org

National Coalition for Consumer Education

National Consumers League
1701 K Street, NW, Suite 1200
Washington, DC 20006
Phone: 202-835-3323
Fax: 202-835-0747
Website: http://www.nclnet.org
E-mail: info@nclnet.org

National Consumer Law Center

1001 Connecticut Avenue, NW
Suite 510
Washington, DC 20036
Fax 202-463-9462
Website: http://www.consumerlaw.org

National Consumers League

1701 K Street, NW, Suite 1200
Washington, DC 20006
Phone: 202-835-3323
Fax: 202-835-0747
Website: http://www.nclnet.org
E-mail: info@nclnet.org

National Council on Economic Education

Website: http://www.ncee.net

National Credit Union Administration
1775 Duke Street
Alexandria, VA 22314-3428
Phone: 703-518-6330
Website: http://www.ncua.gov

National Endowment for Financial Education
Website: http://www.nfec.info

National Foundation for Credit Counseling
801 Roeder Road, Suite 900
Silver Spring, MD 20910
Phone: 301-589-5600
Toll-Free: 800-388-2227
Website: http://www.nfcc.org

National Fraud Information Center/Internet Fraud Watch
1701 K St., NW, Suite 1200
Washington, DC 20006
Toll-Free: 800-876-7060
Fax: 202-835-0767
TDD/TTY: 202-835-0778
Website: http://www.fraud.org

Northwestern Mutual Foundation
720 East Wisconsin Avenue
Milwaukee, WI 53202-4797
Website: http://www.themint.org
E-mail: themint@northwesternmutual.com

Project for Financial Independence
Website: http://www.consultaplanner.org

Rutgers Cooperative Research and Extension
88 Lipman Drive
New Brunswick, NJ 08901-8525
Website: http://www.rcre.rutgers.edu

Securities and Exchange Commission (SEC)
Office of Investor Education and Assistance
100 F Street, NE
Washington, DC 20549-0213
Phone: 202-551-6551
Toll-Free: 800-SEC-0330
Fax: 202-942-9634
Website: http://www.sec.gov/complaint.shtml; http://www.sec.gov/investor.shtml (Investor Information)

Small Business Administration (SBA)
Toll-Free: 800-U-ASK-SBA (827-5722)
TDD: 704-344-6640
Fax: 202-481-6190
Website: http://www.sba.gov
E-mail: answerdesk@sba.com

SmartMoney University

1755 Broadway (2nd Floor)
New York, NY 10019
Website: http://
www.smartmoney.com/university

Social Security Administration

Office of Public Inquiries
Windsor Park Bldg.
6401 Security Blvd.
Baltimore, MD 21235
Toll-Free: 800-772-1213
Website: http://
www.socialsecurity.gov

Teen Consumer Scrapbook

Washington State Attorney
General
Website: http://www.atg.wa.gov/
teenconsumer

U.S. Financial Literacy and Education Commission

Website: http://www.mymoney.gov

USAA Educational Foundation

Website: http://
www.usaaedfoundation.org

Visa—Practical Money Skills for Life Program

P.O. Box 194607
San Francisco, CA 94119-4607
Phone: 800-Visa-511
Website: http://
www.practicalmoneyskills.com
E-mail:
info@practicalmoneyskills.com

Federal Reserve Banks

Federal Reserve Board of Governors

Website: http://
www.federalreserve.gov

Federal Reserve Banks

District #1

Federal Reserve Bank of Boston
600 Atlantic Avenue
Boston, MA 02210
Toll-Free: 800-248-0168, ext. 3755
Phone: 617-973-3755
Website: http://www.bos.frb.org

District #2

Federal Reserve Bank of New York
33 Liberty Street
New York, NY 10045
Phone: 212-720-5000
Website: http://
www.newyorkfed.org

District #3

Federal Reserve Bank of
Philadelphia
10 Independence Mall
Philadelphia, PA 19106-1574
Phone: 800-372-1220
Website: http://
www.philadelphiafed.org

District #4

Federal Reserve Bank of Cleveland
P.O. Box 6387
Cleveland, OH 44101
Toll-Free: 800-537-5990
Phone: 216-579-2478
Website: http://
www.clevelandfed.org

District #5

Federal Reserve Bank of Richmond
P.O. Box 27622
Richmond, VA 23261
Toll-Free: 800-526-2028
Phone: 804-697-8000
Website: http://
www.richmondfed.org

District #6

Federal Reserve Bank of Atlanta
Supervision and Regulation
Department
1000 Peachtree Street, NE
Atlanta, GA 30309-4470
Phone: 404-498-8500
Website: http://www.frbatlanta.org

District #7

Federal Reserve Bank of Chicago
230 South LaSalle Street
Chicago, IL 60604-1413
Phone: 312-322-5322
Website: http://www.chicagofed.org

District #8

Federal Reserve Bank of St. Louis
Banking Supervision and
Regulation—Consumer Affairs
1421 Dr. Martin Luther King drive
St. Louis, MO 63106
Toll-Free: 800-333-0810
Phone: 314-444-8444
Website: http://www.stlouisfed.org

District #9

Federal Reserve Bank of
Minneapolis
90 Hennepin Avenue
Minneapolis, MN 55401
Toll-Free: 800-553-9656
Phone: 612-204-5000
Website: http://
www.minneapolisfed.org

District #10

Federal Reserve Bank of Kansas
City
925 Grand Boulevard
Kansas City, MO 64198
Toll-Free: 800-333-1010
Phone: 816-881-2488
Website: http://
www.kansascityfed.org

District #11

Federal Reserve Bank of Dallas
Banking Supervision Department
2200 N. Pearl Street
Dallas, TX 75201
Toll-Free: 800-333-4460
Phone: 214-922-5508
Website: http://www.dallasfed.org

District #12

Federal Reserve Bank of San
Francisco
Banking Supervision and
Regulation
101 Market Street
San Francisco, CA 94105
Phone: 415-974-2000
Website: http://www.frbsf.org

Resources Within The Department Of The Treasury

Bureau of Engraving and Printing

Office of External Relations
14th and C Sts, SW, Rm. 533 M
Washington, DC 20228
Phone: 202-874-8888
Fax: 202-874-3177
Website: http://
www.moneyfactory.gov

Bureau of the Public Debt

Customer Call Center
Treasury Direct
P.O. Box 7015
Parkersburg, WV 26106
Toll-Free: 800-722-2678
Website: http://
www.publicdebt.treas.gov

Bureau of the Public Debt

Marketing Office
P.O. Box 7015
Parkersburg, WV 26016
Toll-Free: 800-4US-BOND
Website: http://
www.publicdebt.treas.gov

Comptroller of the Currency

Customer Assistance Group
1301 McKinney St., Suite 3450
Houston, TX 77010
Toll-Free: 800-613-6743
Website: http://www.occ.treas.gov

Internal Revenue Service (IRS)

General Information:
800-829-1040
Automated Refund Information:
800-829-4477
Taxpayer Advocate Service:
877-777-4778
TDD Toll-Free: 800-829-4059
Website: http://www.irs.gov

Office of Thrift Supervision
Compliance Policy
1700 G St., NW
Washington, DC 20552
Toll-Free: 800-842-6929
Website: http://www.ots.treas.gov

United States Mint
Customer Service Center
801 9th Street, NW
Washington, DC 20220
Toll-Free: 800-872-6468
Website: http://www.usmint.gov

National Credit Bureaus

Equifax
P.O. Box 740241
Atlanta, GA 30374-0241
Toll-Free: 800-685-1111
Website: http://www.equifax.com

Experian (formerly TRW)
P.O. Box 949
Allen, TX 75013-0949
Toll-Free: 888-EXPERIAN
(397-3742)
Website: http://www.experian.com

Trans Union
P.O. Box 390
Springfield, PA 19064-03090
Toll-Free: 800-916-8800
Website: http://www.tuc.com

Chapter 48

Additional Reading About Credit and Debt

Books To Help You Understand Financial Principles

Cash and Credit Information for Teens: Facts about Earning, Spending, and Borrowing Money, Including Topics Such as Budgeting, Consumer Rights, Banks, Paychecks, Taxes, Loans, Credit Cards, and More
by Kathryn R. Deering (Editor)
Published by Omnigraphics, Incorporated, 2005
ISBN: 9780780807808

Generation Y Money Book: 99 Smart Ways to Handle Money
by Don Silver
Published by Adams-Hall Publishing, 2000
ISBN: 9780944708644

Growing Money: A Complete Investing Guide for Kids
by Debbie Honig and Gail Karlitz
Published by Penguin Young Readers Group, 2001
ISBN: 9780843177022

High School Money Book
by Don Silver
Published by Adams-Hall Publishing, 2006
ISBN: 9780944708743

Millionaire Next Door
by Thomas J. Stanley and William D. Danko
Published by Pocket Books, 1998
ISBN: 978-0671015206

Motley Fool Investment Guide for Teens: 8 Steps to Having More Money Than Your Parents Ever Dreamed Of
by David Gardner, Tom Gardner, and Selena Maranjian
Published by Simon & Schuster Adult Publishing Group, 2002
ISBN: 9780743229968

New Money Book of Personal Finance
by the Editors of *Money Magazine*
Published by Business Plus, 2002
ISBN: 978-0446679336

Personal Finance For Dummies, 5th edition
by Eric Tyson
Published by Wiley, 2006
ISBN: 978-0470038321

Rich Dad, Poor Dad for Teens: The Secrets About Money That You Don't Learn in School!
by Robert T. Kiyosaki and Sharon L. Lechter
Published by Grand Central Publishing, 2006
ISBN: 9780446693219

Savings and Investment Information for Teens: Facts about Making Money Grow, with Information about the Economy, Bank Accounts, Stocks, Bonds, Mutual Funds, Online Investing, and More
by Kathryn R. Deering (Editor)
Published by Omnigraphics, Incorporated, 2005
ISBN: 9780780807815

Online Resources

ABCs of Banking
State of Connecticut, Department of Banking
Website: http://http://www.ct.gov/dob/cwp/
view.asp?a=2235&q=297884&dobNAV_GID=1659

Bankruptcy Judges Warn Young Consumers about Credit Card Debt
Administrative Office of the United States Courts
Website: http://http://www.uscourts.gov/ttb/feb04ttb/bankruptcy

Budgeting for Beginners
Bond Market Foundation
Website: http://http://www.tomorrowsmoney.org/section.cfm/387/429

Cash Crisis: Money Traps That Keep You Broke
by Laura Connerly, University of Arkansas
Website: http://www.uaex.edu/Other_Areas/publications/PDF/
FSHEC-117.pdf

Finding Money to Save
America Saves
Website: http://www.americasaves.org/enroll/findingmoney.asp

Focus on Finances: Preparing for Your Future
Federal Trade Commission and the *Washington Times*
Website: http://www.ftc.gov/bcp/conline/pubs/misc/nie0406.pdf

How to Establish, Use, and Protect Your Credit
Federal Reserve Bank of San Francisco
Website: http://www.frbsf.org/publications/consumer/credit.html

Interest Rates: An Introduction
Federal Reserve Bank of New York
Website: http://www.newyorkfed.org/education/define.html

Knee Deep in Debt
Federal Trade Commission
Website: http://www.ftc.gov/bcp/conline/pubs/credit/kneedeep.htm

Money and Youth
Canadian Foundation for Economic Education
Website: http://www.moneyandyouth.cfee.org/en/index.html

Money Smart Kids
Kiplinger
Website: http://www.kiplinger.com/columns/kids/archive.html

Moneyopolis
Ernst and Young
Website: http://www.moneyopolis.org

Ouch! Cell Phone Bill Surprises
Attorney General of Maryland
Website: http://www.oag.state.md.us/consumer/edge110.htm

Start Now To Teach Pre-College Teens Good Credit Management
By Lucy Lazarony, Bankrate.com
Website: http://www.bankrate.com/brm/news/cc/19980907.asp

Talking to Teens about Money
Consumer Action
Website: http://www.consumer-action.org/english/articles/
talking_to_teens_about_money_english

Teens and Money
Indiana Department of Financial Institutions
Website: http://www.in.gov/dfi/education/MiniLessons/
Teen%20Spending%20Mini.doc

Teens and Their Money
Motley Fool
Website: http://www.fool.com/teens/
teens.htm?vstest=search_042607_linkdefault

Young Money
InCharge® Institute of America, Inc.
Website: http://www.youngmoney.com

Index

Index

Page numbers that appear in *Italics* refer to illustrations. Page numbers that have a small 'n' after the page number refer to information shown as Notes at the beginning of each chapter. Page numbers that appear in **Bold** refer to information contained in boxes on that page (except Notes information at the beginning of each chapter).